W9-BWL-397

WE ALL GO TOGETHER
CREATIVE ACTIVITIES FOR CHILD REN TO USE WITH MULTICULTURAL FOLKSONGS

By
Doug Lipman

FRANKLIN PIERCE COLLEGE
LIBRARY
RINDGE, N.H. 03461

Oryx Press
1994

The rare Arabian Oryx is believed to have inspired the myth of the unicorn. This desert antelope became virtually extinct in the early 1960s. At that time several groups of international conservationists arranged to have 9 animals sent to the Phoenix Zoo to be the nucleus of a captive breeding herd. Today the Oryx population is nearly 800, and over 400 have been returned to reserves in the Middle East.

Copyright © 1994 by Doug Lipman
Published by The Oryx Press
4041 North Central at Indian School Road
Phoenix, Arizona 85012-03397

Published simultaneously in Canada

All rights reserved

No part of this publication may be reproduced or transmitted in any form or by any means, electronic or mechanical, including photocopying, recording, or by any information storage and retrieval system, without permission in writing from The Oryx Press.
Printed and bound in the United States of America

♾The paper used in this publication meets the minimum requirements of American National Standard for Information Science—Permanence of Paper for Printed Library Materials, ANSI Z39.48, 1984.

Library of Congress Cataloging-in-Publication Data

Lipman, Doug.
   We all go together : creative activities for children to use with multicultural folksongs / by Doug Lipman.
      p.   cm.
   For use with individual children or groups, preschool to age 11.
   Includes the music and words.
Includes bibliographies, discographies, and index.
   ISBN 0-89774-764-X
   1. Games with music. 2. Musico-callisthenics. 3. Folk songs—Instruction and study—Handbooks, manuals, etc. 4. Children's songs—Instruction and study—Handbooks, manuals, etc.
5. Intercultural education—Activity programs—Handbooks, manuals, etc. I. Title.
MT948.L57   1994
372.87'044—dc20   93-34071
                                                          CIP
                                                          MN

CURR
MT
948
.L57
1994

To my mother,
who said, "I'll love him no matter what he grows up to be,"

And to my father,
who sang to me and got me singing along.

TABLE OF CONTENTS

PREFACE
THE FIRST ACTIVITY-BASED SONGBOOK

This handbook tells you what you need to know to use folksongs with children—in enjoyable and meaningful activities. The simplest activities are perfect for preschoolers; the most complicated will work for 10- or 11-year-olds.

ANYONE CAN SUCCEED

Whether or not you're experienced with children or with music, this book will give you the necessary concepts and practical suggestions to become a confident leader of musical activities.

If you're a "nonsinger" facing the idea of using music with children for the first time, you will be led step-by-step through the process of matching musical activities with the needs of particular children.

If you're already an experienced music teacher, you'll find many new songs, activities, and variations on what you know—arranged so that you can find activities when you need them.

If you're a classroom or other teacher looking to enliven the curriculum with music, you'll find all the historical and cultural background you need, cross-referenced to enjoyable activities that build social, physical, and cognitive skills.

If you can't read music, don't worry! The melodies in this book are written out for the convenience of those who can read them. If you can't, you have other options for learning the songs—it's the activities that are crucial. Just turn to the section "What If I Can't Read Music?"

Whatever your experience, this sourcebook will give you the songs, activities, ideas, and hints that you need to make musical activities successful and pleasurable.

MULTICULTURAL FOLKSONGS

This book contains 30 folksongs—high quality, lively songs from our folk traditions—with over 140 accompanying activities.

The songs represent African-American, Anglo-American, and Hispanic-American folk cultures. Songs are also included from Bulgaria, England, Ghana, Ireland, Israel, Jamaica, and Korea.

Stressing the educational value of folk music, Hungarian composer Zoltan Kodály called it the "musical mother tongue."

Today, too few children experience the diversity of folksongs from their own culture, much less the variety and vitality of songs from other cultures. When children hear songs from other cultures at all, it's too often only through a recording. Such songs become "cultural novelties," as foreign to children as ethnic costumes they are never allowed to touch or wear.

Using this collection, however, you can not only help children sing songs in many "musical mother tongues," you can also help them participate in the songs—using them, changing them, and coming to know them as familiar treasures from many corners of our diverse world.

ACTIVITIES: THE KEY TO USING FOLKSONGS

To teach a song to young children, you need to know more than just the song itself. You need to know how to use it with children. This means knowing activities that go with the song: games, movements, and new verses.

The activities in this book are divided into three major chapters: Games, Movements, and New Verses. Within each chapter, the activities are presented in order of difficulty. Each chapter starts with the most basic skills, introducing new skills and concepts one at a time.

Each activity uses one of the 30 songs, but each activity is presented where it makes sense in a learning sequence. Using this book, you can choose an appropriate activity first, and then find the song that fits.

What do you say to introduce the song? Should you explain all the rules of a game before you start? What do you do if children suggest verses that don't fit in the rhythm of the song? If your group acted too wild with the last song you tried, what should you do next?

This handbook not only gives you clear, detailed instructions, it also helps you *adapt* the activities to suit your group. An activity isn't quite right for your setting or group? No problem! Many activities have variations to solve space restrictions or other difficulties. In fact, the book contains a whole continuum of activities–from the least challenging to the most.

ACTIVITIES FOR ANY NUMBER OF CHILDREN (OR OTHERS)

Most of the activities in this book can be used with a single child, as well as with a group from two or three to 30 or more. (The only exceptions are some of the games and the

activities for Movements with Others—although you can adapt many of them for larger groups or for just the two of you.)

In addition, dozens of these activities are appropriate—either as written or with minor alterations—for people of any age, from high school students to adults to elders.

To avoid excluding anyone on the basis of age, the activities in this book refer to "players" rather than "children."

For similar reasons (and to avoid the awkwardness of "s/he" or "she or he") players are half of the time referred to as "she," and the other half as "he."

BACKGROUND AND INDEXES

In addition to songs and activities, this book includes the cultural background of the songs, topics for curricular tie-ins, and indexes that let you quickly find a song for a particular use or subject.

If you happen to know how to play the guitar, by the way, you'll find that all 30 songs in this book can be played with just one chord—the E-major chord. (See page xix for how to order a book of simple guitar instructions.)

MUSIC: THE CENTER OF THE CURRICULUM

For the ancient Greeks, music was the subject that united the senses with the intellect, bridging the gap between physical education and mathematics.

For young children, the intellect develops through involvement. Not only are participatory musical activities enjoyable ways to cement group unity and explore various cultures, they are at the very center of a curriculum that integrates the analytical and the intuitive, the cooperative and the individual, the feelings and the intellect, the experiences of joy and of mastery.

If your childhood experience of music focused on "having a good voice" and "not making mistakes," this book will open a new world of possibilities. The healing and educational power of music is available to every child. All that's needed is a collection of good, simple songs and a flexible array of activities to allow children to participate.

At last, teachers, parents and other group leaders have a comprehensive resource for meeting the social, physical, and cognitive needs of young children through music.

ACKNOWLEDGEMENTS

Thank you, Linda Palmström. As my wife and heart's delight, you've made so much of my life possible—including this book.

Thank you, helpers with this project. Marsha Saxton and Robbie Tovey were writing companions. Jay O'Callahan, Marsha Saxton, and Linda Palmström listened while I thought aloud. Wanna Zinsmaster gave many helpful and generous suggestions. My editors at Oryx, Howard Batchelor and Sean Tape, saw this project from conception to completion.

Thank you, those who helped with earlier, unpublished versions of this material: Linda Borodkin, Maureen Kennedy, Lisa Parker, Lorraine Lee, Terry Dash, Elizabeth Koehler Goldfinger, and Tossi Aaron.

Thank you, those who gave me the opportunities to sing with children, including the staff and children at the Massachusetts Mental Health Center, the Lesley College Schools for Children, the Brookline Arts Center, Old South Preschool, Bowen Nursery school, the Manning School (Boston Public Schools), North Shore Nursery School, and innumerable private classes, residencies, and one-time concerts. All of you gave your enthusiasm, your judgement, your love, and your belief in me.

Thank you, my teachers. My father was my first great teacher, helping me love both folksongs and writing. Linda Borodkin just assumed I could do it, taught me what she knew, and learned more with me. Lisa Parker was the first music teacher who encouraged me. Lillian Yaross shared her well-developed approaches to songs. Lillian Yaross, Frances Webber Aronoff, and Lisa Parker each took me under their arms as one of their many educational "children." The teachers at the Kodály Musical Training Institute gave me the musical help I'd been looking for all my life; my debt is especially large to Janos Horvath and Lenke Horvath.

THANK YOU ALL!

AUDIOCASSETTE CREDITS

Doug Lipman : guitar, flute, banjo, dulcimer, piccolo, autoharp, reed organ (melodeon), finger cymbal, mandolin, bottleneck guitar, harmonica, vocals.

Linda Borodkin : guitar, vocals.

Penny Schultz : conga drum, dumbek (Israeli drum), cane rattle, bass drum, vocals.

Vince O'Donnell : fiddle, guitar, vocals.

Debby Saperstone : vocals.

Lee Ellen Marvin : wood block, vocals.

Children's chorus : Karen Lewinnek, Jenny Watkins, Jenna Weiss.

All songs arranged and adapted by Doug Lipman, Linda Borodkin, and Penny Schultz.

Audio producer : Lee Ellen Marvin.

Engineer: Margo Garrison

Recorded at : WGBH Radio, Boston, MA.

WHAT IF I CAN'T READ MUSIC?

Do you have to read music
to use this book?
NO!

The ability to read music has nothing to do with the ability to teach the activities in this book.

Here are four possible ways to use the activities without reading music:

1. Use the tape. A cassette of all thirty songs in this book is available from the publisher. Listen to the tape as many times as you need to!

OR—

2. Get a music-reading friend to sing the songs for you into a cassette tape recorder. The tape recorder will sing them to you over and over until you've learned them!

OR—

3. Use other songs you already know. After you've read through a chapter, you'll know the basic concepts of that kind of activity. Adapt the activities you want to use to fit the songs you already know and like.

OR—

4. Forget about the melodies altogether. Melody (pitch) is just one of the many aspects of music. Sing the words of the songs in this book to a tune you make up yourself. If you even chant these songs without any "tune" at all, you'll still be giving children an experience of rhythm, form, volume, and tempo—not to mention the skills of listening, cooperation, and concentration.

HOW TO USE THIS BOOK

This book can teach you about using folksongs with children. It's also a handbook you can refer to whenever you need a musical activity for a particular purpose.

This section starts with the basic concepts you need to use folksongs with children. Then it tells you how to find, teach, and adapt activities. Finally, it gives you hints about using accompaniments (optional!) and about using the companion audiotape.

BASIC CONCEPTS

To use this book effectively, you need keep only one basic concept in mind: anyone can learn to sing. From that concept, it follows that your job is to give all children enjoyable musical experiences suited to their level of mastery. If you appreciate why folksongs are ideally suited to this process, you will sing them with pleasure and respect. This respect will make the children want to sing them, too—and, as a result, the children will learn to sing.

ANYONE CAN SING!

Anyone can sing.

Anyone can experience the joy of making music with others.

Anyone can lead music activities with children.

Contrary to the familiar belief in "musical talent," it's not true that only some people can learn to sing in tune, read and write music fluently, create melodies, and play instruments. As with any other human ability—such as the ability to read and write words—some people learn more quickly than others. But anyone can learn, and with enough time, effort, and good

help, anyone can reach any desired level of proficiency.

This book is designed to help any adult create musical events that will enable children to enjoy, participate in, and gain mastery in music. No prior musical experience is necessary!

WHY FOLKSONGS?

Music for children needs to meet at least three requirements.

First of all, children cannot be expected to master complicated music right away. They need to begin with music that is simple and short.

Second, children should not be given music that is second-rate. They need and deserve great music.

Third, before they ever get to a music class, children learn about the elements of music through their movement and their speech. They imitate and master many instances of rhythm, pitch, volume, tempo, inflection, and musical form. The songs that children learn, therefore, should build on their existing skills in speech and movement. All too often, music composed for children doesn't fit well with the musical feeling of the movements prescribed for it or with the rhythm and pitch of the words sung to it. This poor fit makes it harder for children to learn musical feeling, rhythm, and pitch!

Folksongs represent a solution to all three of these requirements. Most are brief and simple in form. Because folksongs have come to their present form by being handed down from generation to generation, they have been chosen and enjoyed by generations of people. This longevity speaks for their quality. Further, they have had their "rough edges" smoothed.

Any unnatural movements, rhythms, or inflection patterns tend to be corrected—usually unconsciously—by the people who sing them for pleasure. With folksongs, the words, melody, and traditional movement are all well suited to each other.

Folksongs bring an added bonus as well. Because they have grown out of the needs and desires of their cultures of origin, they form the basis for a naturally multicultural curriculum.

The songs in this book have all been taken from oral traditions. To understand more about the original contexts of the songs, refer to "Background, Curricular Tie-Ins, and Follow-Up Resources." To learn exactly where I learned a particular song and what adaptations I have made, see "Sources of the Songs."

FINDING AND LEARNING SONGS AND ACTIVITIES

This book presents both songs and the activities that go with the songs. As a result, you have several ways to find an activity that matches your goals as a group leader as well as the needs of the group.

Once you have found an activity, you have to learn both the song that it goes with and the activity itself. With some time and effort, anyone can learn any song and any activity in this collection. The instructions that follow aim to make your learning as efficient and enjoyable as possible.

FINDING AN ACTIVITY TO TEACH

You can use this book to "dig right in" and find a song to teach tomorrow. You can start with a song that attracts you, or with a desired type of activity, or with a subject you want to cover.

You can start by finding a particular song—either because you know it already, or are attracted to its words, melody, or cultural background. To do so, browse through "The Songs." You'll find the songs in the same order as on the tape that accompanies this book. With each song, you'll find its words and melody written

out. (Don't panic if you don't read music notation—that's not necessary. Refer to "What If I Don't Read Music?".) You'll find a brief description of the song's background. (For more detail, see "Background, Curricular Tie-Ins, and Follow-Up Resources.") You'll also find the names and numbers of the activities that use the song. For detailed descriptions of each activity, turn to the appropriate section: "Games," "Movements," or "New Verses." Choose the activity that best fits the needs of your situation. Don't forget the possibility of using the song for listening. (See "Teaching a Song—For Listening," below.)

Instead of starting with a particular song, however, you may know that you want to teach a particular type of activity. You may want a game or a movement activity to fit the needs of your group, or you may prefer a quieter "New Verses" activity. In this case, go to the start of the appropriate activity section and read the detailed outline given there. When you find the subsection that most fits the needs of your group, browse among the activities until you find one that appeals to you. Then learn the song used with that activity.

In still another scenario, you may start with a subject or theme for which you want a musical activity. If so, go to the Subject Index at the back of the book. It will refer you to particular activities or to particular songs (in which case you can find activities listed with the song you chose in "The Songs" section).

LEARNING A SONG

Once you've chosen a song to learn, how do you learn it?

Because music is an auditory art, the best way to learn a song is by hearing it. If you're lucky, you'll have a person who is happy to sing the song with you over and over. (That's what the children will have when you teach the song to them!)

If you don't have access to a patient person who knows the song, the next best source is an audiotape of the song—which has endless patience for repeating it! Listen to the tape (available from the publisher) that accompanies this book. Or get someone who reads music (either you or a friend) to sing the song into a tape recorder.

Listen to the song many times. Sing along once you start to get the hang of it. Refer to the written words if there are some you don't understand.

When you can sing along with the taped song, try singing parts of it by yourself. First, play the tape, singing along for an entire verse. Then stop the tape and try to sing what you just sang with help. If you can't do it, go back and listen again. If you do it successfully, go on to the next verse.

Use your effort intelligently. If only one part of the song gives you trouble, focus your attention on just that part. If you need extra help with a single line of the song, for example, play just that line, sing along, rewind, and play it again.

Once you can sing a song after having heard it on the tape, try starting it cold. As you take your morning walk, try to remember the song. Sing another song you know well for a while, then try to start the new song again. If you can't call it up, listen quietly to your own inner memory of the song; it may get "louder." If you still can't call it up, listen to the first line of the song on the tape, then try to sing it from there. After a enough days of this routine, you'll be able to pull the song from your memory at will.

If a song frustrates you, leave it alone for a while. If necessary, substitute another song, or just chant the words when you introduce the activity. Later, give the song another try.

LEARNING AN ACTIVITY

At the same time you're learning the song, you can be learning the activity that goes with it.

For example, if you're learning the new verses activity #20 for the song "Windy Weather," sing a verse by yourself after hearing it on the tape:

Windy weather,
Frosty weather,
When the wind blows,
*We **all blow** together.*

Then try changing the words to the sample words in the activity (which are not sung on the tape):

Rainy weather,
Rainy weather,
When the wind blows,
*We **get splashed** together.*

Finally, try fitting new words of your own into the tune:

Hurricane weather,
Hurricane weather,
When the wind blows,
*We **evacuate** together.*

When you can change the words in this way, you really know the song.

If, for another example, you're learning Movement Activity #25—"We All Stop Together" with the same song, you might try moving along as you sing the song with the tape. Walk around as you sing, stopping and performing a movement at the end of each verse. Your movements can even help you learn the melody, as you develop muscular associations with the song.

In a third case, suppose you're learning Game #11—"The Leaves Blow Together"—also with "Windy Weather." As you sing (with the tape or by yourself), imagine the game. Pretend you're part of a group of children, looking around for a partner at the end of the verse. Try walking around as you sing, then stopping to take hands with an imaginary partner at the word "together."

Once you can sing the song and act out the activity at the same time, you're ready to try it out with people. If you want to maximize your chance of success with a particular group of children, you can first practice the activity on "safer" groups.

For example, you can get another adult to make up verses about kinds of weather, or you can get a small group of very compliant children to try an activity while waiting for a bus or a car pool. Any safe group will do: your family, your neighbors, someone else's family, or a subgroup of the children with whom you want to use the activity.

When I taught nursery school, I would approach a few children during recess, whispering in each one's ear, "I have a secret new game. Would you like to try it?" In this situation, nothing was lost if the children I chose grew bored and ran back to their outdoor activities. A few minutes later, I'd try the game on a new group of three or four children. By the time I taught it to the whole group, nearly every child had already "previewed" it—and knew how it should go. And I had practice in leading it!

HOW TO TEACH SONGS AND ACTIVITIES

Three types of activities are given with the songs: games, movements, and new verses. Each song, however, can be used without this kind of activity, for listening only or for listening and then singing along. Presenting a song for listening requires as much thought and preparation as presenting a participatory activity—but of a different kind.

TEACHING A SONG—FOR LISTENING

Games, movements, and new verses—these are indispensable, participatory ways to present folksongs to children. Equal to these, however, is listening.

To present a song as a listening activity, first make it clear that the children are not to participate in the song. You might say, "I have a song I'd like you to listen to. You can close your eyes if you want. This one is for just me to sing."

If you wish, introduce the song. In your introduction, you can explain why you like the song, any background or words that the children might not know, and what the children might try

to listen for. For example, before singing "Old Joe Clark" you might say:

> You know, in the Appalachian mountains, people love to sing songs that are funny. I like this one because it's about a pretend person who does silly things.
>
> Do you know what a "route" is? It's the way to go somewhere—the route from here to the cafeteria is downstairs and past the gym. If you don't know the route, you might get lost! These songs were made up by people who lived on farms, so they talk about farm things. Can you guess what a hog trough is? It's almost like a big bathtub that pigs eat out of.
>
> Listen to this song, and see if you can imagine the silly things that Old Joe Clark did.

Then sing the song, as beautifully as you can. By beautifully, I mean with love and meaning. You will not sing "Old Joe Clark"—an upbeat, silly dance song—with the same sense of beauty that you'll use for "Arirang," which is a nostalgic, proud and peaceful Korean folksong.

After singing the song, you can go immediately to another song and activity. Or, you can ask questions about the song you just sang: Did you hear what they did to me when I went to Lexington? Did Old Joe Clark seem silly to you? If the group seems ready for it, you might also offer to sing the song again: Would you like to hear that again? If desired, you might go on to a nonmusical follow-up activity, such as "drawing a picture that the song made you think of," writing a story about a nursery-rhyme character who tried to visit Old Joe Clark, or putting on a skit about the day that someone finally got the best of Old Joe Clark.

Once you have sung a song as a "listening song," you have four choices for ways to return to the song. You can ignore the song altogether, leaving it as a one-time listening experience. You can repeat it as a listening experience. You can invite the children to sing it with you. Finally, you can sing it again with another kind of activity: "Do you remember the song I sang you yesterday about Old Joe Clark? Well, some people play a game when they sing it. Today, I'll show you how to play it."

TEACHING A SONG— WITH AN ACTIVITY

Once you have chosen and learned a song and activity, you're ready to teach it to children.

Before you bring an activity to your group, however, notice the activities in the book before and after the one you've chosen. Get an idea of what could make your activity easier or more difficult. This way, you'll be better prepared to make changes on the spot if you've misjudged your group's abilities.

If you have ever had a new child join an existing group, you may have noticed the new child learning the songs and games faster than the group did. In part, the new child learns faster because she can experience the activity as a whole. The new child doesn't have to imagine what the activity would be like, or to discover it, but gets to witness others modeling it for her, learning each part of it in the context of the whole.

Therefore, to teach most efficiently, imitate the experience of the child joining an established group. Demonstrate the whole activity whenever possible. Sing the entire song, not just part of it; only after you have sung it should you break it into smaller pieces. Play the game as completely as possible before stopping to explain it. Take the first turn yourself for making movements or making new verses, before asking the children to try it themselves. To help you do this, specific suggestions for each type of activity are given in the first activities in each subsection.

If you want to point out a word in a song (or a detail of an activity), first sing the song, then ask a question, then sing the song again so the children have a chance to discover it themselves. For example, say, "What does the song say we do when the wind blows?" Then sing,

Windy weather,
Frosty weather,
When the wind blows,
We all blow together.

Say again, "What do we do when the wind blows?" If the group answers incorrectly or doesn't seem to know the answer, sing the song again. If they still don't know, then either the question or the song was too difficult. Your goal is to help the group learn to listen by giving them specific things to listen for—successfully. After they answer correctly, reinforce their achievement: "You are good listeners! You learned that by listening carefully, didn't you!"

In many professional music groups, the leader starts a song by saying, "One, two, three, four." You can give your children similar assistance. When the group is ready to sing along, you can start the song by singing, "Here we go!" Sing these words in the tempo of the song, on the pitch of the starting note, then begin the song itself on the next beat. In this way, the group knows when to start, how fast to sing, and what pitch to start on. If you say "Here we go!" before every song you sing, the group will learn to follow this musical cue—just like a performing jazz band follows the leader's opening "licks."

SO I TAUGHT IT— NOW WHAT?

Once you've taught a song once, you've left the guesswork realm of "I think they'll like this" and entered the real world of "Okay, that's their response. What next?" What you do next depends, of course, on exactly how they responded. Once you have several songs that your group likes, you have the additional problem of deciding when and how often to sing their favorites.

FOLLOWING UP A SUCCESS

If you teach a new song activity and the children not only learn it but seem to like it, you have a success. If they ask to repeat the activity over and over until you're weary of it, you've tapped into a major social, cognitive, or emotional need!

The first follow-up, of course, is to repeat a successful activity. Repeat it the same day, the next day, or the next week—whenever it makes sense, given the demands on your time with the group. Some teachers of music to preschoolers, for example, suggest not repeating a new song until it has "lain fallow" for about two weeks; they claim that after this interval, very young children will respond to the song as if it were an old favorite. Older children may benefit from a fallow time, too, but may also be quick to ask you to repeat "that game we learned yesterday." In any event, don't feel you need to go on to new material too quickly. Only with familiar activities can children achieve the sense of mastery they need.

Repeat your successful activities many times, until they have lost their appeal. Ideally, of course, you'll drop an activity *just before* it gets boring, but in practice you won't always know it's time to drop it until you start seeing the signs of overfamiliarity: lack of interest, attempts to disrupt the activity, or statements like, "Not Old Joe Clark, again!" Don't forget an old activity completely, however. In a tired or overwhelmed moment, an outgrown favorite might have renewed appeal.

When you have a big success, teach other activities that may have the same appeal. If your first chasing game electrifies your group, follow it (after a week or more) with another chasing game. If your group wants to make silly verses to "Old Joe Clark" for hours, look for another silly song, game, or movement activity that will meet the same need. Consider using a successful activity as the center of a web of new activities, each developing the "hit" in a different way: more challenging game forms, activities that explore different aspects of a subject, more elaborate ways to make verses or movements, or ways to put individual children in positions of more and more leadership.

What if you get tired of a song or activity? Your class of preschoolers, for example, may need to repeat a basic choosing game dozens of times. After several years of using the same basic choosing game, you may be sick of it. You can't change the needs of the next class of preschoolers, but you can choose a different song with a similar activity. It will still be a basic choosing game, but it will have a different song, different words, and a different prop. In this way, the children's need for repeating the basic game will not be so completely at odds with your need for variety.

FOLLOWING UP A FAILURE

Believe it or not, your failures are as important as your successes. If you felt sure that your group was ready for a play-party game and they couldn't comprehend it, you've gained the information you need to correct your view of the group. This information is essential to guiding them toward more successes! If you thought they would love a chance to make verses about rainy weather and you found them suddenly trying to remove the carpet from your floor, you've learned something crucial that can guide you toward finding their true interests.

Before deciding for sure that an activity failed, think back. What had been going on the day you tried it? Were you or the children reacting to something that would have made it impossible for them to respond honestly to the song? If you have any reason to believe the activity didn't get a fair hearing, let it sit for a week or so, then give it another try.

If the activity definitely failed, think about *how* it failed. What seemed too hard or too easy for your group? Were they shy about taking turns or impatient to have more turns? Did they use the activity as an opportunity to insult one another? Did they seem de-energized or overenergized? Did they disrupt the activity? If so, how—by leaving, by challenging your authority, by making "bathroom jokes," by getting up and jumping, or by wrestling with one another? The answer to these questions may give you the information you need to choose a more appropriate activity.

If the group was shy about taking turns, for example, it may make sense to repeat the activity several more times. Many groups—especially ones that have never been asked to participate before—need a while to know it's okay to join in.

If, instead, the group was overeager for turns, you may need to try an activity with very short turns, so that no one has to wait too long. Or you may need to rely for a while on activities that everyone does at once.

If the children insulted one another, you may need to address that issue directly. On the one hand, you can help them find appropriate ways to express the feelings that result in insults: anger, fear, humiliation, and experiences of having been insulted in various ways. On the other hand, you should enforce a strict policy of "no putting anyone down in here." If children are not safe from verbal (or physical) aggression, they won't feel safe enough to enjoy what you have to offer.

If they seem to challenge your authority, try introducing activities that give them a chance to be in charge.

If they seem to need more physical activity or physical contact with each other, introduce activities that allow jumping or touching in a structured form.

The activity that didn't work can be a cause for celebration, since it can help you learn the true needs and interests of your group.

MANAGING REPERTORY

Once a group knows more than a handful of musical activities, you won't be able to review them all every time you sing together. How do you know which ones to sing on a given day?

First of all, make a list of the songs that the group knows. This list can be a private one that you keep, categorized perhaps by type of activity. Such a list lets you see at a glance that, although this group knows six games, they know only one movement activity. You can also remind yourself of already learned activities that might be just right for a given mood or topic of study.

The list of songs can also be a public list, kept on the wall for the children to see. For prereaders, the list can even include pictures or diagrams to identify each song. In this way,

children can remind themselves of what songs they know.

Second, let children help choose what to sing. You can read the list of songs they know, and then take a vote or accept requests. I post a list of the children's names, alphabetically by first name. Each day, I choose four or five songs for the group, but each day one child gets a turn to choose a song from the list. The next day, the next child on the list gets to choose one song. If a particular song is never requested, you may need to remind the group of it, or it may be a sign that the song is not right for the group.

Before asking a child to choose a song from the list, you can read the list of songs aloud in an enjoyable way. For example, you can purposely make silly mistakes (read out "Old Joe Shark" for "Old Joe Clark"), read the titles in "code" (e.g., start every word with the same letter: "Mold Moe Mark") and have the children "decode" the song names, or hum the tunes and show mock anger when the children identify them correctly.

By the way, it's okay to teach more than one activity that uses the same tune—if the words are different enough not to cause confusion. After all, generations of children have sung "Twinkle, Twinkle," "Baa, Baa, Black Sheep," and "Now I Know My A, B, C's" without getting confused or even noticing that one melody serves all three.

ABOUT *NOT* USING AN INSTRUMENT— AND WHEN IT HELPS

The most important thing about the guitar or any other instrument is that *you don't need it!*

In contemporary U.S. society, there is a widespread assumption that "making music" implies "playing an instrument." Through the ages, however, people have known that the music made with nothing but the human voice can be the most satisfying. Instruments can add variety and complexity, but they are luxuries. Singing is the only necessity!

Sometimes an instrument is an out-and-out hindrance. When you teach a game, for example, children need you to model the game for them, playing it with them. You can't play a chasing game while playing the piano!

If an instrument is new to you, it may require more of your attention than the children can spare, even during a quiet making-verses activity.

Never use an instrument when it interferes with the singing or the activity! Your voice alone is enough!

In spite of these warnings, an instrument can be a useful tool. An instrument can draw a group to you, supporting the children with an auditory announcement of your presence.

An instrument—be it guitar, autoharp, banjo, piano, or another—can add interest to an activity for listening or for making new verses. It can also add a unifying beat for movement activities. Once children know a game, it can even support their playing it without you: you can sit to one side, playing the instrument (and singing, if desired) as they play the game.

Since the songs in this book require only one chord, you need not be distracted by the need to change chords, which poses the greatest difficulty for most beginners.

Furthermore, the simple-as-pie accompaniments to these songs* are easy enough to teach to older children (generally, ages 10 and up), allowing them to add to their pleasure in songs they have already come to love or to increase their confidence as they teach making-verses activities to younger children.

HOW TO USE THE TAPE

For your convenience, the publisher distributes an audiotape with the melodies of all 30 songs in this collection. You may find the tape helpful for learning the songs (see "Learning a Song"), for learning to accompany the songs, or even for providing individual listening experiences for children.

If you play guitar, the tape will help you tune it, and play along with the songs. (One channel contains a guitar playing very simple accompaniments, all with one chord.*)

The tape is designed as a listening tape for children, too. Play the tape during a car ride or give children a chance to listen individually whenever they want. (Where noise is an issue, provide headphones.)

Please do not use the tape as a substitute for singing the songs with children yourself. It will be much more difficult for them to learn from disembodied voices than from someone they know.

If you are tempted to play the tape for a group of children because you feel you can't sing well, take one of the suggestions given in "What If I Can't Read Music?". It will help the children more if, rather than playing the tape for them, you simply *say* the words of the song with enjoyment. Having children listen to the tape instead of to you conveys the unconscious message that music is for others—or else that music is an electronic commodity, not a human activity. Do not deprive your children of experiencing how their own voices and bodies can create a joyful occasion which is simultaneously cooperative, esthetic, and educational!

---

*To inquire about a book of simple guitar instruction that teaches the E-chord to accompany these 30 songs, please contact Doug Lipman, P.O. Box 441195, West Somerville MA 02144, (617) 391-3672.

GAMES

Children love singing games. They learn them spontaneously from each other and play them voluntarily for hours. Even a game chosen for them by an adult can be greeted with astounding enthusiasm.

To harness this enthusiasm for purposes of teaching, the adult leader must choose games that meet the children's physical, social, and emotional needs as well as the leader's educational purposes.

ADAPTING GAMES TO THE PLAYERS

As the leader, you need to adapt games to the players—not force the players to fit the games.

What does this concept mean in daily practice? First, of course, you must choose a game with care and then introduce it to the group.

Less obviously, however, you must also notice the children's reaction and respond appropriately.

For example, if the game seems too easy, you must find a way to complicate it or else drop it and introduce another. If the game is too demanding, you must simplify it or replace it with a simpler alternative. If the players repeatedly turn an orderly game into a wrestling match, you need to decide what they need that the game lacks, and then provide it. Do they need more physical contact? Are they seeking ways to express affection or hostility? Do they need more opportunities to be in control?

Notice the progression in each section in this chapter from the simplest games to the most complicated. Use these games as models of how to add complications one at a time. If none of these games happens to be exactly right for your group at a given moment, add your own complications. Make a new game from a song that you know; let the song inspire new variations. In cooperation with the players, evolve a new game that is just right for them.

HINTS ABOUT TEACHING GAMES

Groups can learn games easily if you follow these hints for learning, presenting, repeating, and adapting the games you teach.

♪ **Imagine the game before you teach it.** When you learn a game from this book, imagine it from beginning to end. Once it's in your mind—and not just words on the page—you will be able to teach it with verve.

♪ **Demonstrate (don't describe).** Begin by demonstrating what they will do—not by describing it verbally or by reciting the rules.

You will usually be able to start right in as the first player. If you need another player to join you, choose one who is likely to succeed, and then tell her what to do by words, gestures, hand pressure, or any other cues available to you. The others will learn from her success.

Once all can perform an action with you (such as clapping with a partner), then they can try to perform it with one another, without you. If you're not sure whether they're ready, you can interrupt the game one day to say, "Is there any one here who could do what I usually do?" If the volunteer succeeds, the game can proceed without you from then on. If not, you can revert to doing it yourself.

♪ **Repeat favorite games often.** Don't be afraid to let children play the same game many times. If the players like it that much, it's a sign that it meets one or more of their needs. In that case, you are succeeding! Moreover, it's an opportunity for them to reach an important level of mastery.

Listen to the group's preferences. Ask them—individually and as a group—what games they want to play. Even if the games are inappropriate for your setting, you'll gain clues about what other games they might like.

If a group loves a game, give them time to enjoy it. Then, after several sessions, introduce a game that is similar but slightly more difficult. Eventually, the group will have a repertory of games they love.

If *you* get sick of a game, try changing the song. Every group of four-year-olds, for example, needs a "basic choosing game," but one year you can teach Game 1—Juley, You're Amazing, the next you can teach Game 2—The Royal Throne, and the next you can make one up based on a song you already know, such as "Frere Jacques."

♪ **Adapt games to meet the changing needs of the group.** As a group masters a new game, it may make sense to change the rules: "Okay, now that you're so good at finding people, we can make it even harder. We'll have two people hide and sing at the same time!" (See Game 39— How's the Harvest, for example.)

Even before you teach a game, you can adapt it for your group's needs. If you don't have a plastic dinosaur (see Game 3–Colored Dinosaurs), hold up a block or a pebble and say, "This is our magic dinosaur." I've taught dozens of games reusing two basic props: a wooden block and a knotted handkerchief.

Most of the games in this book are themselves adapted from traditional games. They've been changed to be simpler and to avoid emphasizing either winning-and-losing or selecting friends and rejecting the unpopular. Feel free to adapt them further to meet your needs and goals.

THE BASIC GAME SKILLS

Basic game skills include choosing other players, chasing, guessing, hiding, passing objects, and clapping with others. These can happen in various formations, including lines, circles, and the more advanced formations of the play-party games.

In the sections that follow, games are given to establish each basic skill. Suggestions are included to help adjust the difficulty and interest level of each game—to help the leader match the game to the needs of the players.

GAMES FOR CHOOSING
THE BASIC CHOOSING GAME

Many games popular among grade-school children involve a single player—"it"—who has a turn to perform a set of actions and then must choose another player to have the next turn. Preschoolers and kindergartners, however, may be unable to choose another player quickly and simply. For them, choosing another player deserves center stage in its own game.

GAME 1—JULEY, YOU'RE AMAZING
(BASIC CHOOSING)

This game and the next one are identical but use different props and different songs.

> SONG—"Juley" (page 148).
> PROP—a small doll that children can hold in one hand.
> SPACE/FORMATION NEEDED—a seated circle or group, with room to walk entirely
> around the group.

As the leader, hold up the doll, saying, "This is Juliana Brown." Walk around the seated children, holding the doll and singing:

> *Juley, you're amazing,*
> *Oo-oo, oo-oo,*
> *Juley, Juley, Juley,*
> *Walk along, Miss Juliana Brown!*

Choose one of the seated children, and say to him, "Can you do what I just did? I'll help you with the song."

If the child refuses, try another child. When a child agrees, the hand him the doll, saying, "You walk around the circle, and give it to someone else."

Repeat the game with a new player walking around the circle. Continue as desired, or until each player has had a turn.

Keeping the group interested—If the seated players become restless, begin a rhythmic movement and encourage them to join in. Change the movement as often as necessary: for example, clap hands on thighs, in the air, or on the head.

GAME 2—THE ROYAL THRONE
(BASIC CHOOSING)

This game is done just like Game 1, only a different prop and song are used.

> SONG—"I'm Going Home On the Morning Train" (page 135), sung with these words:
>
> > *I'm gonna sit on the royal throne,*
> > *I'm gonna sit on the royal throne,*
> > *I'm gonna sit, you know that I'm gonna sit,*
> > *I'm gonna sit on the royal throne.*
>
> PROP—an oversized plastic or cloth "bracelet" that will easily go on and off a child's
> wrist. Describe it as "a royal bracelet—like a king or queen wears. When I wear
> it, I can sit on the royal throne."

GAME 3—COLORED DINOSAURS
(BASIC CHOOSING, WITH WORD IMPROVISATION)

This game is similar to the first two, except for one added difficulty: the need to choose the last word of the song to fit the chosen child.

SONG—"Down Came a Lady" (page 123), with the words:

Down came a dinosaur,
Down came two,
Down came another one,
And it was colored **red**.

PROP—small plastic dinosaur. Say, "This is a magic dinosaur. When I have it, my shirt turns into dinosaur skin."

Choose a seated child, and sing the color of that child's clothing (red in this case). Say, "You are wearing a red shirt. Now you are a red dinosaur."

GAME 4—WHO'S BEEN HERE SINCE I'VE BEEN GONE?
(BASIC CHOOSING, WITH WORD IMPROVISATION)

This game is similar to the Game 3, but it requires that the player come up with a phrase to sing, not just a single word.

SONG—"Back to Mexico" (page 125), sung with these words:

Who's been here since I've been gone, sugar babe,
Who's been here since I've been gone, sugar babe,
Who's been here since I've been gone,
A friend of mine with **blue shorts** *on, sugar babe.*

PROP—small bean bag or other object. Say, "This is a friendship bag. If you give it to someone, they'll become your friend."

Sing the color and description of the clothing of the child you chose (blue shorts, striped blouse, etc.).

CHOOSING THE NEXT PLAYER

Once players can play one or more of the "Basic Choosing Games," they are ready to play games that use choosing along with other skills.

In these games, children choose the next player, do a simple action with that player, then sit down. These games divide the playing time in two parts: half for choosing, then a second half for the action.

GAME 5—WALK AROUND THE PRAIRIE
(CHOOSING THE NEXT PLAYER, WALKING WITH A PARTNER)

SONG—"I Wish I Was a Cowpoke" (page 130).
SPACE/FORMATION NEEDED—a seated circle or group, with room for two players to hold hands and walk around outside the group.

Walk around the outside of the circle, singing,

I wish I were a cowpoke,
In some cowpoke land,
With a stetson on my head,
And a partner hand-in-hand;

Now choose a player. Holding hands with that player, walk around the outside of the circle, singing:

Walk around the prairie,
Walk around the town,
Walk around the prairie,
And sit the first one down.

Sit down, leaving the player who walked with you to walk alone around the circle singing the first verse. After the words, "A partner hand-in-hand," that player chooses another to walk with, hand-in-hand. At the line, "And sit the first one down," the first player sits down, leaving the second to begin the game again.

GAME 6—TAKE ME DOWN TO WELDON
(CHOOSING THE NEXT PLAYER, CIRCLING TOGETHER)

This game involves a more complicated cooperative action than the preceding one.

SONG—"Weldon" (page 129).
SPACE/FORMATION NEEDED—a seated (or standing) circle with room for two players to hold both hands and turn around inside the circle.

Walk around the inside of the circle, singing,

Take me down to Weldon,
I think I heard them say,
Take me down to Weldon,
I think I heard them say.

By the end of these four lines, choose a player to be your partner, asking, "Do you want to rally with me?" Once you find a player who gives a "yes" answer, take both hands with the player, forming a two-person circle inside the larger circle. Walk around your small circle, singing,

Rally, rally, rally,
I think I heard them say,

Rally, rally, rally,
I think I heard them say.

At the end of this verse, sit down in the big circle, saying to the player you rallied with, "Now you walk around by yourself, and choose someone to rally with."

GAME 7—THE ANIMAL PARTY
(CHOOSING THE NEXT PLAYER, DANCING TOGETHER)

In this game, the melody does not change to indicate the shift in action; the only cue for this shift is in the words.

> SONG—"There Was A Little Frog" (page 159).
> SPACE/FORMATION NEEDED—a seated (or standing) circle with room for two
>   players to hold both hands and turn around inside the circle, and to walk
>   outside the circle.

During verse 1, walk around the outside of the circle, choosing a partner:

> 1. *Where will the animal party be, uh-huh, uh-huh?*
>   *Where will the animal party be,*
>   *Down in the swamp in a hollow tree, uh-huh, uh-huh.*

During verse 2, dance with your partner in the center of the circle (you can hold hands or elbows, or dance without touching):

> 2. *The first to come were two little ants, uh-huh, uh-huh,*
>   *The first to come were two little ants,*
>   *Fixing around to have a dance, uh-huh, uh-huh.*

During verse 3, you and your partner walk separately around the inside of the circle (alternatively, you can leave the circle and walk outside it). By the end of the verse, join the circle, letting your partner go back outside the circle to become the next leader:

> 3. *Then they went on their honeymoon, uh-huh, uh-huh,*
>   *Then they went on their honeymoon,*
>   *And so my story ends quite soon, uh-huh, uh-huh.*

Initially, you can play this one at a time with the group members. Once they have enough experience to enable two group members to play with each other, you can drop out.

GAME 8—GETTING TO KNOW YOU
(CHOOSING THE NEXT PLAYER, WITH SPECIFIED MOVEMENTS)

In this game, the partners perform movements that are more complicated than those in the previous games.

> SONG—"Juley" (page 148).
> SPACE/FORMATION NEEDED—a seated (or standing) group or circle.

Say, "Who'd like to play a game with me?" Choose a partner, then stand facing him. Sing, doing the indicated actions with your partner:

words	actions
1. *I'd like to get to know you,*	1. Partners shake hands.
2. *Oo-oo, oo-oo*	2. Partners hold both palms toward each other and clap hands four times, once on each "oo."
3. *Really, really, really,*	3. Partners join hands in a two-person circle and walk around it once.
4. *Walk along, Miss Juliana Brown!*	4. Partners drop hands and trade places; new leader walks up to new partner; repeat.

Initially, you can play this one at a time with the group members. Once they have enough experience to enable two group members to play with each other, you can drop out.

Variation—more couples each time. The first time through, play as described above. The second time, however, both players choose new partners from among those who have not yet played. During subsequent repetitions, there will be two couples playing, then four, then eight, and so on. This method is a quick way to get a very large group involved.

PARTNER CHOOSING GAMES

In these games, all players choose partners at once. The pairs of players then perform some specified action together.

GAME 9—GET YOURSELF A PARTNER (CHANGE PARTNERS, DO MOVEMENTS)

SONG—"Weldon" (page 129).
SPACE/FORMATION NEEDED—enough room for all to walk around.

Say, "Get yourself a partner!" and sing the verse:

> *Get yourself a partner,*
> *I think I heard them say,*
> *Get yourself a partner,*
> *I think I heard them say.*

If any players haven't chosen partners, help them. When all have partners, say, "When you hear me say, 'Rally,' you clap hands with your partner." Sing the refrain once through, which is:

> *Rally, rally, rally,*
> *I think I heard them say,*
> *Rally, rally, rally,*
> *I think I heard them say.*

Without pause, sing the verse again:

Get another partner, (etc.)

Variation—At any point, you can say, "I know a new way to rally! Clap elbows with your partner!" As desired, you can suggest new motions for partners to do together–or even request ideas from the group.

GAME 10—CHARLIE HAD A PARTNER
(CHANGE PARTNERS, MAKE SHAPES)

SONG—"Charlie over the Ocean" (page 133).
SPACE/FORMATION NEEDED—enough room for all to walk around.

Say, "Be my echo!" then sing this verse (the group echoes each line):

Charlie had a partner,
Charlie and me,
Charlie went walking,
Across the sea.

Say, "When we sing it this time, get a partner and follow me." Sing the verse above, walking in a circle (with a partner, if there's an odd number of players). Then, without pause, begin the second verse (the group echoes, as in the previous verse):

Can you make a circle,
Two by two?
Find a way to make one,
Both of you.

Say, "Make a circle with your partner. Use any part of your bodies!" Each pair of players makes a single circle with their arms, legs, fingers, or whatever they choose. After waiting for the pairs to solve the problem, say, "Look at those circles! Now, get a new partner!" Then begin the song again, singing both verses.

Variation—other shapes. To make the game more challenging, you can substitute another shape for the circle (square, triangle, line, etc.).

GAME 11—THE LEAVES BLOW TOGETHER
(CHANGE PARTNERS, HOLD HANDS AND RUN, JOIN WITH ANOTHER PAIR)

SONG—"Windy Weather" (page 136).
SPACE/FORMATION NEEDED—enough room for all to walk around.

Sing,

Windy weather, frosty weather,
When the wind blows, we all go together.

Say, "Do you know what you'll do when you hear the word 'together'? You'll find another person and hold hands! Let's practice once: 'Together!'"

Once all have found partners, say, "Good job! Now, I'll see if I can fool you. Let go of your partner." Sing the song again. At the word "together," all should grab partners (the same partner or another) again.

Once you are satisfied that all can get partners, say, "Are you ready for a harder way? This time, while I'm singing the song, you pretend you're a leaf blowing gently around the room."

Once the group can succeed at being leaves and then finding partners, say, "From now on, when you hear the word, 'together,' get a *different* partner—one you haven't had yet."

Repeat the game as desired, or until all have been partners with every player.

Variation—expanding leaf piles. To make the game more challenging, gradually increase the number of players holding hands. Begin with individuals "blowing" around the room, as above. At the first "together," have each individual join another to make a pair. When the song begins again, however, partners continue to hold hands while "blowing"; at "together," each pair joins onto another pair. At the next "together," each group of four joins with another group of four. In a short time, there will be a single pile of "leaves" blowing around the room.

Variation—calling out a number. After each word "together," the leader calls out a number, such as "three!" The "leaves" then form into groups of three. Each time, the leader can call out a different number. To end, the leader can call out the number that will unite the whole group.

PARTNER-STEALING GAMES

In these games, all have partners—except a "single player." The single player steals a partner, leaving someone else as the single player.

When I teach these games, I insist that each player gets only one turn to be a single player. This rule prevents the hurt feelings that can sometimes result from "never being chosen" by others or from being forced to repeatedly take the role of the single player.

My rule, however, makes these games more difficult: when only one player remains who has not had a turn, the single player must choose the *partner* of that player. If it were not for the confusion created by this requirement, these games would actually be easier than the Partner Choosing Games.

These partner-stealing games all start with each player having a partner. A partner choosing game such as Game 8 (Getting to Know You, Variation—more couples each time) can be played first (leaving every player with a partner), or the leader can begin by saying, "Everyone get a partner."

GAME 12—STEAL A PARTNER BEFORE I GO
(STEAL PARTNERS)

This game and the next are identical, except for the song and the opportunities for group participation while it's sung.

> SONG—"Back to Mexico" (page 125).
> SPACE/FORMATION NEEDED—enough room for all to stand in pairs, with walking
> space between each pair.

If there is an even number of players, you can be the first "single player." If not, find the one player who has no partner and say, "You are lucky! You get to choose *anyone* to be your partner, when the song ends. While we sing, you walk around, looking to see who you might choose."

Sing,

> *I'm going back to Mexico, sugar babe,*
> *I'm going back to Mexico, sugar babe,*
> *I'm going back to Mexico,*
> *Steal a partner before I go, sugar babe.*

After the song, you may have to say, "Choose a partner now."

At this point, the one whose partner was chosen becomes a single player. Say to this new single player: "Now *you* walk around; at the end, you can choose any partner except your old one."

If a single player chooses a partner whose own partner has already had a turn, you'll have to help out. Say something like, "Oh, Jenna's partner had a turn already, so you can't pick Jenna. You can pick Mario, Jason, or Sabriah."

The game continues as desired, or until all have had a turn to be the single player.

Variation—adding group participation. Once the group has learned the basics of this game, you can ask the standing players to participate in the song. All can join in by singing the words "sugar babe," or by clapping along. You can add variety by changing the clapping to thigh-patting or foot-tapping, etc. Or, the players can clap hands (or do another motion) with their partners.

GAME 13—GETTING NEW HORSES (STEAL PARTNERS)

This game is identical to the previous game, except for the song and the group participation in the singing.

SONG—"Hill and Gully Rider" (page 150), sung with the words:

> *Hill and gully rider, hill and gully,*
> *Hill and gully rider, hill and gully,*
> *Got my horse and come down, hill and gully,*
> *But my horse done stumbled down, hill and gully,*
> *And the night-time come a-tumbling down, hill and gully.*

If desired, make a brief story about how you came down a mountain in twilight; your horse stumbled and left you alone; then you needed a new horse! So you take a Horse now (a partner); this leaves another Rider (your Horse's partner) without a Horse. This Rider becomes the new leader, and begins the game again. At the end of the session, conclude the story by saying that everyone is down the mountain safely.

For group participation in the song, all can sing the response "hill and gully" after each line.

GAME 14—LOST MY PARTNER AND I CAN'T DANCE JOSEY (STEAL PARTNERS, WITH PARTNER MOVEMENTS)

This game and the next one add actions for the partners to do together. The partner-choosing rules from the beginning of this subsection still apply.

> SONG—"Hold My Mule" (page 143).
> SPACE/FORMATION NEEDED—enough room for everyone, in groups of two, to
> turn around.

Like the others in this section, this game begins with all players having partners. It can follow a partner-choosing game; or you can say, "Everyone get a partner"; or you can sing this introductory verse:

> *Get your partner if you want to dance Josey,*
> *Get your partner if you want to dance Josey,*
> *Get your partner if you want to dance Josey,*
> *Hello, Susan Brown-ie-o.*

As the single player walks among the standing couples, sing,

> *Lost my partner and I can't dance Josey,*
> *Lost my partner and I can't dance Josey,*
> *Lost my partner and I can't dance Josey,*
> *Hello, Susan Brown-ie-o.*

After the singing, have the single player choose a partner, leaving the chosen player's partner as the next single player. Before the game begins again, however, all the standing players join hands with their partners and rotate in circles of two, singing,

> *Chicken on the fence post, we'll dance Josey,*
> *Chicken on the fence post, we'll dance Josey,*
> *Chicken on the fence post, we'll dance Josey,*
> *Hello, Susan Brown-ie-o.*

At this point, the circles stop, the single player walks among the others, and all sing "Lost my partner and I can't dance Josey. . . ."

Variation—changing the movement. The movement performed during the verse "Chicken on the fence post . . ." can be changed or varied. For example, partners can interlock elbows and rotate, perform a clapping movement together, or hold hands and jump up and down.

GAME 15—GRANDSTAND PARTNERS (STEAL PARTNERS, PERFORM HAND-CLAPPING PATTERN WITH PARTNER)

This activity is set up the same as the previous three games.

> SONG—"Stewball" (page 144).
> SPACE/FORMATION NEEDED—enough room for all to stand in pairs, with walking
> space between each pair.

The first single player walks among the standing partners, as you sing the following (the group answers with the words in parentheses):

> The races (uh-huh)
> They ended (uh-huh)
> And the people (uh-huh)
> Clapped their hands (clapped their hands),
> And somebody (uh-huh)
> Took my partner (uh-huh)
> Back to the (uh-huh)
> Grandstand (grandstand).

At this point, the single player chooses a partner, leaving another player without a partner. All sing the refrain, clapping with their partners:

> O   R   O L   O   B   B   B
> *Bet on Stewball, and you might win, win, win,*
>
> O   R   O L   O   B
> *Bet on Stewball, and you might win.*

(The letters above the words refer to the clapping motions. "O" stands for "own," which means clap your own hands together. "R" means clap right hands with your partner; "L" means clap left hands. "B" means clap both hands with your partner, i.e., your palms clap against your partner's palms.)

Begin the verse again. As you sing, the new single player walks among the standing partners.

Variation—simplifying the clapping. The clapping movements can be simplified. For example, partners can clap both hands for the entire refrain. For variety, they can clap elbows, knees, or other body parts.

OTHER CHOICES

In this game, players must choose something other than another player. For other activities involving choices, see "Making Verses" and "Making Movements."

GAME 16—WHAT'S YOUR CHOICE? (MAKE CHOICES)

SONG—"Sit Down" (page 121).
SPACE/FORMATION NEEDED—enough room for all to stand together, with two distinct areas (such as opposite walls) to run or walk to.

Point to one side of the room, singing,

> *What's that yonder that I see?*
> *Looks just like the city to me.*

Point to the opposite side of the room, as you continue the song:

What's that yonder that I see?
Looks just like the country to me.

Say, as you point to the appropriate sides of the room, "If you like the city better, go to that side of the room. If you like the country better, go to the other side."

At this point, if desired, you can give time for players to discuss why they chose what they did. Some helpful ground rules for players: say why you made your choice, not what's wrong with the other choice; no putting down what someone else said; give as many specific details as possible (e.g., say "I like to go to the theater and use the main library" rather than, "there are more good things to do in the city.") As leader, of course, you should observe these ground rules, too; in this game, it's more important to encourage choices and discussion than to correct grammar or dubious opinions.

To end, sing the refrain with movements, as on page 86.

Begin the game again with a new pair of choices.

Variations—other choices. This game encourages talk about values. Any opposites can be used (hot weather, cold weather; being rich, being poor), or any two examples of one category (sneakers or leather shoes; two colors; two television programs; two neighboring communities).

This game relates easily to curricular subjects: Which of these two countries we've studied would you rather live in? Which farm animal would you rather be? Which geometric shape do you think is more beautiful?

Players can contribute choices, too. An individual can suggest two choices, or the leader can ask for a suggestion of one thing that someone likes. If someone says, "I like to eat!" the leader can say, "What's your favorite food?"

If the answer is "Ice cream!" the leader can say, "What's someone else's favorite food?"

When the answer is given, "Pizza," the leader can sing the verse again, offering a choice between ice cream and pizza.

CHASING AND RACING GAMES

Chasing games—including playground favorites like "Drop the Handkerchief," "Duck, Duck, Goose," and "Red Rover"—have many exciting qualities: physical exertion, competition, and the thrill of chasing and being chased.

To adapt chasing games for indoor use, you need only learn a few basic strategies. Even three-year-olds can play chasing games—in a living room!

THE BASIC CHASING GAME

Just like the basic choosing game, the basic *chasing* game begins with you, the leader, walking around a seated circle, then choosing another player. The basic chasing game, however, adds a simple chase at this point. Then, in both games, the chosen player becomes the new leader.

Chasing is much more easily demonstrated than described. If you remain the leader for each turn, therefore, no explaining is required, and there's no need to worry about one child chasing another out of the room. For this reason, it may make sense to remain the leader for days or even weeks. Get ready for some physical activity!

Once the children are fully comfortable with the chase, you can say to a child who just chased you, "Can you be the leader once?" If the child succeeds, the leader's role can pass from child to child; if not, you can quietly take the next turn.

GAME 17—LOST MY HANDKERCHIEF
(BASIC CHASING GAME)

This game and the next are identical but use different props and different songs. Note that the players jump rather than run, making these games safer for indoors.

> SONG—"Kitty Kasket" (page 134).
> PROP—a handkerchief or other piece of cloth. If the handkerchief is knotted in the center, it drops rather than floats.
> SPACE/FORMATION NEEDED—a seated circle or square, with room to walk entirely around the group.

As the leader, hold up the handkerchief, and say, "This is my handkerchief. I hope I don't lose it again today!" Walk around outside the seated players, holding the handkerchief and singing:

> *Kitty, kitty kasket,*
> *Green and yellow basket,*
> *Lost my handkerchief yesterday,*
> *It's all full of mud, so I tossed it away.*

At the words "tossed it away," drop the handkerchief in the lap of one of the seated players, and say to her, "It's a jumping race! You have the handkerchief. Please don't pick it up and chase me with it!"

By now, the player has probably picked up the handkerchief and stood up.

Say, "Oh, oh! She's going to jump after me! Please don't chase me!" Keep prompting the player, while jumping up and down around the outside of the seated group.

When you and the player return to the player's place, let the player catch you (if she hasn't already), as you say, "Oh! You got me! You did it! Now, give me the handkerchief back. Thank you; now you sit down."

Begin the process again, this time choosing a new player.

About getting the player to chase the leader—A tone of mock terror will get even a very shy child to jump after you. Try screaming something like, "Oh, no! She's going to get me! What will I do now? She almost has me!" For once, the power to inspire fear is given to the child, if only in fun. If the child refuses to chase you, of course, just choose another.

Getting the child to chase you seems to work best if you jump backwards, so that you're always facing the child who's chasing you.

If the child forgets and starts running after you, remind her by saying, "It's a jumping race! She's jumping after me!"

GAME 18—CATCHING THE MORNING TRAIN
(BASIC CHASING GAME)

As in the previous game, make the chase a "jumping" race.

SONG—"I'm Going Home On the Morning Train" (page 135), sung with these words:

> *I'm gonna catch the morning train,*
> *I'm gonna catch the morning train,*
> *I'm gonna catch, I'm gonna catch,*
> *I'm gonna catch the morning train.*

PROP—toy train
SPACE/FORMATION NEEDED—a seated circle or square, with room to walk entirely
around the group.

After singing the song, choose a seated player, then pass the plastic train to her. She gets up and chases you once around the circle, back to her place. You sit in her place, she becomes the new leader, and the game begins again.

Variation: To make the game more challenging, the leader can drop the prop behind the chosen player, rather than pass it to him.

GAME 19—WHOSE COLORS AM I NAMING?
(BASIC CHASING GAME, WITH WORD IMPROVISATION/QUICK
RESPONSE)

All the following games can be played with a "jumping" chase (as described in Game 17—Lost My Handkerchief), or with running, walking, or crawling chases. For more types of chasing, see Game 20—Can't Catch Me, below.

This game adds a "quick response" for the seated player—to recognize the colors of her clothing as sung by the leader.

SONG—"Kitty Kasket" (page 134).
SPACE/FORMATION NEEDED—a seated circle or square, with room to walk or run
entirely around the group.

Walk around the outside of the circle, but do not touch anyone. Instead, sing the unique colors of a seated player's clothes:

> *Kitty, kitty kasket,*
> *Blue and white basket,*
> *Lost my handkerchief yesterday,*
> *It's all full of mud, so I tossed it away.*

When the player dressed in blue and white recognizes herself, she starts to chase you around the circle. You may have to sing the song several times until the "blue and white" player recognizes her description.

Variation—nonsense rhymes. You can include descriptions of clothing that are easier to recognize (but harder to learn to sing) by changing the word "basket" and its nonsense rhyming word, "kasket" (see also Rhyming Verses):

> *Kitty, kitty kirt,*
> *Red and purple shirt . . . (etc.)*

Or:

> *Kitty, kitty kess,*
> *Polka dot dress . . . (etc.)*

For very young children, the singing and recognition may be enjoyable in itself, with no need for the chase!

GAME 20—CAN'T CATCH ME
(BASIC CHASING GAME, WITH VARIATIONS: MOVING CIRCLE, CHANGING THE CHASE, AND WORD IMPROVISATION)

This game adds opportunities for several new variations.

> SONG—"Charlie over the Ocean" (page 133).
> SPACE/FORMATION NEEDED—a circle, with room to walk or run entirely around the group.

This basic chasing game is played without a prop. As leader, you skip outside the circle, singing:

> *Charlie, over the ocean,* (group echoes each line)
> *Charlie, over the sea,*
> *Charlie caught a blackbird,*
> *Can't catch me.*

At the words "Charlie caught a blackbird," touch the next player, who leaves the circle to chase you once around the ring—and then becomes the next leader, as you sit in the player's place.

Variation—moving circle. Traditionally, this game is played with a moving circle. All join hands in the ring and skip to the right; the leader skips outside the circle in the opposite direction.

Variation—changing the chase. All the basic chasing games can be played with a "jumping race," as described in Game 17, as well as with the traditional running, which, of course, is usually safest in a gym or outdoors. Jumping races can be enjoyed safely in tighter quarters. Crab-walk or hands-on-toes races can be even more contained.

Try teaching a particular song with a single type of chase. When you want to introduce another form of movement, teach a new game.

For more advanced players, however, change the type of chase from turn to turn. The leader can simply yell out, "hopping race!" before starting to sing.

Variation—singing the type of chase. In a still more demanding form of the game, the leader can dictate the type of race by singing the name of an animal whose movement is to be imitated. For example, you might sing,

> *Charlie, over the ocean,* (group echoes each line)
> *Charlie, over the sea,*
> *Charlie caught a black snake,*
> *Can't catch me.*

You and the chosen player would now have to crawl around the circle like snakes.

GAME 21—RACING ROUND THE TRACK
(BASIC CHASING GAME, WITH PLAYERS RACING IN OPPOSITE DIRECTIONS AROUND THE CIRCLE)

This game includes a true race around the circle, not a chase. For possible variations, see "Variation—Changing the Chase" in the previous game.

> SONG—"Stewball" (page 144).
> SPACE/FORMATION NEEDED—a circle, with ample room to walk or run entirely around the group.

In this racing game, the leader ("Molly") walks outside the circle singing the "call" from this song, while the group sings the "response" (in parentheses):

> *Old Mistis (uh-huh)*
> *Bet millions (uh-huh)*
> *And old Masta (uh-huh)*
> *Bet pounds (bet pounds)*
>
> *That old Stewball (uh-huh)*
> *Could beat old Molly (uh-huh)*
> *On the first (uh-huh)*
> *Running round (running round).*

After the group sings "running round," Molly touches another player and begins to race around the circle in either direction. The other player ("Stewball") must race in the opposite direction, trying to arrive back at Stewball's place before Molly. As they race, the group sings:

> *Bet on Stewball, and you might win, win, win,*
> *Bet on Stewball, and you might win.*

After the race, "Stewball" becomes the next "Molly."

Caution: If players race by running, there's a danger of collision halfway around. For younger children in a confined space, let the race be "run" on knees, with hands on knees, or in some other slower fashion.

GAME 22—CHE CHE TAG
(CHASING GAME, WITH ONE PLAYER CHASING ANOTHER IN ANY DIRECTION FOR THE COUNT OF TEN)

In this game and the next one, one player chases another but not around the circle.

> SONG—"Che Che Ku Le" (page 138).
> SPACE/FORMATION NEEDED—leader facing group, in an unobstructed space for chasing.

As leader, you sing the song and perform the indicated movements; the group echoes each line, imitating the movements as they sing:

Che che ku le (tap hands on head);
Che che kufi sa (tap hands on shoulders);
Kofi sa langa (tap hands on hips);
Ka ta chi langa (tap hands on ankles);
Kuma de de (fall to the ground).

When all are waiting on the ground, call out suddenly the name of one of the players, who gets up and runs from you. Immediately, the group starts to count to ten. At the word "ten," (or earlier, if the player is caught) you both stop, then return to the group. All stand again, and the player you chased becomes the new leader.

GAME 23—CATCHING THE RABBIT
(CHASING GAME, WITH ONE PLAYER CHASING ANOTHER
IN AND OUT OF THE STANDING CIRCLE)

SONG—"Old Mr. Rabbit" (page 153).
SPACE/FORMATION NEEDED—a circle of standing players, with about a foot
between each player, and room to walk or run entirely around the group.

As leader, you are the Farmer; you start in the center of the circle. The Rabbit starts outside the circle. As all sing and clap the following verse twice through, you chase the Rabbit in and out of the circle:

Old Mister Rabbit,
You got a mighty habit,
Of jumping in my garden,
And eating all my cabbage.

At the end of the second time through the song, the Rabbit becomes the new Farmer, a new player is chosen as Rabbit, and the game begins again.

Note: Sing the song all the way through, even if the Rabbit is caught early. This puts more emphasis on the singing and less on the chasing. As in all these games, choose a new leader each time, whether the leader caught the player being chased or not.

Variations—Vary the time of the chase by singing the song three times through, or only once.

To make the chase more unusual and less wild, require that both players crouch and freeze each time the word "cabbage" is sung.

You can use this counting-out rhyme to choose the new Rabbit. Point to a different player with each beat; the final player pointed to will be the new Rabbit.

I called my dog
And put him on the track;
Dog lost the rabbit
And came right back.

You can also vary the type of movement allowed in the chase: hopping on one foot, walking backwards, or other variations.

ONE CHASES MANY

In the basic chasing games (described earlier), one player chases one other player. Everyone else remains stationary and may even serve as road markers for the two chasing players.

In the games in this section, however, there are times when everyone moves. This variation makes greater demands on the players' ability to organize themselves in space!

BASIC TAG GAME

The easiest possible tag game makes each element simple and clear: where the goal (safe place) is, where the tagging player starts, where the rest of the players start, and how long the chase can last.

To add to the interest without becoming more difficult, the basic tag game can add imagery (for example, the chasing player pretends to be a monster) or humorous dialogue between the chaser and the others.

For spaces where running is unsafe, crawling and other "slowing" methods can be substituted. For details, see the Basic Chasing Games, especially Game 20—Can't Catch Me.

GAME 24—DO YOU WANT THE WIND TO BLOW? (BASIC TAG GAME)

SONG—"Windy Weather" (page 136).
SPACE/FORMATION NEEDED—a section of open wall (safe for children to crash
    into if they misjudge their speed) adjacent to a clear area for chasing.

Point to the section of open wall, saying, "This is the safe place. The Wind can't touch you if you're touching this wall. Everyone come over to the safe place!" Using a counting-out rhyme or other method, choose a volunteer to be the "Wind," saying "You are the Wind. You stand over here [at the opposite end of the chasing area] in the Wind's Cave."

Join the group of children at the wall. "If we're feeling brave, we can go over to the Wind's Cave." Walk toward the Wind's Cave, joined by any who wish, and sing:

> Windy weather,
> Frosty weather,
> When the wind blows,
> We all go together.

Say, "Now the Wind says,

> Do you want the wind to blow today?

"We say, 'No!'" (All shout, "No!")

Repeat the song. Then the Wind asks the question again, and again the group answers, "No!"

Before singing the song the third time, say, "This time we're going to answer 'Yes.' When the Wind chases us, run back to the safe place!"

After the chase, the game begins again with a new player as the Wind.

When playing with preschoolers, try to get the Wind to chase you, instead of the other children. As soon as everyone shouts, "Yes," say, "Oh, no! The Wind is going to touch me!" Then back away from the Wind toward the safe place, giving a running commentary: "Oh, oh! She's catching me now. She got me!" This makes it less scary for the others and guarantees that the Wind will get the satisfaction of tagging at least one person!

GAME 25—DOWN CAME A MONSTER
(BASIC TAG GAME, WITH WORD IMPROVISATION)

This game adds a chance for the chaser to improvise some humorous dialogue.

SONG—"Down Came a Lady" (page 123).
SPACE/FORMATION NEEDED—a section of open wall (safe for children to crash into if they misjudge their speed) adjacent to a clear area for chasing.

This game is identical to the previous game, except that the chaser is "the monster," and the players sing this song three times:

Hello, monster,
How are you?
Nighttime is coming,
So whatcha gonna do?

The Monster responds with an improvised description of what he will do at nighttime, such as:

I'm gonna get my pajamas on now.

or:

I'm sneaking downstairs for a glass of water.

The third time, the Monster says,

I'm coming to get you!

The Monster chases the other players to the wall. A new monster is chosen, and the game begins again.

OTHER TAG GAMES

The following three games vary the elements of the chase. The first two change the nature of the "safe place"; the third changes the method of tagging.

GAME 26—COLOR TAG
(TAG GAME, WITH WORD IMPROVISATION AND VARYING "SAFE PLACES")

SONG—"Charlie over the Ocean" (page 133).
SPACE/FORMATION NEEDED—a circle or group, surrounded by a clear area for chasing. Optionally, there can be walls of different colors or walls with large swatches of different colors on them.

Sing the song (all echo each line):

Charlie, over the ocean,
Charlie, over the sea,

Charlie caught a yellow bird,
Can't catch me.

After the final line is echoed, chase the players as they all run to touch a yellow object. When all have been caught or are safely touching a yellow object, the game begins again with a new leader. Each new leader sings a different color of bird, requiring the group to find objects of that color.

If the group needs extra time to locate the safe objects, always sing the verse twice—or start the leader some distance away from the group.

Variation—wall tag. If there are walls of different colors or with colored swatches on them, sing one of those colors; then all run to the appropriate wall.

Variation—object tag. Sing the name of an object in the playing area:

. . . Charlie caught a <u>chair</u> . . .

All run to touch the object named. For beginning readers or students with limited English, label the objects. To teach another language, label and sing them in Spanish or whatever language you are teaching.

GAME 27—CABBAGE TAG
(TAG GAME, WITH "STOOPING" TO BE SAFE)

SONG—"Old Mr. Rabbit" (page 153).
SPACE/FORMATION NEEDED—a clear area for chasing.

One player, the "Gardener," tries to catch the others, as all sing, over and over:

Old Mister Rabbit,
You've got a mighty habit,
Of jumping in my garden
And eating all my cabbage.

At the word "cabbage," any player in danger of being tagged may stoop, placing both hands on the ground on an imaginary "cabbage." The Gardener may tag only standing players; players may stand up any time, but may stoop only as the word "cabbage" is being sung. When a player is tagged, announce to the group: "Sabrina is the new Gardener!" and begin the song again.

If the Gardener has too hard a time catching anyone, limit the number of "stoops" per player; for example, each player might have a maximum of three stoops to use.

Variation—line of gardeners. To make the game cumulative and cooperative, have each tagged player join on to one of the Gardener's hands, until a long line of Gardeners are chasing a single "Rabbit."

GAME 28—PARCH
(TAG GAME IN WHICH YOU TAG PLAYERS BY THROWING SOFT OBJECTS AT THEM)

SONG—"Back to Mexico" (page 125).
PROPS—one or more "sticks" of paper-towel tubes, toilet-paper tubes, sponges, foam cylinders, or other appropriate items.

SPACE/FORMATION NEEDED—a clear, bounded area for chasing and for throwing "sticks."

Say, "Do you know what 'parch' means? It means almost burned, until something is stiff and dry. When you hear me say 'parch,' make your body stiff and parched. 'Parch!' Good. We'll play a game where one of you can say 'parch' as soon as you have all these Sticks."

Hold the Stick (or Sticks), and sing, naming one of the players:

> *Never seen the likes since I've been born, sugar babe,*
> *Never seen the likes since I've been born, sugar babe,*
> *Never seen the likes since I've been born,*
> *Picking up sticks in **Jonathan's** corn, sugar babe.*

After the song, drop the Sticks. Say, "Everybody run from Jonathan!" All players but Jonathan run to the edges of the play area. Say, "Jonathan, pick up all the Sticks! As soon as you have them all, holler 'parch'!" When Jonathan hollers "parch," say, "Everybody parch, right where you are!"

Say, "Jonathan, you can throw a Stick at someone, but you can't move your feet." If he hits someone, say to that person, "Turn to ashes and collapse!" (Turning to ashes can be done dramatically, if preferred.) When all the "Sticks" are thrown, say, "Bring all the Sticks to Jonathan. Now Jonathan's the new leader."

MANY CHASE ONE

Like the "One Chases Many" games just given, these chasing games usually require more space or more physical control than do one-on-one chases or races.

GAME 29—RACE WITH THE DOLLAR
(TAG GAME IN WHICH MANY CHASE ONE)

SONG—"Stewball" (page 144).
PROPS—a "dollar," which can be a coin, a disk, a stone, or even a block.
SPACE/FORMATION NEEDED—a section of open wall (or other goal) adjacent to a
    clear area for chasing. Players stand across from the goal in a side-by-side line,
    with both hands in front, palms together.

Hide the "dollar" between your hands (hold them in front of you with palms together) and sing (the group sings the responses in parentheses and joins in the refrain):

> *It was a big day (uh-huh)*
> *In Dallas (uh-huh)*
> *Oh, don't you wish you (uh-huh)*
> *Was there (was there),*
>
> *Oh, you'd-a bet your (uh-huh)*
> *Last dollar (uh-huh)*
> *On that iron (uh-huh)*
> *Gray mare (gray mare).*

refrain:

> *Bet on Stewball, and you might win, win, win,*
> *Bet on Stewball, and you might win.*

As you walk up and down the line, holding your hands over each of the players hands, surreptitiously drop the Dollar into someone's hands. At any point during the refrain, the player with the Dollar (who is now "Stewball") tries to slip away from the group and make it to the goal before another player can catch her.

If you reach the end of line before Stewball slips away, walk back down the line in the other direction. After receiving the dollar, Stewball can run immediately, or wait for a more opportune moment.

To play in a confined space, have the players kneel in line and race on all fours.

Variation—larger groups. This game works as described with a group size from four to about 15 players. For larger groups, play with more than one leader and more than one dollar.

RACES
BASIC RACING

In chasing games, one player tries to catch another. In racing games, players run against each other to reach a finish line or other goal.

In the simplest races, two players race toward a visible goal.

In the following game, one player chooses between two goals, one close and the other farther away.

GAME 30—SHORT OR LONG
(BASIC RACING GAME, WITH CHOICE OF TWO FINISH LINES TO RACE TOWARD)

SONG—"Round the Corner" (page 137).
SPACE/FORMATION NEEDED—a clear area for chasing with two possible finish lines, one farther than the other.

As leader, "count out" the seated or standing players while singing (all join in on "Around the corner, Sally"):

> *Oh, will you race me short or long?*
> *Round the corner, Sally.*
> *Oh, will you race me short or long?*
> *Round the corner, Sally.*

"Counting out" means pointing to or touching each player in turn while singing the song–as if playing "Eeney Meeney Miney Mo" or "One Potato, Two Potato."

The last player "counted" (the one you point to at the last word of the song) has to answer the question with "long" or "short." As soon as the player responds, you both race to the appropriate finish line.

After the race, return and begin again. To maximize the number of players who get to race, you can choose a new leader *and* a new second player each time.

COOPERATIVE RACES

Most traditional racing games end by producing an individual winner—with many losers. These cooperative races, on the other hand, offer a different kind of challenge. They require players to work together so that many or all may win.

GAME 31—TRAINS RACE TO A TIE
(COOPERATIVE RACING GAME: CROSS THE FINISH LINE JUST AS THE SONG ENDS)

SONG—"Train Is A-Coming" (page 155).
SPACE/FORMATION NEEDED—a clear area for a slow race, with a line to cross (or wall to touch) that's big enough for all to reach at once.

Each player is a "train." All begin at one starting line and shuffle toward the finish line singing:

> *Train is a-coming, oh, yeh,*
> *Train is a-coming, oh, yeh,*
> *Train is a-coming, train is a-coming,*
> *Train is a-coming, oh yeh.*

The goal is to cross the finish line just at the last word of the song, "yeh." All trains must move forward at all times, however slowly.

If you want a longer race, sing more verses, such as:

> *You better get your ticket, oh, yeh . . .*
> *Whistle is a-blowing, oh, yeh . . .*
> *Train going home now, oh, yeh . . .*

Variation—cooperative tasks. Give partners a cooperative task to perform in exactly the time it takes to sing one verse (or two). For example, give two players a flat board or book to hold between them, on which they must balance a marble. They must carry the marble across the room on the book, dumping the marble into a basket just as the verse ends.

To make this task easier, make the book bigger or substitute a wadded up piece of paper for the marble.

GAME 32—CIRCLE HOPPING
(COOPERATIVE RACING GAME: HOP FOR THE AGREED-ON NUMBER OF VERSES)

SONG—"Hold My Mule" (page 143).
SPACE/FORMATION NEEDED—a clear area or a circle for hopping.

Players decide on how many verses of "Hold My Mule" to sing (and decide which verses they'll sing). Then they hop around as they sing the verses they chose:

Hold my mule while I dance Josey,
Hold my mule while I dance Josey,
Hold my mule while I dance Josey,
Hello, Susan Brown-ie-o.

Had a glass of buttermilk and I danced Josey . . .

Wouldn't give a nickle if I couldn't dance Josey . . .

My shoe's untied and I can't jump Josey . . .

Briar in my heel and I can't jump Josey . . .

Chicken in the bread pan, can't dance Josey . . .

A winner is any player who hops for the entire singing without putting down the other foot. There can be many winners, of course, and the players who don't win can keep hopping.

Variations. You can require players to keep inside a circle or other marked area. Alternatively, instead of letting players hop individually in any direction, you can require them to hop on a line or around a circle. For even more cooperation, let them form pairs, lines, or circles, holding hands (or holding the hips or shoulders of the players in front of them); they must follow their partner or the leader of their line, all aiming to hop the whole time without putting down the other leg. Teams or whole classes can aim to set records for the number of verses successfully hopped through! For teaching time calculation, have children time their singing of one verse, then add or multiply to estimate how many minutes their chosen number of verses will last.

GUESSING AND HIDING GAMES

Children of all ages love to find what is hidden. They are thrilled to hide and to have others seek them. Even sophisticated older children can be captivated by the puzzle of a guessing game.

Why do children love these games so much? We know that one of an infant's major milestones is the development of *object permanence:* the ability to conceive of the continued existence of hidden objects. Later, this ability leads to the social milestone of understanding that parents will return after an absence. Children's delight in guessing and hiding games may stem from the playful challenge to these elemental cognitive structures.

Some of these games are very quiet and require little room. Hide-and-seek, on the other hand, usually demands more space and movement—although preschoolers will often enjoy it in very limited spaces, even with only one hiding place! The use of blindfolds can make such games challenging for older children, even when room for movement is very limited.

THE BASIC GUESSING GAME

In the most basic musical guessing game for groups, one player leaves the area while a prop is hidden under a seated player's legs. The first player returns and tries to guess who has the prop. This game is most easily played in a seated circle on the floor, but also works with the players seated in a circle of chairs or even in rows of desks. Ideally, the guesser can wait around a corner or in an adjoining room while the prop is hidden, but the guesser can also just face away from the group at the edge of the room.

To teach this game, stay seated with the group. Although it's helpful for you to demonstrate the role of the guesser, it's even more important for you to help the group hide the prop. Of course, a second adult (if available) can help by being the first guesser.

GAME 33—WHERE'S THE GOLDEN APPLE? (BASIC GUESSING GAME.)

This game and the next one are identical but use different props and different songs.

> SONG—"Sleep, Bonnie Bairnie" (page 158).
> PROP—a yellow or gold foam ball. Another color ball will do, or any small yellow or gold object.
> SPACE/FORMATION NEEDED—a seated circle or square, with room to walk entirely around the group; plus a place for one child to wait.

Sit down with crossed legs, "tailor style" (sitting on the floor with each foot tucked under your opposite thigh; this requires you to cross your shins), with the group. Hold up the prop and say, "This is my Golden Apple. I'm going to hide it like this." Put the prop in the space formed by your folded legs, then cover it with your hands. If you have a second adult in the room, say, "Justine will be the first guesser. Justine, go around the corner. Don't look!"

If there's no second adult, say, "Who wants to be the one to guess who has it?" Choose the first guesser yourself, or use a counting-out rhyme (such as "Eeney Meeney Miney Mo" or "One Potato, Two Potato"). It helps the others if you choose the player most capable of learning this game from your oral instructions.

Once the guesser has gone around the corner say, "Who wants to hide it first?" You can choose someone randomly or use this counting-out rhyme (point to a different child with each beat):

> One, two, three, four,
> Apple at the castle door.

Put the Golden Apple in the lap of the child you pointed to on the word "door." Hold your hands in your own lap as if you have the Apple, and say, "Pretend you have it, everybody!"

Now call to the guesser: "Come on in!" Once the guesser is standing outside the circle, say, "Don't guess yet; wait till we sing the song." Sing, as the guesser waits outside the circle (or walks around the circle looking for the hidden Golden Apple):

> Sleep, bonnie bairnie, behind the castle,
> Bye, bye, bye, bye.
> You shall have a golden apple,
> Bye, bye, bye, bye.

Say, "Okay, take your first guess. Who do you think has the Apple?" Once the guesser names or points to a seated child, say to the seated one, "Show her! Pick up your hands so she can see if you have it!"

If the guess was correct, say, "You got it on the first guess!" If not, say, "Walk around and look at everybody. Don't guess till we're done singing!" Sing the song again. After three incorrect guesses, say to the group, "Okay, it's time to show her who really had it. Show her!" The one with the Apple will hold it up for the guesser to see.

Say to the one who had the Apple, "You're the next guesser. Go around the corner until we call you. Don't look!"

Choose a new child to hide the Apple, as before. Each time, the one who hid the Apple becomes the next guesser. For the last turn of the day, choose the first guesser to be hider. After the Apple is found say, "You had a turn to go out and guess already, so we'll stop here for today."

With a small group, every player can have a turn every time.

GAME 34—WHO HAS THE LEMON?
(BASIC GUESSING GAME)

This game is played just like the previous one, but a different prop and a different song are used.

SONG—"Al Citron" (page 124), sung with these words:

Al citron de un fandango sango, sango, sabaré,
Sabaré de la randela con su triki triki tron.

PROP–a small yellow ball or other yellow object

Hold up the prop and say, "This is a pretend citron. *Citron* is a Spanish word for a fruit like a lemon, but bigger."

For a counting-out rhyme to choose the next hider, you can use the following rhyme (point to a different child with each beat):

Lemon, apple, peach and pear,
Hide the citron under there.

GUESSING A PERSON

Because people are the most important objects in the life of a child, they are the easiest to identify. In the games that follow, a player must identify a person using senses other than sight. Obviously, such games work best with a group of children who know each other.

To eliminate the sense of sight, the guessing player can simply close his eyes. Alternatively, you can give him a blindfold, which makes it less tempting to peek. On the other hand, blindfolds can be slightly scary for young children, and blindfolds that touch the hair might be suspected of spreading head lice. If you use a blindfold, therefore, you may prefer a simple half-mask (held on by an elastic string) to a tied handkerchief or an oversized hat.

GAME 35—WHO CRIED?
(GUESSING-A-PERSON GAME)

In this game and the next, a person is guessed by the sound of her voice.

SONG—"Dance a Baby Diddy" (page 151).
PROP—blindfold (optional)
SPACE/FORMATION NEEDED—a seated (or standing) group or circle.

Say, "Who wants to close your eyes and guess who is crying?" Choose the first guesser, then say, "Would you like to wear a blindfold or just keep your eyes closed?" Sing the song:

> Dance a baby diddy,
> What can Daddy do wid'e?
> Sit on my lap, give it some pap,
> And dance a baby diddy.

Say to the others, "Raise your hand if you want to be the one who cries." Point to a player, saying, "Pretend to cry like a baby." Ask the guesser, "Can you guess who it was?" After the guesser says the name of a player, say, "Open your eyes and see!" Have the same player cry again. Let the player who cried become the new guesser, and begin again.

Note: Don't be surprised if some children are reluctant to pretend to cry. The idea that "big children don't cry" is still strongly (if subtly) reinforced in our culture, especially for boys. Accept any child's refusal without fuss, but don't give up the game. Many children will first try the game the sixth or tenth time you play it—and then play it with relish.

Variation. Play in a circle of chairs, with the guesser in the middle. Spin the guesser around, then guide the guesser to a seated player. If desired, have the guesser actually sit in the lap of the player to be guessed.

GAME 36—WHO'S THE MOUSIE?
(GUESSING-A-PERSON GAME)

This game adds two complications: the circle moves around the guesser, and the person being guessed must sing a precise response within the song.

> SONG—"There Was a Little Frog" (page 159).
> PROP—blindfold (optional).
> SPACE/FORMATION NEEDED—a standing circle of players, with one player in the center.

Sing the song:

> There was a little frog who lived on a hill,
> Uh-huh, uh-huh.
> There was a little frog who lived on a hill,
> Who rustled and tussled like Buffalo Bill,
> Uh-huh, uh-huh.

Say, "Can you sing the 'uh-huh'?" Sing again, letting the group respond with "uh-huh, uh-huh." After a verse or two, say, "Is there someone who can sing the "uh-huh" by yourself?" Choose one of those whose hands are raised, saying, "This time, let Shayne sing 'uh-huh' by herself." (Note: if this solo singing is too difficult for your group, do not go on with the game. Sing a few verses of the song, then try again another day.)

Once the players can sing solo on "uh-huh," say, "I have a guessing game. Who wants to be the frog and try to guess who the Mousie is?" Choose a first guesser, and say to him, "You're the Frog. Would you like to wear a blindfold, or just keep your eyes closed?" Place the Frog in the center of the circle, saying, "You stand still. I'll tell you when to guess."

Lead the players around the circle as you sing the first verse. At the last "uh-huh," stop the circle. Touch the player who is standing directly behind the guesser, saying, "You're the Mousie! You sing 'uh-huh' by yourself on the next verse." Standing still, sing this verse, letting the Mousie sing the response:

> *The frog took Mousie on one knee,*
> *Uh-huh, uh-huh,*
> *The frog took Mousie on one knee,*
> *And said, "Oh, Mouse, will you marry me?"*
> *Uh-huh, uh-huh.*

Say to the Frog, "Now guess. Who just sang?" After the guess, say, "Open your eyes and see!" Start again with Mousie as the new Frog.

Hint: If the person directly behind the Frog has already had a turn, let the next player in the circle be Mousie instead.

GAME 37—WHOSE FACE IS THIS?
(GUESSING-A-PERSON GAME)

This game involves guessing a person by touch rather than by sound.

> SONG—"Poor Lonesome Cowhand" (page 156).
> PROP—blindfold (optional).
> SPACE/FORMATION NEEDED—a seated or standing circle (or line) of players, with one player in the center.

Sing to the group:

> *I'm a poor, lonesome cowhand,*
> *I'm a poor, lonesome cowhand,*
> *I'm a poor, lonesome cowhand,*
> *A long way from home.*

Tell this little story to set the mood:

> There was once a poor cowhand who was all alone. It was night. There was no moon, no stars. The cowhand was stumbling along in the dark—and felt . . . a person's face! It was someone the cowhand knew! It was someone who could be a partner for the cowhand!

Ask, "Who would like to be the Cowhand?" Choose a volunteer and ask, "Would you like to wear a blindfold, or just keep your eyes closed?" Stand the Cowhand up in the center of the circle (or in front of the line). Sing the song, as above.

Say, "We're going to find you a partner. See if you can tell who it is." Walk the Cowhand to one of the others. Say, "Touch your partner's face very gently. Try to figure out who it is." While the cowhand is touching the Partner's face, hair, and shirt, sing,

> *I don't have a partner,*
> *I don't have a partner,*

I don't have a partner,
To ride the range with me.

Ask, "Who do you think it is?" After a guess or two, say, "Open your eyes and look!" Let the Partner be the new Cowhand, and begin again.

GUESSING A WORD

Many other kinds of guessing games work well with a song added. This kind of word-guessing game, however, *must* have a song. In this type of game, players choose a word with two or more syllables, then form one group for each syllable. Each group then sings a given song using their syllable as the only word of the song. The guesser then walks among the groups as they sing, trying to guess the word from its sung syllables.

For such a game to work, the players need to know what a syllable is, and they also need to know the chosen song well enough to sing it with any syllable. For such players, however, the game is easier than it sounds.

GAME 38—WHAT WILL WE EAT IN THE SUKKAH?
(WORD-GUESSING GAME)

SONG—"HaSukkah" (page 154).
SPACE/FORMATION NEEDED—enough room for everyone to sit or stand in two (or three or four) groups while one person walks among the others. Rows of desks can work fine.

Make sure the group is already familiar with the melody. Review the song with the words they know.

Say, "Do you remember what Jewish people do in a sukkah during the holiday of Sukkot? They eat their meals in it. We're going to think of a food from the fall harvest that we'd like to eat in a sukkah. Then someone will have to guess what it is. Who wants to be the guesser?"

Choose a guesser, and send her out of the room. With the group, decide on a harvest food, such as apples. Divide the players into two groups. One will sing "aa" and the other will sing "pull." Rehearse each group separately, then get both to sing simultaneously.

Call the guesser back into the room, and say, "We're going to sing the name of a food with two syllables. The far half of the group will sing one syllable; the near half will sing the other syllable. You have to guess what word those two syllables make. Ready?"

If the guesser hasn't guessed after several times through the song, you can have each group sing separately, in turn. Choose a new guesser and food, and repeat.

Variation—use a different song. To make a new game of this type, choose a different song that your group knows well (e.g., "Down Came a Lady," page 123). Then just choose a category of word that fits with the content of the song (e.g., the name of the person who "came down"). Now your groups will each sing one syllable of a person's name to the tune of "Down Came a Lady."

Variation—finding game. In this game of auditory discrimination, first whisper one syllable of the chosen word into the ear of each player (or pass out cards with one syllable written on each). Each player starts to sing the song with his assigned syllable and walks around the room seeking others singing the same syllable. When two players singing the same syllable find each other, they link arms. At the end, there will be one large group for each syllable in the word.

Alternatively, let each player seek out another who is singing a different syllable. Then the pair (in the case of a two-syllable word) can join together to form a "word." For three-syllable words, of course, each player must find two others.

THE BASIC HIDING GAME

In the basic hiding game, one person hides while everyone else seeks.

A confined space with only a few possible hiding places is an advantage for young children just learning this game. For older children, a shortage of hiding places speeds up the game; if they threaten to lose interest, add challenge with a handicap such as blindfolds or with a complicating variation.

Music can have two functions in the basic hiding game. A song (like the familiar chant of counting by fives) can mark how long the seekers wait while the hider hides. In addition, if the hider sings a solo response, the song can speed up the game by giving an auditory clue about where to look.

GAME 39—HOW'S THE HARVEST? (BASIC HIDING GAME)

SONG—"Arirang" (page 139).
SPACE/FORMATION NEEDED—a seated or standing group of players, with one or
    more hiding places.

Say, "This song is from Korea," and sing,

> *Arirang, Arirang, arariyo,*
> *Arirang Valley, how well you grow.*
> *In our village the harvest is good,*
> *All through the land there will be plenty of food.*

Say, "This is a hide and seek game. One of us will go to Arirang valley and look for food. The rest of us will find him. Who wants to be the first to hide?" Choose a player to be the first hider, and then say, "After we finish the song, we'll sing, 'How's the harvest?' You'll sing back, 'There's lots of food here!' Then we'll try to find you. Ready?"

Sing the song as the hider finds a hiding place (if the space is limited, you can have the group close their eyes while the hider hides). Sing "How's the harvest?" as a simple one- or two-note call. After the hider sings back, "There's lots of food here," say, "Let's find him!" After the group has found the hider, bring them back to the starting place by saying, "If you want to be the next one to hide, come back here!" Choose the next person.

Variation—move as a group. Have the group hold hands in a circle or line as the hider hides. Say, "Everyone needs to have food in Arirang valley. So we'll go looking for her together. Keep holding hands as we go looking!" This variation provides plenty of opportunity for honing skills of cooperation!

GAME 40—FINDING THE COWHANDS
(BASIC HIDING GAME, WITH CUMULATIVE HIDING)

SONG—"Poor Lonesome Cowhand" (page 156).
SPACE/FORMATION NEEDED—a seated or standing group of players, with one or
more large hiding places (big enough to hold nearly the whole group).

Say, "Can you imagine being a cowboy or cowgirl, out on the big lonesome prairie—and getting lost? Here's what you might say, if you were one of the many cowhands who spoke Spanish." Sing,

> *Soy un pobre vaquero,*
> *Soy un pobre vaquero,*
> *Soy un pobre vaquero,*
> *O no, O no, O no.*

(If desired, sing the English words, "I'm a poor, lonesome cowhand . . . ," or alternate the Spanish and English verses.)

Choose a first hider. Say, "This is a hide-and-seek game—but we're all lonesome cowhands. Rory will hide somewhere in these two rooms. That will be the cowhand camp. We'll keep singing while we look for him. If you find Rory, do you know what you do? You stop singing the song and hide with him. Don't tell anyone you found him, just join him in the camp."

At the end of the game, the entire group will be hiding with the first hider. Call them back by saying, "If you want to hide like Rory did, come back here!"

FINDING HIDDEN PEOPLE AND OBJECTS

There are thousands of games that involve finding a person or thing that has been hidden. Two samples are included here.

In the first game, one person seeks another. In the second, the classic "hot and cold" game is given a musical dimension.

GAME 41—WALKING MY LOST DOG
(ONE PERSON SEEKS ANOTHER)

SONG—"Wake Me, Shake Me" (page 127).
PROP—blindfold (optional)
SPACE/FORMATION NEEDED—a seated (or standing) group or circle.

Say, "Can you tell what I do every morning?" Sing,

> *Wake me, (bark, bark)*
> *Shake me, (bark, bark)*
> *Don't let me sleep too late (bark, bark).*
> *Gotta walk my dog in the morning*
> *Swing on the garden gate (bark, bark).*

Sing again, if necessary, until the group responds with "walk my dog." Say, "Can you join in on the 'bark, bark'?" Sing again to practice the response.

Choose a player to be the Owner who will "walk the dog." Ask, "Would you like to wear a blind-fold or just keep your eyes closed?" Choose another player as the Lost Dog, whose solo will be "bark, bark."

The blindfolded Owner tries to find the Lost Dog, listening for the solo "bark" by the Lost Dog as all sing the song. Both players must remain inside the circle. When the song has been sung three times (or twice, if desired), begin again by letting the Lost Dog become the new Owner and by choosing a new Lost Dog. If the Owner succeeds in touching the Lost Dog, of course, just finish the verse you are singing, then begin again in the same way.

Variation—other animals. Let the lost animal be a cat or bird, make machine noises (telephone rings, refrigerator hums), or even play a musical instrument.

If desired, have more than one pair of players in the center, each Owner seeking a different Lost Animal while all the Lost Animals make their noises at once during the appropriate part of the song. You might change the verse to "Gotta walk my pets in the morning," or, if you're using machine noises, "Gotta do my chores. . . ."

GAME 42—HOT AND COLD SINGING (FINDING AN OBJECT WITH MUSICAL CLUES)

SONG—"It's a Shame" (page 126).
PROP—a piece of paper or filecard: the "homework."
SPACE/FORMATION NEEDED—a seated (or standing) group or circle. A hallway or
    other place for the guesser to wait (optional).

Make sure the group knows the song. If necessary, use it for making verses (page 105) to give practice singing it.

Show the group the Homework (a distinctive piece of paper or colored file card). Say, "I know some of you have lost your homework one time or another. This is the Homework you've been looking for! Who wants to guess where we hide it?"

Choose one player to leave the room; choose another to hide the Homework in a place evident to the rest of the group. Call the guesser back into the room; say, "We'll sing. The louder we sing, the closer you are to the Homework. If we sing softly, that means you're going away from it. Are you ready?"

Lead the group in singing

> *It's a shame to lose your homework on a Sunday,*
> *It's a shame to lose your homework on a Sunday,*
> *When you got Monday, Tuesday, Wednesday, Thursday, Friday,*
> *Saturday,*
> *It's a shame to lose your homework on a Sunday.*

If the group has trouble giving good clues through singing louder or softer, you may have to use body movements to "conduct" the singing.

When the Homework is found, choose another guesser and another hider, and repeat. (Alternatively, let the guesser become the next hider.)

FINDING A SOUND

Since games in this special category use simultaneous sounds, they can be adapted easily for use with songs. An easy form of the game uses a song with two simultaneous melody parts, as in the example given here. In other forms, players sing the same melody but with one of two different syllables or sounds (e.g., half sing, "Arff, arff, arff," and the other half sing "Meow, meow, meow"). See also page 30, Variation—finding game.

GAME 43—FINDING YOUR PART
(FINDING A SOUND GAME)

SONG—"Atse Zetim Omdim" (page 146).
PROP—a piece of paper for each player with either the word "melody" or the word "ostinato" written on it; or else the words "La" or "Atse Zetim Omdim" (optional).
SPACE/FORMATION NEEDED—enough room for all to walk around.

Make sure that everyone knows the song and can sing either part independently. This may require using several other activities with this song first.

Assign each player to sing either the melody (the "la, la" part) or the ostinato (the "atse zetim omdim" part). Assign the parts by whispering into each player's ear, or by passing out appropriately labeled pieces of paper.

Say, "You each will sing the part I assigned to you. Walk around the room. When you find someone who is singing your same part, link elbows. Keep going until we have two big lines!"

LINE AND CIRCLE GAMES

Lines and circles are basic geometric shapes. They are also basic shapes for group activities. Preschoolers love to create spontaneous "parades," exploring the power of the line that in adult life becomes the procession or the picket line. Circles, on the other hand, echo the natural formation around a fire or other point of interest. Children love to create circles and to explore what circles can do.

Some children focus on the destructive power of these formations: a circle can be pulled down by one person; a line is subject to the "domino effect." Over the generations, traditional games have evolved to meet these fascinations halfway. If your students love pulling a circle down, try giving them structured chances to explore the dependency involved in a circle or line—whether through "all fall down" games, thread-the-needle games, or cooperative challenges like the "lap sit."

THE BASIC LINE-FORMING GAME

No game is more useful than the basic line-forming game. Use it to form a line anytime—with a sense of ritual and fun.

When I was in third grade, I remember lining up to leave the classroom. This procedure seemed to take 10 minutes and was accompanied by scoldings from our teacher, which had the effect of making us less cooperative the next time, making the process take longer and require further scoldings.

Whether you need a line for another game or to walk to another part of a building, why not use a game to form it? Once you have a line, you can let the leader curve around to the end, and you'll have a circle. If you need to escort children to individual locations, lead them in a line—then reverse the line-forming process to "drop off" children along the way.

GAME 44—MAKE A TRAIN
(BASIC LINE-FORMING GAME)

This game and the next one are identical but use different songs and different ways to hold on to the next person.

> SONG—"Train Is A-Coming" (page 155).
> SPACE/FORMATION NEEDED—a seated (or standing) group or circle, with room to
>   walk entirely around the group.

Walk around the group, singing,

> *Train is a-coming, oh, yeh,*
> *Train is a-coming, oh, yeh,*
> *Train is a-coming, train is a-coming,*
> *Train is a-coming, oh, yeh.*

Point to or touch a player, saying, "Do you want to join the train?" If the player says, "no," just choose another. If the player says, "yes," take his hand. Walk around the group together, singing again.

Repeat until all willing players have joined the line. If desired, take the completed "train" on a short expedition around the room.

Hints: With three- or four-year-olds, a second adult may be needed to help each new player join the end of the "train." Once the group is familiar with this game, however, you can speed up the line-forming process by choosing two or more children at once.

GAME 45—LEAVING CHEYENNE
(BASIC LINE-FORMING GAME, WITH SUNG NAMES)

> SONG—"Good-bye, Old Paint" (page 140), sung with these words:

> *Come on, big* **Mark** [sing the name of the chosen child]*,*
> *I've saddled old Fan.*
> *Good-bye, old Paint, I'm leaving Cheyenne.*

Play as "Make a Train," but sing the name of each chosen child. If desired, have each child imitate the holding of reins by grabbing the belt or shirttail of the person ahead.

To speed up the process, name several players in each verse:

> ***Lisa, Bob, and Leora****,*
> *I've saddled old Fan . . .*

GAME 46—THE GINGER GAME
(LINE-FORMING GAME, WITH OBJECT PASSING)

This game forms lines of four players and adds the passing of an object down the line.

> SONG—"So He Planted Ginger" (page 132).
> PROP—a soft object, such as a knotted handkerchief, bean bag, or stuffed animal.
> SPACE/FORMATION NEEDED—a seated (or standing) group or circle, with room to walk entirely around the group.

Before starting, give the prop to a seated player, saying, "You are the River. We'll need you later." Now say to the group, "I am the Planter. I planted some ginger, and it grew so quickly, I didn't know how to keep it short." Walk around the group, singing,

> *So I planted ginger, ginger grows so quickly.*
> *So I got a Nanny Goat to graze on the ginger.*

Stop and choose a player to be the Nanny Goat. Then say, "You're the Nanny Goat. Grab on behind me! When I say 'Nanny will not graze on ginger,' let me see how you stand when you don't want to help me. Good!" Continue singing:

> *Nanny will not graze on ginger,*
> *Ginger grows so quickly.*

Say, "Oh, no! How will I get the Nanny to help me. I know!" Begin to walk, with the Nanny following behind you. Sing,

> *So I got a magpie, to stay and talk to Nanny.*
> *So I got a magpie, to stay and talk to Nanny.*

Choose another player to be Magpie, who joins the line behind Nanny. Encourage each player to find a defiant way to stand as the appropriate line is sung:

> *Magpie will not talk to Nanny,*
> *Nanny will not graze on ginger,*
> *Ginger grows so quickly.*

If desired, find a dejected way to stand during the final line of the song.

Repeat the process as you add a Beech Tree to the line:

> *So I went to Beech Tree, to give a nut to Magpie.*
> *So I went to Beech Tree, to give a nut to Magpie.*
> *Beech Tree won't give nut to Magpie,*
> *Magpie will not talk to Nanny,*
> *Nanny will not graze on ginger,*
> *Ginger grows so quickly.*

At last, choose the River (the one holding the prop) to join the line:

> *So I went to River, to give a drink to Beech Tree.*
> *So I went to River, to give a drink to Beech Tree.*

At these words, the River gives the prop to Beech Tree:

River gave a drink to Beech Tree,

(If you gesture to River and Beech Tree as you sing, the players will probably catch on. Repeat the line if they miss it the first time.) Continue passing the prop up the line as you sing each appropriate line:

Beech Tree gave a nut to Magpie,
Magpie sat and talked to Nanny,
Nanny went and grazed on ginger,
Ginger grows so quickly!

At the last line, you get the prop (as Planter) and hold it up triumphantly. All sit down and begin again with a new River and a new Planter.

Variations—multiple lines. For a faster game, have two or more props and a matching number of Planters choosing simultaneously. To increase the number of lines quickly, have each player in the first line become a Planter in the second.

Variation—passing the prop without hands. For an entertaining, cooperative, physical challenge, the prop must be passed without using hands. Older children may even be able to use firm objects like beach balls or tennis balls.

SINGLE LINE GAMES

Once you have formed a line with one game, you can enjoy the line with another. In the following games, children can explore the properties of lines: they can spiral, intersect themselves, twist themselves up, and provide a formation for follow-the-leader. These games are a meeting between music and geometry!

GAME 47—WINDING THE OLIVE TREE
(SPIRAL LINE GAME)

SONG—"Atse Zetim Omdim" (page 146).
SPACE/FORMATION NEEDED—a line of players, with enough room to form the line into an approximate circle.

Form a line with all the players holding hands and facing in the same direction, with you at one end (you can use games 44 or 45 to form the line). Say to the player at the other end, "You are the Olive Tree! You have an important job: to stand still. Don't turn around! Everyone else, when I touch you on the shoulder, you stand still, too."

Walk forward, leading the line around the stationary Olive Tree (in the natural direction, with all players facing in), singing,

Olive trees are standing,
Olive trees are standing (repeat as needed).

If desired, sing part or all of the time in Hebrew:

Atse zetim omdim,
Atse zetim omdim.

You can also sing the second melody part ("la, la . . ."), if you wish.

Lead the line toward the person standing next to the Olive Tree so you can tap her on the shoulder and make her stop. Each time you lead the line around the tree, tap the next player away from the Olive Tree. Your goal is to stop each of the players after they take their place in the spiral, but before they become too crowded and lose their balance. The end result after you have tapped all the players is a tightly formed spiral with all the players standing still, facing inside toward the Olive Tree.

When all are stopped, ask the Olive Tree, "Would you like us to unwind or fall down?" If the answer is "fall down," say, "Careful! Let's not let anyone get hurt. Fall down slowly!" Lead the spiral in a controlled "fall." To unwind, on the other hand, resume the song but lead the line in the opposite direction, encouraging the players to begin walking when the person next to them moves away, until you have a straight line again.

Variation–unwinding from the inside. A quicker but more demanding way to unwind begins with the center player. Disengage yourself from the spiral, then say, "We can do a trick, but you have to keep holding hands. Raise your hands up, but don't let go of the people next to you. Ready? Hold your hands up high." Reach in and take the available hand of the Olive Tree, and lead him under the most convenient pairs of joined hands, directly to the outside of the spiral. As the line follows your lead, the spiral straightens out from the inside.

GAME 48—BESSIE DOWN
(THREAD-THE-NEEDLE LINE GAME)

This game and the next one involve "threading the needle," in which the end of the line passes, in turn, through each pair of joined hands. In this game, the players return to their original positions after each pass; in the next, each pass of the line leaves an additional player with crossed arms.

SONG—"Hill and Gully Rider" (page 150).
SPACE/FORMATION NEEDED—a line of players, with enough room to walk behind and in front of the line.

Form a line with all the players holding hands and facing in the same direction, with you at one end. (You can use games 44 or 45 to form the line.) Stretch the line out straight, then stop. Say, "In Jamaica, they love to 'bessie down.' That means to crouch down and keep walking!"

You have one free hand and one hand joined with the second player in line. Hold up your joined hands, bend down enough to walk forward under the arch, and return to your starting position, singing,

Hill and gully rider, hill and gully.
Hill and gully rider, hill and gully.
And a bend down, low down, hill and gully.
And a low down, bessie down, hill and gully.
And you better mind you stumble down, hill and gully.

You will need to allow your loosely held hand-grip to rotate back to a relaxed position.

Without pause, walk under an arch made by the hands of the second and third players in line, pulling the second player under the arch, too. (If they don't raise their joined hands, touch the appropriate hands and say, "Lift your hands as high as you can. We're coming through!") Again, the line returns momentarily to the starting position.

Repeat, pulling the second and third players under an arch made by the third and fourth players hands. Continue, leading players under each arch in turn. Repeat the song as needed.

Variation—going over the hands. For a more challenging game, lower each pair of joined hands and lead the line in stepping over them. If the hands are held close to the ground, even young children will be able to join in. For more challenge, hold the hands higher. Traditionally, Jamaican players hold their joined hands so high that players have to jump over them!

GAME 49—TANGLE
(THREAD-THE-NEEDLE LINE GAME WITH ARM-CROSSING)

In this game, the players "thread the needle," but do not go all the way under their own hands. As a result, they end up turned backwards, with their own hands crossed in front of them.

SONG—"Che Che Ku Le" (page 138).
SPACE/FORMATION NEEDED—a line of players perpendicular to a wall, with enough room to walk behind and in front of the line.

Form a line with you at one end and with all the players holding hands and facing in the same direction. (You can use games 44 or 45 to form the line.) Say to the last player in line, "You have an important job. You have to put your free hand on the wall, and leave it there!" Position the line so that the last player can lean one hand on it, with the line roughly perpendicular to the wall.

Say, "In this game, you keep holding hands—even if it means you end up tangled up!" Lead the line between the last player and the wall, under the player's arm, singing,

> *Che che ku le* (group echoes each line)
> *Che che kufi sa*
> *Kofi sa langa*
> *Ka ta chi langa*
> *Kum a de de.*

Repeat the song as needed. As the line finishes going under the last player's arm, say to the last player, "Don't turn under your own arm—let yourself get tangled." At this point, the line should return to its original position—except that the last player is now "tangled": facing the opposite direction, with his own arms crossed in front of his chest.

Repeat, leading the line under the next pair of joined hands (between the last player and the next-to-last). Now two players will be tangled.

Repeat, leading the "untangled" portion of the line through one arch after another, until you are the only player who is not "tangled."

Variation—shaking out the tangles. You may add this "epilogue" to the game. At the end, turn around, reaching your free hand under your joined hand, as though you were being "tangled," too. Slowly guide your end of the line back toward the player who's touching the wall (walk backwards). Grab the hand that's touching the wall; now you have a circle in which all are facing out with their own arms crossed over their chests.

Say, "Do you want to shake the tangles out?" The group should respond, "Yes!" Sing the song again, jumping up and down. Keep jumping more energetically until the circle disintegrates. You have jumped the tangles out!

GAME 50—YOU DO IT, TOO
(FOLLOW-THE-LEADER LINE GAME)

SONG—"Round the Corner" (page 137).
SPACE/FORMATION NEEDED—a line of players, with enough room for the line to
"parade" around.

Form a line with you at one end and with all the players facing your back. Say, "I'm the leader. Do what I do!" Lead the line, singing as you walk,

> Oh, what I do, you do it, too,
> Round the corner, Sally.
> But don't you stop until I do,
> Round the corner, Sally.

At the final word, stop suddenly in a dramatic position (e.g., with your arms stretched over your head). If necessary, say, "Everyone do what I'm doing!" If desired, repeat several times with you as the leader, assuming a different dramatic position each time.

When the group can follow you easily, say to the person behind you in line, "Samantha [use the player's name], it's your turn to be the leader. At the end, find your own way to freeze." Go to the end of the line. After Samantha's turn, she goes to the end of the line, and the next in line becomes the leader. Repeat until each player has had a turn to lead.

Variation—multiple lines. Once the group can do the game easily, form multiple lines (you might use the "multiple line" variation of the Ginger Game—game 46—to do so). Each line of four will be led by a different player; after only four repetitions, each player will have had a turn to lead.

FORMING A CIRCLE

The easiest way to form a circle starts with a line. The leader of the line can walk toward the line's other end, then grab the last player's hand. Bingo!

The next game forms a circle by starting with two players holding hands, then adding players to the circle one at a time.

GAME 51—CIRCLE TWO IN WELDON
(FORM-A-CIRCLE GAME)

SONG—"Weldon" (page 129).
SPACE/FORMATION NEEDED—a seated (or standing) group, with room to form a
circle of all the players.

Say, "Raise your hand if you would like to be my partner!" Choose a volunteer; join both hands with the volunteer; and spin around in a circle of two, singing,

Circle two in Weldon, I think I heard them say,
Circle two in Weldon, I think I heard them say.
Rally, rally, rally, I think I heard them say,
Rally, rally, rally, I think I heard them say.

Say, "Raise your hand if you want to join the circle next!" Add a new player to the circle, singing,

Circle three in Weldon, I think I heard them say,
Circle three in Weldon, I think I heard them say.
Rally, rally, rally, I think I heard them say,
Rally, rally, rally, I think I heard them say.

Repeat until all have joined the circle.

Variation—add two or more players at once. Instead of adding one player, add two or more each time. If you add three players each time, you give practice counting by threes. Start with three (for example), and then "Circle six," "Circle nine," until all the children have joined the circle.

Variation—each player chooses the next. Instead of choosing each new player yourself, have the most recent player to join the circle choose the next to join.

SINGLE CIRCLE GAMES

Like lines, circles are basic geometric shapes whose properties children love to explore. If children pull down others in the circle, you may have to limit any behavior that threatens the safety of others. But be sure to give them enough opportunities to play "falling down" games. If necessary, organize additional sessions just for those who love this form of group interaction.

The following simple games highlight properties of a circle: the interdependence of its members, and its abilities to spin, to expand and contract, and to turn itself inside-out.

GAME 52—BELIEVE I'M FALLING DOWN (FALLING CIRCLE GAME)

SONG—"Old Joe Clark" (page 141).
SPACE/FORMATION NEEDED—a standing circle of players, with hands joined.

Say, "When you hear the word, 'down,' we're going to fall down—carefully. Are you ready?" Sing as all stand still,

Walk around, Old Joe Clark,
Goodbye, Betty Brown;
Walk around, Old Joe Clark,
Believe I'm falling down.

At the last word, "fall" down slowly. Say, "Do you want to play it again?" If necessary, practice again with a stationary circle. If the players insist on falling down violently, present slow falling as a challenge: "You did a great job of crashing down. But it's much harder to fall down slowly. I don't know if you're able to do it. Want to try?"

When the group is ready for more challenge, say, "This time, let's walk around the circle." Repeat as desired!

GAME 53—FASTER AND FASTER
(SPINNING CIRCLE GAME)

SONG—"Windy Weather" (page 136).
SPACE/FORMATION NEEDED—a standing circle of players, with hands joined.

Say, "Would you like to make our circle go around fast?" If some players seem fearful, say, "You can watch first, if you want."

To the remaining players, say, "Watch me to know how fast to go. We'll start out slow." Guide the circle around, singing,

> Windy weather,
> Frosty weather,
> When the wind blows,
> We all go together.

Gradually increase the speed. To end, let go hands and stop singing. In the traditional form of this game from Dublin, everyone ends up on the floor in a heap.

GAME 54—THE HUM HUDDLE
(SINGLE CIRCLE GAME)

SONG—"Windy Weather" (page 136).
SPACE/FORMATION NEEDED—a standing circle of players, with hands joined, and
with space behind all the players.

Say, "Here's a new game. Watch me to know what to do." As you sing the first line, take small steps backwards (the others should imitate you, causing the circle to expand):

> Windy weather,

As you sing the second line, step forward, making the circle smaller:

> Frosty weather,

During the next two lines, release hands and step backwards, greatly expanding the circle:

> When the wind blows,
> We all go together.

Immediately after the word "together," hum the last note of the song, and make small shuffling steps toward the center. When you meet in the center, keep humming until you run out of breath. Join hands and begin again. This activity is great practice for learning to sing the same pitch as everyone else.

GAME 55—THE GREAT TURN-AROUND
(SINGLE CIRCLE GAME)

SONG–"Down Came a Lady" (page 123).

Start the circle moving as you sing, using the name of the player next to you:

> *Down came a possum,*
> *Down came a hound,*
> *Down came **Marsha**,*
> *And she was turned around.*

Say to Marsha, "Guess what you do! You let go of hands and turn around. Now grab hands again." Marsha has now rejoined hands in the circle, but she's facing out—while all the others still face in.

Repeat with the player next to Marsha, singing his name.

When all are facing out (including you!), say, "Keep holding hands!" Let go of the player on one side of you. Walk forward and pull the circle into a line, singing,

> *Down came a possum,*
> *Down came a hound,*
> *Down came **everyone**,*
> *And we were turned around.*

Guide the line until you can rejoin hands with the last player. Now you have a circle again—with everyone facing in!

Variation—two or more at a time. Once the group can play this game easily, speed the process by singing two or more names in each verse:

> *Down came **Timmy** and **Sami**,*
> *Down came a hound,*
> *Down came **Susan** and **Andy**,*
> *And they were turned around.*

Mathematical concept. This game can be thought of as illustrating an abstract mathematical concept, the distributive property of operations. In this game, the "operation" is "turning someone around." First we apply this operation to each player individually; then we apply it to the whole circle at once. The net result is the same. (Actually, it's almost the same. We have in fact reversed the order of the circle, so this operation yields a different result when performed on the whole than when performed on each part individually. If, on the other hand, we multiply by two a series of numbers to be added, we would get the same result as if we had added them first and then multiplied the whole by two.)

GAME 56—SIT IN OUR LAPS (SINGLE CIRCLE GAME)

SONG—"Dance a Baby Diddy" (page 151).
SPACE/FORMATION NEEDED—a standing circle of ten or more players, with hands on the waist of the person ahead.

March around the circle, singing,

Dance a baby diddy,
What can we do wid'e?
Sit on my lap, give it some pap,
And dance a baby diddy.

Dancey, baby, dancey,
How it shall gallop and prancey,
Sit on my knee, gently on me,
And dancey, baby, dancey.

As you march, adjust the circle so that the gap between players is equal to about one-half arm's length.

Say, "Stop where you are. If we win this game, we all win! All at once, sit in the lap of the player behind you. If we do it at the same time, we might win!"

If all fall, gravity wins. A skilled group can even walk in the seated position. Don't forget to keep singing as you waddle!

GAME 57—THE TRAIN LEAVES THE ROUNDHOUSE (FORM-A-LINE-FROM-A-CIRCLE GAME)

SONG—"Train Is A-Coming" (page 155).
SPACE/FORMATION NEEDED—a standing circle of players, with hands joined.

For this game, you should not be part of the circle. From outside the circle, say, "You are the roundhouse. I am the train. Hold your joined hands up high. The train is coming through the roundhouse!" Walk in and out of the arches formed by the raised hands, singing,

Train is a-coming, oh, yeh,
Train is a-coming, oh, yeh,
Train is a-coming, train is a-coming,
Train is a-coming, oh, yeh.

At the last word, stop. Face the last arch you passed under. Say to the two players forming it, "You are now part of the train. Get on board!" Say to the others, "Oops! The roundhouse just got smaller. Fix the hole in it!"

Take hands in a line of three. Lead the line in and out of the arches, singing, as before.

Each time the verse ends, two more players join the train, and the ever-smaller circle reconnects. When all are part of the train, you can "take a trip" around the room.

Variation—multiple lines. To make the game go faster, have more than one leader begin. At the end, all the trains can hook up into one big train or proceed to separate areas as small groups—to snack tables, for example.

RHYTHM GAMES

This chapter gives only a small sample of the thousands of singing games that are based on maintaining a rhythmic activity. Children have originated and adapted a huge variety of rhythm games, including ball-bouncing games, jump-rope games, and clapping games. The simple games that follow emphasize teaching children to keep a steady beat. The pounding and passing games, in particular, start with the easiest possible activity and progress step by step to the level of a traditional stone-passing game.

THE BASIC POUNDING GAME

In many parts of the world, children play complex games that involve pounding stones (or other objects) on the ground, then passing them to other players.

The next activities reduce the traditional games to their simplest possible form: pounding an object over and over on the ground, followed by passing it to the next player.

GAME 58—SUKKAH POUNDING
(BASIC POUNDING GAME)

SONG—"HaSukkah" (page 154).
PROP—a plastic hammer or other object suitable for pounding on the floor.
SPACE/FORMATION NEEDED—a seated group, circle, or line. Children will discover
   that it's easiest if they sit cross-legged.

Hold up the plastic hammer, and say, "I'm going to help build a sukkah. That's the special little booth—like a house—that Jewish people build for the holiday called Sukkot." Pound the hammer on the floor in front of you as you sing,

> *HaSukkah, mah yafah,*
> *Umah tov lashevet bah,*
> *HaSukkah, mah yafah,*
> *Umah tov lashevet bah.*

After the song, say, "Who would like to help build a sukkah, like I just did?" Pass the hammer to a volunteer, and begin the song again.

GAME 59—WASHING THE HANDKERCHIEF
(BASIC POUNDING GAME)

SONG—"Kitty Kasket" (page 134).
PROP—a bean bag, small plastic ball, or other object suitable for pounding on the
   floor. (For more advanced groups, you may want one bean bag for each
   player.)
SPACE/FORMATION NEEDED—a seated group, circle, or line.

Hold up the bean bag, and say, "My handkerchief got muddy, but I can use this Rock to wash it in the river." Pound the Rock on the floor in front of you as you sing,

> *Kitty, kitty kasket,*
> *Green and yellow basket,*
> *Lost my handkerchief yesterday,*
> *It's all full of mud, so I tossed it away.*

At the last word, "away," pound the Rock once on the floor in front of the player next to you in the circle—then leave it there. Say to that player, "Now you do what I did. Ready?"

Repeat until each player in the circle has had a turn.

Variation—multiple rocks. Once players are skilled using one Rock, introduce a second one half-way across the circle (or down the line). Another day, try using three, four, or more. The ultimate challenge is to have as many Rocks as players!

STONE-PASSING GAMES

In the games below, players pass stones or other objects around the circle. Once they are adept at the basic forms of these games, you can introduce one of the following variations (based on actual games from various cultures).

Variation—multiple stones. All the games can be played with two or more stones in use at once. If you omit the circle changes in *Pass the Oatmeal* and *Hot Cabbage,* all the games can even be played with one stone for each player.

Variation—sing faster. Gradually increase the tempo of the song until it's too fast to continue.

Variation—forfeits. If someone misses a hand-off, have that person pay a "forfeit"—such as performing a silly action or doing a necessary task (e.g., erasing part of the blackboard). To keep forfeits from feeling punitive, keep them from being too unpleasant, or limit them to one per player. You can also substitute forfeits for circle changes in *Pass the Oatmeal* and *Hot Cabbage,* below.

Variation—stop and change directions. The Leader can call out, "Get ready to STOP!" At the word, "Stop," each player with a stone, instead of passing it, hits it on the ground. The song begins again, but the players pass the stone(s) in the other direction. Let the role of Leader be taken by different players—even by the one who missed or ended up with the stone at the end of the song.

Variation—pass to anyone. Players of a Haitian game can pass, not just to the adjacent player, but to anyone in the circle. If, when using multiple stones, anyone ends up with a pile of too many stones to pass, that player is declared "gage" ("it"), and the game begins again.

Note on teaching—imaginary stones. When teaching any of the following games, it may help your group to rehearse the song first with *imaginary* balls, stones, etc., so that the group gets a feel for when to pound.

GAME 60—PASS THE OATMEAL
(STONE-PASSING GAME, WITH SECOND CIRCLE)

This game and the next adapt a traditional elimination game (like "Wonder Ball") to send players to a second circle.

> SONG–"Wake Me, Shake Me" (page 127).
> PROP–a bean bag, plastic ball, or other object suitable for pounding on the floor.
> SPACE/FORMATION NEEDED–a seated circle, with room for a second circle of
> equal size.

Hold up the plastic ball, and say, "This is my oatmeal. I love to get up in time to eat my oatmeal in the morning! I'll pass it all around the circle." Pound the ball on the floor in front of you once, then pass it on to the next player as you sing,

x   x

Wake me, shake me . . .

You pound the ball at the first "(x)," then pass it at the second "(x)." Say to the player who just received the ball, "You do what I did: pound it first, then pass it to Jaimie." The ball continues around the circle as all sing:

x   x

. . . Don't let me sleep too late.

x   x

I gotta eat my oatmeal in the morning,

x   x

Gotta swing on the garden gate.

At the word, "gate," say to the player who just received the ball, "You get to go to the Kitchen! You start another circle over there." Begin the game again, starting with the next player in line. When you reach the word "gate" again, send another player to the Kitchen. Repeat until all players have joined the second circle.

Hints—entertaining the second circle. To keep the players in the second circle interested, encourage them to sing the song. If the players in the first circle gain the knack of when to pass the Oatmeal, you can join the second circle. Whichever circle you're in, you can model different movements for the Kitchen players to do in rhythm with the ball passing: clap hands, tap head, or pat knees or floor.

Variation—passing in the second circle. If the group is large, you can reduce the wait in the second circle by introducing a ball to pass around in that circle. For an endless game, start with two circles, and let the player "eliminated" from each circle change to the other circle.

GAME 61—HOT CABBAGE
(STONE-PASSING GAME, WITH SECOND CIRCLE)

This game is identical to the previous one, except that players in the second circle choose when to sing the "fatal" word, "cabbage."

> SONG—"Old Mr. Rabbit" (page 153).
> PROP—a bean bag, plastic ball, or other object suitable for passing around the circle.
> SPACE/FORMATION NEEDED—a seated circle, with room for a second circle of
>   equal size.

Hold up the plastic ball, and say, "This is my vegetable. When the song says, 'cabbage,' it turns into a cabbage and the farmer catches me with it. We'll pass it around until the word 'cabbage.' Ready?"

Start passing the ball around the circle, singing,

Old Mister Rabbit,
You got a mighty habit,
Of jumping in my garden
And eating all my tomatoes.

Old Mister Rabbit,
You got a mighty habit,
Of jumping in my garden
And eating all my cabbage.

Send the player who ends up with the ball on "cabbage" to start a second circle, the Singer's Circle. Join that player in the Singer's Circle; together, choose a list of up to four vegetables—such as "broccoli, scallions, cabbage"—always ending with "cabbage." As the players in the first circle pass the ball, sing the verse three times, ending with "broccoli" the first time, "scallions" the second time, and "cabbage" the third. This way, the players in the first circle do not know when to expect the word "cabbage."

Repeat until all but two players have joined the Singer's Circle.

GAME 62—TRIKI
(STONE-PASSING GAME)

This game adds a rhythmic variation and may be played with multiple stones.

> SONG—"Al Citron" (page 124).
> PROP—a bean bag, plastic ball, or other object suitable for pounding on the floor.
> (You may want one for each player.)
> SPACE/FORMATION NEEDED—a seated circle.

Hold up the bean bag, and say, "The children in Mexico love games in which they pass stones around the circle." Pass the Stone around the circle as you sing,

x   x   x   x   x
Al cit-ron de un fan-dan-go sango, san-go, saba-ré,

x   x   x   x   x
Saba-ré de la ran-de-la con su tri-ki tri-ki tron.

To pass the Stone around the circle, strike the Stone on the ground in front of the player next to you, at the first "(x)." Each player, in turn, receives the Stone at one "(x)," and passes it on at the next "(x)."

If desired, add more Stones until everyone has one. Each player must then grab a new Stone between the "(x)'s" and pass it on at the next "(x)."

Variation—adding the "Triki" part. When the players are comfortable with the simple version above, sing the song yourself, pretending to pound and pass the Stone on. At the final three words of the song, actually tap the Stone three times:

x   x   x
. . . con su tri-ki tri-ki tron.

As you tap, you will perform a different movement with each of the three taps: 1) tap the Stone in front of the next player, but keep it in your hand; 2) tap it in front of the player on your other side; and 3) tap it in front of the next player and leave it there.

Say, "Did you hear the tricky part?" Demonstrate the end again, if necessary. Say, "Try clapping the end of the song with the tricky part." When the group can clap the new rhythm well, pass the

Stone as you sing. When you are convinced that each player understands the new "fake-fake-pass" sequence at the end, introduce more and more Stones until each player has one. Getting the end right is exhilarating!

OTHER RHYTHM GAMES

The two games below each introduce a genre of rhythm games: clapping games and jump-rope games. Each genre could certainly merit its own chapter. Once these examples get you started, learn others from teachers or from children, or invent them yourself.

GAME 63—PASS A CLAP
(CLAPPING GAME)

SONG—"Round the Corner" (page 137).
SPACE/FORMATION NEEDED—a seated or standing circle (or line) of players.

Sing the song to the group:

> *Oh, around the corner we will go,*
> *Round the corner, Sally.*
> *Oh, around the corner we will go,*
> *Round the corner, Sally.*

Say, "Can you clap this with me?" Sing the song again, clapping along.

Say, "Sometimes, on sailing ships, the orders are passed from the captain to the bosun (the officer who repeats what the captain says) to the sailors. Let's pass one way of clapping, along the line. You keep clapping while I do something different." Clap over your head, as all clap normally and sing the song again.

Say, "This time, Dora [name the child next to you] will do what I did. Everyone else, clap normally." Join the group in normal clapping as Dora claps with her hands over her head, and all sing the song again.

Say, "Now the next person claps the new way. Keep passing it along!"

Variation—multiple claps. After the group understands how to pass a clap along the line, add a second new way of clapping before the first one has passed to the end of the line. Now, while the fourth or fifth player is clapping over her head, you will be clapping on the floor in front of you. Eventually, you may be able to pass along a new way of clapping with each repetition of the song.

GAME 64—CHARLIE OVER THE JUMP ROPE
(STATIONARY-ROPE JUMP-ROPE GAME)

SONG—"Charlie over the Ocean" (page 133).
SPACE/FORMATION NEEDED—two children holding the ends of a jump rope, and
        one player ready to jump, with the remainder of the players in a group (or line)
        seated (or standing) nearby.
PROP—six feet or more of rope; jump-rope handles are not required.

As the first jumper, show the rope-holders how high to hold the rope for you (even one inch off the floor will do!). Say, "Hold the rope this high off the floor. I'm going to jump over it." Jump back and forth across the stationary rope as you sing:

Charlie, over the ocean, (the group echoes each line)
Charlie, over the sea,
Charlie caught a blackbird,
Can't catch me.

If the group does not know the song, instruct them to echo each line.

After your turn, choose one of the rope-holders to be the next jumper, and choose another player to become a rope-holder. Repeat.

Each player becomes a rope-holder, then the jumper, instructing the holders how high to hold the rope. The jumper then rejoins the group (at the end of the line, if the group's in line).

PLAY-PARTY GAMES

Play-party games—which are based on square dances, but without instrumental music or a caller—are by far the most complex games in this collection. Drawing on skills from partner-choosing games and circle games, they range from slight elaborations on the circle games to highly challenging sequences of coordinated movements.

Four of the songs in this collection have been part of the authentic play-party tradition. In addition to some of the traditional games used with those songs, this chapter includes a few simplified versions of them—just enough to allow the gradual introduction of new figures.

Please note that the spoken instructions are only for the purposes of teaching the games. Once they've been learned, it's only necessary to sing the words of the songs.

ABOUT THE TWO ROLES

Most play-party games involve two distinct roles, one traditionally enacted by males, the other by females. Many contemporary game-leaders are quite comfortable calling the roles "boys" and "girls" or "men" and "women."

Two difficulties sometimes interfere with the use of these roles. First, children of certain ages often resist physical contact with the opposite sex, and they are doubly resistant to instructions that explicitly mention contact between the sexes, such as "boys promenade the girls." Second, some adults (including me) often prefer that the game roles be neutral, rather than reinforcing sex-role stereotypes.

As a result, some leaders avoid teaching these games to children at the "resistant" ages. Others teach them only to same-sex groupings. Still others teach them anyway, declaring to their students, "Outside, you can play by whatever rules you want to. In here, you have to treat all people the same. 'Cooties' are neutralized while you're in here." Each leader will have to make a judgement, based on the players, the setting, and the leader's values.

Some of the difficulties inherent in the "male and female" roles can be partially surmounted by changing the names of the roles. Some leaders refer to "number 1's and number 2's," others prefer "A's and B's." To me, these names (though quite neutral) suffer from being hard to remember: I can't readily associate "number 2" with promenading on the side of my partner that's closer to the center of the circle.

Therefore, I prefer other names for the roles. As arbitrary as they are, they still give me something to imagine that's more vivid in my mind than numbered dancers. Since the "woman's" role involves promenading outside, I sometimes call the two roles "in's and out's." Other times, I use arbitrary but vivid terms that I hope will have positive associations for the players: "lions and dragons," "racers and stunt-drivers," "unicorns and ponies," or even "Lakers and Celtics" (or two other sports teams).

Most of the following games involve partner changes. Please note that they can be played until players have returned to their original partners. If, on the other hand, you stop at any other point, players will have new partners for the next game. In addition, if you are using neutral roles, you may want players to switch roles with their partners before beginning the next game. Switching roles adds confusion, however, so you'll need to balance the benefits of comfort with one role against the benefits of experience with both.

CIRCLES OF PARTNERS

The section Games for Choosing (above) presents games that help players learn to choose and change partners. Line and Circle Games, on the other hand, give ways to help players form circles. When both skills have been mastered and players are ready for a new challenge, you can combine them in the games that follow.

The first game involves choosing partners in a circle. In the second game, the figures performed by individuals in the first game are now performed by couples. In the third game, the only additional figures (circle right and left, go into the center and back) should be familiar from other circle games.

All three games below reinforce the square-dance conventions of circling left (when circling in only one direction), and of progressing to the right (as when the lead couple dances first with the couple on their right, then with the next couple beyond them, and so on to the right around the circle of couples).

GAME 65—TWO IN THE MIDDLE
(CHOOSING PARTNERS IN THE CIRCLE)

SONG—"Hold My Mule" (page 143).
SPACE/FORMATION NEEDED—a standing circle of players, with hands joined and with one player in the center.

As the player in the center, say, "Now I find a partner while we sing!" Lead the group in singing,

> *Choose your partner and come dance Josey,*
> *Choose your partner and come dance Josey,*
> *Choose your partner and come dance Josey,*
> *Hello, Susan Brown-le-o.*

You are now in the center with a partner. Say, "We join hands with our partner, and we can 'dance Josey' any way we want to." Sing, as you dance with your partner in any way you choose (while the outer circle stands still and sings),

Two in the middle and can't dance Josey,
Two in the middle and can't dance Josey,
Two in the middle and can't dance Josey,
Hello, Susan Brown-ie-o.

Circle left in the center, as you say, "Now we make our little circle just walk around," and sing

Circle left and can't dance Josey . . .

Say, "Each of us in the center finds our own partner," and sing the first verse again as you both get partners. When there are two couples in the center, say, "We each join hands with the partner we just chose. The two partners have to find some way to 'dance Josey.'" Sing as they do,

Four in the middle and can't dance Josey . . .

Next, repeat the "circle left" verse, while all four make a single circle in the center.

Repeat the entire set of three verses by having each of the four center players find a partner. You'll have "eight in the middle," then "16 in the middle," etc. When you run out of players in the circle, just have everyone find a partner from somewhere. End with "circle left," and you'll have a circle of partners, ready for another play-party game. By the way, this gives great experience of the mathematical concept of the "powers of two."

GAME 66—MOVE IT ROUND
(PAIRS OF COUPLES DANCE IN THE RING)

SONG—"Stewball" (page 144).
SPACE/FORMATION NEEDED—a standing circle of partners (each player faces in, standing next to a player identified as his partner).

Take your partner into the center of the circle, and say, "We're the first Lead Couple. When everyone sings, 'You find you a new one,' we join hands with the next couple, and bring them into the center of the circle." Sing this part of the verse (the second half) as you bring the couple that was originally on your right into the ring:

And you find you (uh-huh)
A new one (uh-huh)
And you move like (uh-huh)
Anything (anything).

Say, "Now the four of us circle around together." Sing the refrain twice as your circle of four walks around to the left in the center of the ring:

Make a circle, and move it round, round, round,
Make a circle, and move it round.
Make a circle, and move it round, round, round,
Make a circle, and move it round.

Take your partner and rejoin the outer circle, saying, "We get out of the center now," and sing the first part of the verse,

Oh, you leave that (uh-huh)
Old couple (uh-huh)
In the center (uh-huh)
Of the ring (of the ring),

Say to the couple remaining in the center, "You're the new Lead Couple. Get the next couple in the circle, join hands with them, and bring them into the center of the circle." Sing the second half of the verse again, as the second couple brings the third couple into the ring,

And you find you (uh-huh)
A new one (uh-huh)
And you move like (uh-huh)
Anything (anything).

Repeat the refrain, with these two couples making a circle of four together and walking it around to the left. Sing the entire verse as the current Lead Couple leaves the center, and the remaining couple brings yet another couple into the center. Continue until each couple has had a turn to be the Lead Couple.

Variation—forming a Sicilian Circle. After the Lead Couple circles with the next couple, have them keep their hands joined and return to the big circle as a group of four. The next Lead Couple will then be the couple who was originally third. In this way, only half the couples get to be Lead Couples. At the end of the game, however, you will have the formation known as a Sicilian circle (a large circle made of small circles of two couples each). This formation is needed for Game 77—Euchre Ring.

GAME 67—ROUND THE CIRCLE
(PARTNER CHANGE AROUND THE RING)

This game introduces the concept of moving from partner to partner around the ring. This concept is essential to the games that follow. When teaching it, you may wish to introduce some of the "role terms" described above in the section, The Two Roles. If so, the "in's" (traditionally, "men") are the ones who progress from partner to partner counter-clockwise around the circle (to their right when facing the center), and the "out's" (traditionally, "women") progress clockwise (to the left).

SONG—"Round the Corner" (page 137).
SPACE/FORMATION NEEDED—a standing circle of partners (each player faces in, standing next to a player identified as her partner).

Make sure the circle is large enough to avoid crowding during the game. Say, "Turn and face your partner! Take hands with your partner, and the two of you circle to the left together." Sing as you circle to the left within each circle of two,

Oh, around the circle is the game,
Round the corner, Sally.

(Circling with your partner can be considered a form of the swing. For variations, see the next section, The Promenade and the Swing.)

Say, "Now reverse directions!" All circle to the right within their circles of two, as you sing,

> *Oh, back we go, the way we came,*
> *Round the corner, Sally.*

Say, "Get back exactly where you started. You are facing along the big circle. Now step back from your partner four small steps!" (Make sure there is enough room so that the players don't bump into each other.) Sing as you back up,

> *Oh, back 'em up and stop 'em dead,*
> *Round the corner, Sally.*

Say, "Now go forward, and walk right past your partner! Don't turn around!" Sing as you walk forward,

> *Oh, wave goodbye and walk ahead,*
> *Round the corner, Sally.*

Say, "Everybody stop! Look who's ahead of you! It's not your partner—it's your *new* partner. Get ready to circle left!" Repeat the game with new partners. If time allows, it's fun to repeat until all reunite with their original partners, halfway around the circle.

THE PROMENADE AND THE SWING

Two easy play-party figures are the promenade and the swing. Since they involve touching a partner—traditionally of the opposite sex—they exist in several forms, ranging from hands-only contact to arm-on-body contact.

In the traditional settings of the play-party games, the "waist swing" and "waist promenade" were often frowned upon by adult onlookers. In certain grade-levels of contemporary schools, they may be resisted by the players themselves.

In the promenade, partners walk side by side, holding hands in some way. The simplest promenade position is just holding near-hands, side by side. Slightly more complicated is the "skater's position": both hands joined in front of you, your left hand in your partner's left hand, and your right hand in your partner's right. Adult square dancers generally prefer two-handed positions in which one partner's right hand (traditionally, the man's) is held behind the other's body, either at the waist or above the shoulder.

The simplest swing is the two-handed turn described in "Round the Circle," above. Variations include crossing the two hands (the partners' hands and bodies, seen from above, look like a figure eight), the elbow swing, and several variants of ballroom position, the familiar position used for the waltz and similar dances. In all cases, the fun of swinging depends on interaction with your partner—matching speed and "weight" in order to turn around together.

GAME 68—PROMENADE THE CORNER
(PARTNER CHANGE WITH PROMENADE AROUND THE CIRCLE)

SONG—"Old Joe Clark" (page 141).
SPACE/FORMATION NEEDED—a standing circle of partners (each player faces in, standing next to a player identified as his partner).

To establish each player's role (see The Two Roles), say, "Raise your partner's near hand. If you have your right hand raised, you're an 'In.' If you have your left hand raised, you're an 'Out.' All the 'In's' raise both hands over your head! All the 'Out's' touch your toes! Now you know who you are. Are you ready for the game?"

Say, "Join hands in the big circle, and circle to the left!" Sing (to the first half of the tune of the verse),

> *Circle left with Old Joe Clark,*
> *Circle left and gone;*

Say, "Now circle back to the right!" Sing (completing the verse),

> *Circle back the other way,*
> *With the golden slippers on.*

Say, "Now, turn and join two hands with your partner. Notice where you are right now; you'll have to come back to this same place. Okay, circle left with your partner in a little circle of two!" Sing (to the first half of the tune of the verse),

> *Swing your partner round and round,*
> *Swing around, I say;*

Say, "Everybody stop where your partner was. That is, keep turning until you've traded places with your partner." Sing (completing the verse),

> *Now leave your partner where you were,*
> *And look the other way.*

Say, "Turn your back on your partner. You should see another person facing you. Take that other person's two hands, and promenade together, side by side. The 'In's' walk on the inside of the circle as you promenade." Watch me and my partner! Demonstrate the promenade with a partner.

Say, "Okay, everybody try it." Sing (to the tune of the refrain),

> *Promenade, Old Joe Clark,*
> *Promenade, I say,*
> *Promenade, Old Joe Clark,*
> *I ain't got long to stay.*

Say, "Now, stop! The 'Out's' go one step ahead of the 'In's' and and turn to face the center of the circle; the 'In's' back up into the circle and turn to face the center—and everybody holds hands again in the big circle. You have new partners. Let's check: In's, raise your right hand—that should be the hand holding your new partner. Out's, raise your left hand–that hand should be the one holding your new partner. Any problems? Let's start again!" Start over, singing "Circle left, Old Joe Clark . . ." Repeat as desired or until all have returned to their original partners.

Variation—types of swings. Instead of circling left with your partner, use an elbow swing (hook right elbows and turn clockwise around your partner), or another form of swing. Show several swings to your group and ask which they prefer to use. If some prefer a more vigorous elbow swing but others feel safer using a two-handed swing, make a rule guaranteeing the ability to choose the safer-feeling swing: "If your partner offers you an elbow, you can give an elbow or two hands. If your partner offers you two hands, then you have to give two hands back."

GAME 69—DOUBLE SWING
(PARTNER CHANGE WITH ELBOW SWING AND PROMENADE AROUND THE CIRCLE)

SONG–"Weldon" (page 129).

SPACE/FORMATION NEEDED–a standing circle of partners (each player faces in, standing next to a player identified as her partner).

Establish roles as in Game 68—Promenade the Corner.

Say, "Circle to the right in one big circle!" Sing this verse as all circle right,

> *Let's go down to Weldon,*
> *I think I heard them say,*
> *Let's go down to Weldon,*
> *I think I heard them say.*

Say, "Now circle back the other way!" Sing the refrain as all circle left:

> *Rally, rally, rally,*
> *I think I heard them say,*
> *Rally, rally, rally,*
> *I think I heard them say.*

Say, "Watch me and my partner. We take our right elbows and make an elbow swing." Demonstrate the elbow swing, in which you and your partner lock right elbows and circle clockwise around each other.

Say, "Okay, everybody try it. Swing your partner!" Sing the verse as all elbow swing their partners:

> *Swing your partner in Weldon,*
> *I think I heard them say,*
> *Swing your partner in Weldon,*
> *I think I heard them say.*

Say, "Now, stop the swing, back where you started. Turn your back on your partner. You should be facing someone else's partner. That's your corner: the person next to you who is not your partner. Swing your corner!" Sing the refrain as all swing the corner with an elbow swing,

> *Rally, rally, rally . . .*

Say, "Stop the swing, and promenade the one you're swinging. That's your new partner. The 'In's' walk on the inside of the circle as you promenade together." Sing the verse as all promenade counter-clockwise around the circle:

> *Fare thee well in Weldon,*
> *I think I heard them say,*
> *Fare thee well in Weldon,*
> *I think I heard them say.*

Say, "Now, stop! The 'Out's' go one step ahead of the 'In's' and turn to face the center of the circle; the 'In's' back up into the circle and turn to face the center—and everybody holds hands again in the big circle. You have new partners. Let's start again!" Start over, singing "Let's go down to Weldon . . ."

Repeat as desired or until all have returned to their original partners. Note that each time through the figures, each player will have a different corner.

GAME 70—HONOR TO YOUR CORNER (PARTNER CHANGE WITH TWO-HANDED SWING, PROMENADE, AND BOW)

SONG—"I Wish I Was A Cowpoke" (page 130).
SPACE/FORMATION NEEDED—a standing circle of partners (each player faces in, standing next to a player identified as his partner).

Establish roles as in game 68—Promenade the Corner.

Say, "Everybody join hands with your partner. Now promenade around the circle." Sing the verse, as all promenade their partners:

> *I wish I was a cowpoke,*
> *In some cowpoke land,*
> *With boots on my feet,*
> *And a lariat in my hand.*

Say, "Everybody stop. Drop hands. Bow to your partner." All bow to partners as you sing the first line of the refrain (the sung directions are addressed to the "In's," whose partners are on their right):

> *Honor to your right*

Say, "Now turn your back on your partner until you face someone else. That's your corner: the person next to you in the circle who is not your partner. Bow to your corner!" Sing the second line of the refrain as all bow to corners,

> *Honor to your left*

Say, "Now take two hands with your partner, and turn your partner around once." As all turn once around with partners, sing the third and fourth lines of the refrain,

> *Swing your right-hand partner,*
> *And promenade to the left.*

Say, "Now turn your back on your partner, and find your corner. That's your new partner. Promenade!" Sing the verse as all promenade. At the end of the verse, sing all four lines of the refrain, as all complete the appropriate actions: honor to partner, honor to corner, swing partner, and find the corner to promenade. Promenade the corner while singing the verse. Repeat as desired, or until all return to their original partners.

GAME 71—HAYSTACK ON MY SHOULDER
(PARTNER CHANGE WITH TWO-HANDED SWING, PROMENADE, AND BOW)

This game is a variation of the previous game, adding the "haystack on my shoulder" figure.

SONG—"I Wish I Was A Cowpoke" (page 130).
SPACE/FORMATION NEEDED—a standing circle of partners (each player faces in, standing next to a player identified as her partner).

Begin like the previous game, "Honor to your Corner." As all promenade partners at the beginning of the game, however, sing this verse, instead:

I want to be a farmer,
And join the farmer band,
Where the farmers walk together
In some farmer's land.

Say, "Join hands in one big circle. Step toward the center until we are almost shoulder-to-shoulder. Circle to the left!" Sing the first two lines of the refrain as all circle left in one close-packed circle:

Circle to the left,
Circle to the left

Say, "Now I'll show you how to put a haystack on your shoulder." Holding hands in the circle, put your right hand over your head, turning to your left to face left around the circle. Move your right hand (still joined to the next player's) in front of your head, and place it on your own left shoulder. You will have ducked under your own right hand. Your left hand (still joined to the player in front of you) will extend in front of you (when all are in the haystack position, your left hand will rest on that player's left shoulder). Your right hand will rest on your left shoulder, holding the hand of the player who is now behind you.

Undo your own haystack by ducking back under your own right hand, and leave the circle (to help those having difficulty with the haystack figure). Say, "Are you ready to put a haystack on your shoulder? Everyone lift your right hand over your head. Now look at your own left shoulder. Back under your right hand, and put it on your left shoulder." If any are having difficulty, gently guide them into the right position by lifting their right hands and turning their bodies a quarter-turn to the left. Sing (once the game is learned, players will get into the haystack position during these last two lines of the refrain):

With a haystack on my shoulder,
Circle to the left.

Say, "'Granger' is another word for a farmer. Farmers still have an association called 'the Grange.' Keep the haystack position, and walk straight ahead around the circle!" Sing the first three lines of this verse as all walk forward,

I want to be a granger,
And with the grangers stand,
With a haystack on my shoulder,

Say, "Now duck under your right arm again to straighten out the circle." Sing, as all undo the haystack position,

> *And a pitchfork in my hand.*

Say, "Let go hands, and bow to your partner." Sing the refrain, as all do the motions indicated in the words (see the previous game for details):

> *Honor to your right,*
> *Honor to your left,*
> *Swing your right-hand partner,*
> *And promenade to the left.*

Begin the game again with the new partners. Repeat as desired, or until all have returned to their original partners.

ADDING THE ALLEMANDE AND THE DO-SI-DO

The next two figures, the allemande and the do-si-do, are easy enough to learn that it's often possible to learn them in the same game. If needed, however, devise your own games that introduce only one new figure at a time.

In one of the many historical ironies of dance terminology, the term "allemande" comes from the French for "German." In other words, North Americans have naturalized an English dance figure that the French thought was typically German!

The allemande consists of a turn by one hand around another player. To allemande right, for example, both players grab right hands and circle clockwise (the obvious direction) once around—returning to their starting positions. Similarly, to allemande left, grab left hands and walk forward (counter-clockwise) once around.

The thrill of a good allemande, like the thrill of a good swing, depends on "giving weight" to the opposite player. For this reason, many dancers use an "arm wrestling" grip instead of a "handshake" grip. The "arm wrestling" grip allows the players to stay closer together and to adjust how much they each lean back against the other player. When both players make subtle adjustments and arrive at a mutually comfortable amount of "weight," the turn is fast and almost effortless. Good dancers can easily allemande twice in two lines of "Old Joe Clark," whereas beginners may find it challenging to make it around once. The secret of a snappy allemande is to expend your effort in leaning back, not in walking forward.

For most people living in the United States or Canada, the do-si-do (from the French *dos a dos:* "back to back") is the most familiar square-dance figure. In it, two facing players pass by the right shoulders, walk a few steps to their right (thus passing back to back), and back up to their starting positions. In effect, they have each circled around the other. Except for the start and end of the figure, they do not face one another when performing the traditional do-si-do, however: each player begins facing one wall of the room and continues to face that wall throughout the figure. Few contemporary dancers use the arm-position familiar from cowboy movies: arms crossed in front of the chest. Most leave their arms in a comfortable walking position. Some add a twirl, turning two or more times around to their own left as they make a small circle to the right around the opposite player.

GAME 72—DOUBLE ALLEMANDE
(PARTNER CHANGE WITH PROMENADE, ALLEMANDE, AND DO-SI-DO)

SONG—"Old Joe Clark" (page 141).

SPACE/FORMATION NEEDED—a standing circle of partners (each player faces in, standing next to a player identified as his partner).

Establish roles as in Game 68—Promenade the Corner.

Say, "Turn your back on your partner. Do you see your corner? That's the person next to you who is not your partner. Watch me allemande left around my corner." Demonstrate the allemande left. Say, "Are you ready to try it? Give your left hand to your corner. Hold on! Pull back a little bit—enough to balance each other gently. Now each of you walk forward all the way around your corner. That's an allemande *left*; you used your left hand. Let's try it with the song." Sing (to the first half of the verse) as all allemande left the corner:

> Left hand 'round your corner, now,
> Left hand 'round, I say,

Say, "Now turn your back on that person. Face your partner. Give your other hand—your right hand—to your partner. Allemande right, the other way around." Sing (to the second half of the verse) as all allemande right the partner:

> Right hand 'round the partner, now,
> I'm a going away.

Say, "Now face your corner again. You're going to walk behind each other, and end up back where you are. Watch me and my corner." Demonstrate the do-si-do. Say, "Do-si-do means 'back to back.' Look at what wall you're facing. You'll never stop facing that wall. Touch your own right shoulder. Walk past your corner, passing right shoulder to right shoulder. Slide by each others' backs; now back up to where you started. Let's try it again with the song." Sing (to the first half of the verse) as all do-si-do corners:

> Do-si-do your partner, now,
> Do-si-do, I say

Say, "Now face your partner again. Do-si-do your partner!" Sing (to the second half of the verse) as all do-si-do partners:

> Do-si-do your partner, now,
> Ain't got long to stay.

Say, "Get back to where you started. Look at your corner again. Now take your corner and promenade." Sing the refrain as all promenade the corner:

> Promenade your corner, now,
> Promenade, I say,
> Promenade your corner, now,
> I ain't got long to stay.

Say, "The person you're with is your new partner! Let's start over with this new partner. Allemande left your *new* corner!" Begin again, singing, "Left hand 'round your corner. . . ." Repeat as desired, or until all have returned to their original partners.

THE GRAND RIGHT-AND-LEFT

The grand right-and-left, a classic square-dance figure, requires the cooperation of an entire circle of players. All the players must perform a sequence of turns simultaneously, alternate the hands they extend to oncoming players, and keep track of their direction around the circle. As a result, the grand right-and-left can be grandly exhilarating, or else grandly confusing.

Two of the games that follow can be be played in forms that include the double-L swing, a basic variation of the grand right-and-left. In the grand right-and-left, each player pulls by each oncoming player, then goes on to the next player in the circle. In the double-L swing, players turn once-and-a-half around the player they meet, and then proceed as in the grand right-and-left. The extra turn makes the figure more dizzying than the grand right-and-left, but the extra time spent on the turns makes it easier to find and redirect players who have lost their way. In this sense, the double-L swing can sometimes be easier for a group than the basic grand right-and-left.

The first game in this series teaches a figure called "rights and lefts," in which two players pull by each player in the ring—sort of a grand right-and-left for two moving players at a time. This figure makes an excellent introduction to the skills used later in the full grand right-and-left.

GAME 73—RIGHTS AND LEFTS
(CHOOSING PARTNERS, WITH "RIGHTS AND LEFTS" FIGURE–LIKE A GRAND RIGHT-AND-LEFT IN WHICH ONLY TWO PLAYERS MOVE AT ONCE)

SONG-"Hold My Mule" (page 143).
SPACE/FORMATION NEEDED—a standing circle of players, with one player in the center.

As the player in the center, say, "Grab hands with the players next to you, and circle right." Sing, as all join hands and walk around the circle to the right:

> *Chicken on the fence post, can't dance Josey,*
> *Chicken on the fence post, can't dance Josey,*
> *Chicken on the fence post, can't dance Josey,*
> *Hello, Susan Brown-ie-o.*

Say, "Now I can choose any partner to join me in the center." Walk around the inside of the circle as you sing, choosing one player as your partner. Bring your chosen partner into the center of the circle with you before the end of the verse:

> *Choose your partner and come dance Josey,*
> *Choose your partner and come dance Josey,*
> *Choose your partner and come dance Josey,*
> *Hello, Susan Brown-ie-o.*

Say, "Now the two of us join the circle and do 'rights and lefts.' We turn right hands with each other and pull by." Demonstrate with your partner. Join the circle, then take your partner's right hand in your right hand, using a "hand-shake" grip. Keeping right hands joined, walk forward, pulling your partner by you. Now you have changed places with your partner, and your partner is behind you; stop.

Say, "Wait a minute! Now we're headed in opposite directions. That's right. I leave my partner behind. He's headed one way, I'm headed the other. We each reach out our left hands to the person we meet. Guess what we do now? We pull by the person we meet by the left hand." Pull by the next player in the circle by the left, making sure your partner does the same with the appropriate player. Your partner is getting farther and farther away from you as you head around the circle in opposite directions.

Say, "Now we each see someone else ahead of us. Our right hands are free. What do we do? That's right; we pull by that person by the right. We just keep going in our own directions around the circle, left past one person, then right past the next. Everyone else stand still until we come to you!" Sing as you and your partner each alternate right-hand pull-by's with left-hand pull-by's around the circle:

> Chew my gum while I dance Josey,
> Chew my gum while I dance Josey,
> Chew my gum while I dance Josey,
> Hello, Susan Brown-ee-o.

Keep going until you meet your partner, halfway around the circle from where you entered it. If you need more music to fill the time it takes you, sing other nonsense verses, such as these:

> Shoestring's broke and can't dance Josey . . .
>
> Crank my Ford while I dance Josey . . .
>
> Briar in my heel and I can't dance Josey . . .
>
> Stumped my toe and I can't dance Josey . . .

When you come to your partner, say to him, "Now I join the circle again, and you stay in the center. After we circle, you get to choose another partner and do the whole thing again. Ready?" Begin the game again with "Chicken on the fence post. . . ." Repeat as desired or until *every* player has had a turn to be the center player.

The teaching instructions for the remaining games are abbreviated. Once you understand the figures, use the games described above as models and create your own instructions.

GAME 74—THE GRAND RIGHT-AND-LEFT
(GRAND RIGHT-AND-LEFT FIGURE, WITH CIRCLE AND PROMENADE)

This game and the next one are identical, except that the second uses the double-L swing in place of the grand right-and-left.

SONG—"There Was A Little Frog" (page 159).

SPACE/FORMATION NEEDED—a standing circle of partners (each player faces in, standing next to a player identified as her partner).

During this verse, all join hands and circle to the right:

> *Circle right around the ring, uh-huh, uh-huh,*
> *Circle right around the ring,*
> *Ducks are dancing on the wing, uh-huh, uh-huh.*

During this verse, circle left:

> *Circle back the other way, uh-huh, uh-huh,*
> *Circle back the other way,*
> *Mice are marching in the hay, uh-huh, uh-huh.*

Say, "This is the grand right-and-left. Face your partner! Give your partner your right hand; now pull by. Keep going the same direction. Stick out your left hand. There should be someone coming toward you. Grab that person by the left hand and pull by. Now there should be someone else coming toward you with a free right hand. Pull by! Keep going in the same direction around the circle!"

Do the grand right-and-left figure until partners meet, halfway around the circle, singing,

> *Pull 'em left and pull 'em right, uh-huh, uh-huh,*
> *Pull 'em left and pull 'em right,*
> *Cows are singing in the night, uh-huh, uh-huh.*

If you need more verses, think of more animals that can be "singing in the night": cats, owls, mules, dogs, and so on.

When partners meet, cross hands and promenade around the circle, singing,

> *The cat is dancing with the hen, uh-huh, uh-huh,*
> *The cat is dancing with the hen,*
> *Ducks are rolling home again, uh-huh, uh-huh.*

If desired, play the game again.

GAME 75—THE DOUBLE-L SWING
(DOUBLE-L SWING—A GRAND RIGHT-AND LEFT FIGURE, BUT WITH ONE-AND-A-HALF TURNS—WITH CIRCLE AND PROMENADE)

SONG—"Back to Mexico" (page 125).
SPACE/FORMATION NEEDED—a standing circle of partners (each player faces in, standing next to a player identified as his partner).

Circle right to this verse:

> *Around the mountain I must go, sugar babe,*
> *Around the mountain I must go, sugar babe,*
> *Around the mountain I must go,*
> *If anything happens, let me know, sugar babe.*

Circle left to this verse:

> *What you gonna do when the weather gets cold, sugar babe,*
> *What you gonna do when the weather gets cold, sugar babe,*
> *What you gonna do when the weather gets cold,*
> *Do like a ground hog, hunt me a hole, sugar babe.*

At the point where the players would begin the grand right-and-left figure, say, "This is the double-L swing. Give your right hand to your partner, and turn all the way around each other, back to where you are now. Don't let go of hands; keep turning even more, until you have changed places with your partner. Now, do you see another person coming toward you? Give that person your left hand, and turn all the way around that person. Hold on and keep going until you've changed places again. You're slowly working your way around the circle. Try it!" Sing, as all begin the double-L swing:

> *Rights and lefts around the ring, sugar babe,*
> *Rights and lefts around the ring,*
> *Turn 'em 'round like anything, sugar babe.*

If you need more verses, sing some of these:

> *What you gonna do when the money gives out . . .*
> *. . . Sit on the corner with my mouth in a pout. . . .*
>
> *Got no money, but I will have some . . .*
> *. . . Just you wait till payday comes. . . .*
>
> *I'll be blamed if I can see . . .*
> *. . . How my money got away from me. . . .*

When partners meet in the circle and promenade, sing,

> *Now we're going through the sticks, sugar babe,*
> *Now we're going through the sticks,*
> *Puffing and a-blowing like a Hudson six, sugar babe.*

GAME 76—LET'S GO DOWN TO WELDON
(GRAND RIGHT-AND-LEFT PLUS DOUBLE-L SWING, WITH CIRCLE AND PROMENADE)

SONG–"Weldon" (page 129).
SPACE/FORMATION NEEDED–a standing circle of partners (each player faces in, standing next to a player identified as her partner).

Circle right to this verse:

> *Let's go down to Weldon,*
> *I think I heard them say,*
> *Let's go down to Weldon,*
> *I think I heard them say.*

Circle left to the refrain:

> *Rally, rally, rally,*
> *I think I heard them say,*
> *Rally, rally, rally,*
> *I think I heard them say.*

Grand right-and-left to the verse:

> *My friends all live in Weldon,*
> *I think I heard them say,*
> *My friends all live in Weldon,*
> *I think I heard them say.*

Continue the grand right-and-left as you sing the refrain.

Do the double-L swing with this verse (sing the refrain, too):

> *Once and a half in Weldon . . .*

Promenade partners around the ring, as you sing this verse (sing the refrain, too):

> *Let's have fun in Weldon . . .*

Players return to their places in the ring ("In's" turn to face the center of the circle by backing into the ring; "Out's" turn to face the center as they step ahead of their partners), turn their backs on their partners, take their corners, and promenade, singing this verse (and the refrain):

> *Fare thee well in Weldon . . .*

After the promenade, reform the ring. The one you promenaded is now your new partner. Begin again, and continue as desired.

If you need extra verses to sing at any point in the game, use some of these, or make your own:

> *Twenty-five miles to Weldon . . .*

> *Treat 'em all alike in Weldon . . .*

> *Keep a-hooking in Weldon . . .*

> *Ain't got long in Weldon . . .*

THE SICILIAN CIRCLE

The Sicilian circle formation consists of one large circle, formed of many small circles. The small circles each have two couples in them. As a result, a Sicilian circle is sometimes described as "couple facing couple around the ring."

In a Sicilian circle dance, couples progress around the ring, just as individual players do in many of the games above. As a result, not only does each couple have one "man" and one "woman" (see the section The Two Roles for alternate terms), but each couple dances in one of two possible roles: "headed clockwise around the big circle," and "headed counter-clockwise around the big circle." To prevent undue confusion, don't teach the following game until players are comfortable with the two basic roles.

Many games and dances use the Sicilian circle formation. The following traditional play-party game is simple enough to be an introduction to the formation.

GAME 77—EUCHRE RING
(SICILIAN CIRCLE FORMATION; PAIRS OF COUPLES CIRCLE RIGHT AND LEFT, THEN PASS THROUGH WITH FULL TURN, GO ON TO THE NEXT COUPLE)

SONG—"Old Joe Clark" (page 141).
SPACE/FORMATION NEEDED—a Sicilian circle: a large ring made of small rings, each small ring consisting of two couples.

This game is similar to 67—Round the Circle, but with couples instead of individuals (and omitting the forward-and-back figure). To form a Sicilian circle, play the "Forming a Sicilian circle" variation of Game 66—Move It Round.

Say, "Stand next to your partner, in promenade position. You should be facing another couple. One couple is facing counter-clockwise around the ring; let's call them the Lead Couples. Raise your hand if you're a Lead Couple. The other couple is facing clockwise. Let's call you the Other Couple. Raise your hand if you're an Other Couple."

Each small ring (two couples holding hands in a circle of four people) circles to the right, as all sing the first half of the verse:

> Four hands round in the euchre ring,
> Four hands round, I'm gone,

All reverse direction to circle left in the small rings, singing the second half of the verse:

> Four hands round in the euchre ring,
> With the golden slippers on.

Say, "End your circles right back where you started. The Lead Couples should be facing counter-clockwise around the ring. Raise your hands, Lead Couples! Good! Now look at that couple facing you. Walk right up to that couple. You can't go straight through them, so pass by the right shoulder of the person directly ahead of you, just like in a do-si-do. When you get past that person, stop! Look ahead of you: there's a new couple headed toward you. That's the couple you'll dance with next. But first, take your partner's near hand. Turn your partner around, one full turn. Now, grab hands with the new couple. You'll start the game over with them!"

Having walked through the "pass through" figure, have the players dance it, saying, "Go back to where you started the game. As we sing, you'll pass through the couple you're facing, turn once around with your partner, and face a new couple." Sing the refrain:

> Fare you well, my darling girl,
> Fare you well, I'm gone,
> Fare you well, my darling girl,
> With the golden slippers on.

Repeat the game as desired, or until the original pairs of couples are together again.

MOVEMENTS

Moving playfully is as natural to children as eating and breathing. Moving while singing is as natural as singing itself.

Movement activities help children develop their repertory of movement possibilities, their control over their own movements, their understanding of their movements, and their rhythmic abilities.

For a movement activity to succeed, you (as the leader) must match it to the group members' social abilities as well as to their physical skills.

When teachers of young children think of movements with children, they often think first of "fingerplays," or else of a room full of children pretending to be galloping horses or stampeding elephants (with swinging "trunks" formed by their two arms). This chapter gives you ways to succeed at both of those kinds of activities and to introduce you to an even richer and more nourishing menu of movement possibilities.

PULSE

The most important element of most music is the pulse—the beat.

The pulse of music is both fundamental and powerful. Nearly all music in the world has a regular, underlying beat that synchronizes musicians and listeners. When we join the music by singing or moving to the pulse, we also unite with others. Frances Aranoff, a great music teacher, quotes her own teacher as saying, "When you learn to join in by walking to a pulse, your steps seem to chant to you, 'You're right! You're right! You're right!'"

Young children learn to "move with the beat" in two distinct phases. In the first phase, they learn to make movements that have a pulse—at a rate they choose themselves—and to sing along with their own movements. In the second phase, they learn to change the rate of their movements to match a pulse that someone else has set.

The most basic movement activities for a group, therefore, give players a chance to move to a pulse (beat) they choose and give them cues about matching their movements to a pulse chosen by someone else. Once players can match the group's pulse with a single, repeated movement, they are ready to try keeping the pulse with a sequence of movements. Then, once they have mastered sequential pulse movements, they can go on to movements that do not occur in time with a steady pulse, but in more complicated rhythms. At the same time, they can begin to explore movements through space and with other players.

THE ELEMENTS OF MOVEMENT

In the sections that follow, the various elements of movement are each introduced in conjunction with a particular group of activities. Thus, the concept of "changing the feeling of a movement" is introduced under Repeated Pulse Movements, and the concept of "imitative movements as distinguished from abstract movements" is introduced in the section on Sequential Pulse Movements.

In fact, each of these elements is present in *every* kind of movement. Any kind of movement can be altered to be done with a different feeling or changed from imitative to abstract—or done in a different rhythm or speed or with a different part of the body. The elements are introduced in the various sections only for the convenience of appearing near clear examples.

REPEATED PULSE MOVEMENTS

A repeated pulse movement is a movement that gets repeated over and over in time with the pulse (beat) of a song. Examples include steadily clapping the hands, tapping the head, or hopping around the room. Because the movement does not change, the player can direct his full attention to timing the movement.

The activities in this section give you a chance to sing in time with the movements of each player, in turn. This means that, at least for that one turn, each player will get a chance to experience the satisfaction of moving in time to the music. Once they've experienced being "in time," players have a greater chance of being able to speed up or slow down to be in time with the group.

All the following activities can be done with a group seated on the floor or on chairs, in almost any formation. If the group is in a circle or semi-circle, however, the children have the advantage of being able to see each other. This set-up helps them know what to do and how fast to do it.

To stay interesting, movements need to be varied in some way. In the following activities, players suggest the variations themselves, whether it's which part of the body to move, the exact movement to make, or different ways to perform a given movement.

CHANGING THE PART OF THE BODY

This kind of suggestion is the most concrete for players to make. After all, the parts of their own bodies are concrete objects that they have with them at all times. Even players who don't share a language with the leader can make suggestions by simply moving or by pointing to the part of their body they wish to move. As a result, these activities can help players learn the names of body parts, as well.

MOVEMENT ACTIVITY 1—WHAT GOES AROUND? (PLAYERS SUGGEST WHICH PART OF THEIR BODIES TO MOVE IN A CIRCULAR PATTERN)

SONG—"Old Joe Clark" (page 141).

Sing the refrain, moving one or both arms in front of you in a small circle (as though washing an invisible window):

> *Round and around, Old Joe Clark,*
> *Round and around I say,*
> *Round and around, Old Joe Clark,*
> *I ain't got long to stay.*

Say, "Can you move your arms round and round, like I did? Try it!" Sing and move as before, as all join you.

Say, "Who can think of another part of your body you could move around and around? Raise your hand, so I know who to listen to." When you point to a player who has raised her hand, you may have to repeat the question, "What part of your body could you make go round and round?" Reinforce the name of the body part by saying it aloud, whether the player spoke the name or only used a gesture: "Your head! Great idea! Let's move our heads around and around!" Sing the refrain again, moving your head in a small circle as all join in.

To maximize the music learning in this activity, be sure to match the speed and energy of your movement to the speed and energy of the player who suggested "the head." This matching will require singing the song with a different tempo (speed), and perhaps with a different energy-level (volume, tone of voice) as well. Your goal is to match the song to the movement of the player whose turn it is. If the player does not demonstrate the movement before you start to sing, you may need to say, "Show me how!" Once the player begins the movement, start singing with a matching tempo.

Repeat, taking a suggestion from another player. If the group is small enough, give each player a turn.

MOVEMENT ACTIVITY 2—WHAT TO CLAP WITH
(PLAYERS SUGGEST WHICH PART OF THEIR BODIES TO USE FOR CLAPPING)

This activity is similar to the previous one, but involves clapping instead of moving in a circular pattern.

> SONG—"Al Citron" (page 124).

Sing, as you clap your hands,

> *Al citron de un fandango sango, sango, sabaré,*
> *Sabaré de la randela con su triki triki tron.*

Say, "What was I doing with my hands? That's right, clapping. Try it with me." Sing and clap again as all clap along.

Say, "What other part of your body could you use to clap with?" Choose a player whose hand is raised. Say, "Ruperto says we can clap our feet. Show us how, Ruperto. Let's try it!" Sing and clap your feet, matching Ruperto's speed and energy.

Repeat with another player. Repeat as desired, or until all have had a turn.

MOVEMENT ACTIVITY 3—WAKE MY BODY IN THE MORNING
(PLAYERS SUGGEST WHICH PART OF THEIR BODIES
TO HAVE "WAKE UP AND DANCE")

This activity is similar to the previous one, but includes a small story and free-form "dancing" with the various parts of the body.

> SONG—"Wake Me, Shake Me" (page 127).

Tell this little story:

> One morning, we were all sleepy. Our arms were sleepy; our legs and head were sleepy. Let me see your whole body be sleepy.
> Suddenly, the fingers woke up and started dancing. The rest of the body stayed asleep, but the fingers danced and sang.

With your arms still relaxed and motionless, move your fingers around as you sing,

> *Wake me, shake me,*
> *Don't let me sleep too late,*
> *Wake my fingers in the morning,*
> *Swing on the garden gate.*

Continue the story, adding the appropriate motions:

> The fingers got so tired that they fell back asleep, but the toes heard the song. The toes woke up, and they began singing and dancing:

> *Wake me, shake me,*
> *Don't let me sleep too late,*
> *Wake my toes in the morning,*
> *Swing on the garden gate.*

> The toes danced and danced until they got tired and fell back asleep.

Say, "What part of our bodies do you think woke up next?" Call on a player and take his suggestion, such as "our tongue." Tell how the tongue danced, singing and moving your tongue as appropriate. (The sound produced by singing while moving your tongue is delightfully silly!)

Continue the story, incorporating the suggested parts of the body. When you are ready to stop, finish the story this way:

> Finally, the whole body woke up. The whole body said, "Well, if we can't sleep, we might as well dance!" So the whole body began to dance and sing at once:

> *Wake me, shake me . . . wake my whole body in the morning. . . .*

> The body danced and danced all day long. At last, it was tired, and it got sleepy again. The fingers fell back asleep. The toes fell back asleep. The arms fell back asleep. The head fell back asleep. Even the tongue fell back asleep. The entire body fell back asleep, and slept soundly until the morning.

CHANGING THE MOVEMENT

Movements from real-life situations may not be as easy to bring to mind as body parts, but they can inspire the imagination. In the activities that follow, players suggest different movements that would be used for an actual activity, such as building a hut or quieting a baby.

MOVEMENT ACTIVITY 4—HOW TO BUILD A SUKKAH (PLAYERS SUGGEST MOVEMENTS THAT WOULD BE USED IN BUILDING A BOOTH)

SONG—"HaSukkah" (page 154).

Sing the song as you clap:

> HaSukkah, mah yafah,
> Umah tov lashevet bah,
> HaSukkah, mah yafah,
> Umah tov lashevet bah.

Say, "On the Jewish holiday called Sukkot, some Jewish people build a special booth—like a little house—and then sit in it, sing songs, pray, and eat their dinner. It reminds them of how, long ago, Jewish people were wandering across the desert and didn't have real houses. So, now, on Sukkot they make the walls of wood, but for a roof, they just put branches on top.

"I know one thing we'd have to do to build a sukkah: saw the branches for the roof. Help me saw!"

Rhythmically pretend to saw, as you sing the song again.

Say, "What else would we have to do to make a little house?" Call on a player for a suggestion. If a player says, "Carry the branches," for example, encourage her to find a rhythmic way to pretend to carry the branches, then sing the song in her tempo as all join in the movement. (If she starts walking around and you want the group to remain seated, you can ask her to find a sitting-down way to pretend to carry them.)

Repeat as desired, or until every player has had a turn.

MOVEMENT ACTIVITY 5—HOW TO SOOTHE A BABY (PLAYERS SUGGEST MOVEMENTS THAT WOULD MAKE AN UPSET BABY FEEL BETTER)

This activity and the next three activities are similar to the previous one, but involve different songs and different types of movements.

SONG—"Sleep, Bonnie Bairnie" (page 158).

Ask, "How could we soothe a baby? How could we make a baby feel better, if it's feeling bad?" Answers might include rub its back, rock it in our arms, rock it in a cradle, or stroke its forehead. Sing, as all pantomime the chosen action:

> Sleep, bonnie bairnie, behind the castle,
> Bye, bye, bye, bye.
> You shall have a golden apple,
> Bye, bye, bye, bye.

For maximum musical learning, encourage the pantomime to occur in time with the pulse of the song. If a child pantomimes stiffly and statically, you might model a fluid, rhythmic way of performing the same movement.

MOVEMENT ACTIVITY 6—PLANTING A TREE
(PLAYERS SUGGEST MOVEMENTS THAT WOULD BE USED TO PLANT A TREE)

This activity is similar to 4—How to Build a Sukkah, but it involves a different song and a different type of movement.

SONG—"Atse Zetim Omdim" (page 146).

Say, "Jewish people have a holiday for planting trees. In Israel, February is the time when the trees start to wake up after the winter. So they have a holiday to be happy that the trees are waking up, and to plant new trees. In the land of Israel, they have a special kind of tree, the beautiful kind that olives grow on. So they sing, 'Olive trees are standing.' Help me sing!" Sing the song:

> Olive trees are standing,
> Olive trees are standing.
> La, la, . . .

Say, "What do you do when you plant a tree?" If a player says, "Dig a hole," for example, say, "Keith says, 'Dig a hole.' Good! Show us how, Keith. Everyone try it Keith's way." Sing the song again, matching Keith's tempo and energy, as all imitate Keith's movement.

Repeat as desired, or until everyone has had a turn.

MOVEMENT ACTIVITY 7—WAYS TO SAY GOODBYE
(PLAYERS SUGGEST MOVEMENTS THAT ARE PART OF SAYING GOODBYE)

This activity is similar to 4—How to Build a Sukkah, but it involves a different song and a different type of movement.

SONG—"Back to Mexico" (page 125).

Ask, "What do people do when they're leaving one another?" Some answers might be wave, give hugs, shake hands. Have a player model one of the movements, as all do the movement and sing:

> I'm going back to Mexico, sugar babe,
> I'm going back to Mexico, sugar babe,
> I'm going back to Mexico,
> Say goodbye before I go, sugar babe.

MOVEMENT ACTIVITY 8—HOEING ON A PRISON GANG
(PLAYERS PANTOMIME MOVEMENTS DONE BY PRISON GANGS)

This activity is similar to 4—How to Build a Sukkah, but it involves a different song and a different type of movement.

SONG—"Stewball" (page 144).
PROP—a long object that players can grasp by the end and lift up and down, such as a broomstick or a cardboard tube (optional).

Say, "When African-American prisoners were given hard jobs to do, they sometimes used music to make the jobs easier. They would stand in a line with their hoes, and they'd all raise their hoes together—it sometimes felt like the song was helping them do the lifting. Then they'd hit the ground with their hoes all at the same time, and they weren't just hoeing for the prison warden, they were making music for themselves."

Stand up, and pretend to hoe. Let your "hoe" strike the ground at each word in boldface type:

> It was a **big** day (uh-**huh**)
> In **Dal**-las (uh-**huh**)
> Don't you **wish** you (uh-**huh**)
> Was **there** (was **there**),
>
> You'd-a **bet** your (uh-**huh**)
> Last **dol**-lar (uh-**huh**)
> On that **i**-ron (uh-**huh**)
> Gray **mare** (gray **mare**).

Say, "Line up across the room. Let's pretend we're prisoners hoeing our way across a field together." Sing the song again, pretending to hoe in unison. If desired, continue the song with the refrain and other verses.

Variation—props. Give one or more players a broomstick, cardboard tube, or other prop to represent a hoe. Striking the hoes on the ground will produce a sound; encourage the group to make the sound in unison.

Variations—other prison movements. Another movement similar to hoeing is chopping a felled log into sections. A line of prisoners would stand on one side of the log, raising and striking their axes into the log in time to the song.

Other movements (such as picking cotton or cutting cane) were performed in time to the same song, but with less precision. For example, when cutting stalks of sugar cane or sorghum, prisoners would find individual ways to relate their movements to the music. Each player can mime grabbing the stalk, cutting it near the bottom with a big knife, and throwing the stalk into a big bag worn over the shoulder.

CHANGING THE FEELING

In some movement activities, the fun can be in performing the same action with different emotions. Changing the feeling can also be used as a variation for any of the previous movement activities.

MOVEMENT ACTIVITY 9—THAT DARNED HANDKERCHIEF! (PLAYERS PANTOMIME WASHING A HANDKERCHIEF, PERFORMING THE ACTIONS WITH VARIOUS EMOTIONS)

SONG—"Kitty Kasket" (page 134).

Sing:

> Kitty, kitty kasket,
> Green and yellow basket,

Lost my handkerchief yesterday,
It's all full of mud, so I tossed it away.

Say, "My handkerchief got all muddy! But I didn't toss it away, I washed it. Who can show me how to wash a handkerchief in a sink?" Have a player demonstrate a simple washing movement. Sing the song, encouraging all to join in the movement.

Say, "How would you wash your handkerchief if you were mad at the handkerchief for being dirty?" Have a player demonstrate angry washing; sing, encouraging all to join in the movement.

Suggest different possible emotions, such as:

♪ You love the handkerchief so much!
♪ You're afraid the handkerchief might get ruined in the water.
♪ You're sleepy.

If desired, have players suggest other possible feelings.

Variations—other parts of the body, other images. Ask players to pretend to wash their handkerchiefs with their feet. How about with their noses? What other part of the body could they use?

Alternatively, ask, "How would you wash your handkerchief if it were very heavy?" After all have tried it with the song, suggest other images:

♪ If it were very light
♪ If it were huge (or tiny)
♪ If you were washing it in mud (or in air)

CHANGING THE WORDS

While changing parts of the body, movements, or even feelings, you can also change the words of the song. This variation adds another level of difficulty, of course.

For more on techniques of eliciting verbal suggestions from players, see the chapters on New Verses.

MOVEMENT ACTIVITY 10—JOBS ON A TRAIN (PLAYERS SUGGEST MOVEMENTS THAT MIGHT BE DONE BY SPECIFIC WORKERS ON A TRAIN)

SONG—"Train Is A-Coming" (page 155).

Ask, "What does the engineer do to drive the train?" If a child says, "He pulls on a big stick," for example, you might reply, "Good! That big stick is called a throttle. Pretend you're an engineer—who might be a man or a woman, by the way—and pull on the throttle while we sing."

Sing, as all pretend to pull on the throttle:

The train has an engineer, oh, yeh,
The train has an engineer, oh, yeh,
Train has an engineer, train has an engineer,
The train has an engineer, oh, yeh.

Say, "Who else is on board the train?" If a child says, "The conductor," you might reply, "Yes! What does the conductor do?" If the response is "punches the tickets," then say, "Great! Show me how to punch the tickets. Everyone try it!" Sing, as all pretend to punch the tickets:

The conductor punches tickets, oh, yeh . . .

Repeat as desired, or until all have had a turn to suggest a train job.

Variations—other actions, other ways to do them. You can also ask for other actions for the same jobs. If you have just acted out passengers pulling on the stop cords, you can ask, "What else do passengers do on a train?"

In addition, you can ask what other parts of the body could be used to perform the same movement. After "pulling on the throttle," say, "What other part of your body could you use to pull on the throttle?"

Alternatively, you can ask for other feelings to apply to the same movement: "How would you pull on the throttle if you felt angry?"

SEQUENTIAL PULSE MOVEMENTS

In the previous movement activities, Repeated Pulse Movements, players repeat one action over and over for the entire verse of the song. In Sequential Pulse Movements, however, players perform a sequence of different actions.

In the simplest sequential pulse movements, each action is repeated two or more times, then followed by another action, which is also repeated several times. More difficult activities change actions on every beat, without repeating them first.

MOVEMENT ACTIVITY 11—WAVING THE LULAV (PLAYERS PRETEND TO WAVE PALM LEAVES IN EACH OF FOUR DIRECTIONS)

SONG—"HaSukkah" (page 154).
PROP—A Lulav (an actual bouquet made of a palm branch, a willow branch, and the bough of a leafy tree) or an imitation made from cardboard or another material (optional).

Face east, holding an actual or pretend Lulav bouquet. Sing the first two lines of the song without moving:

HaSukkah mah yafah,
Umah tov lashevet bah,

Continue to sing as you wave the Lulav (or pantomime doing so) toward the east on each "x":

x   x   x   x
Ha-Suk-kah mah ya-fah,

Without pausing, turn 90° to your right to face south, and repeat the action on each "x":

x   x   x   x

U-mah tov la-shev-et bah.

Turn 90° more to face west, and repeat the same action, beginning the melody again:

x   x   x   x

Ha-Suk-kah mah ya-fah,

Turn 90° more to face north, and repeat the action again:

x   x   x   x

U-mah tov la-shev-et bah,

Now wave the Lulav four times toward the sky:

x   x   x   x

Ha-Suk-kah mah ya-fah,

Finally, wave it four times toward the ground as you finish singing the song:

x   x   x   x

U-mah tov la-shev-et bah.

Say, "Do you know what I was just doing? I was 'waving the lulav.' A 'lulav' is a bouquet made of a palm branch, a willow branch, and the branch of a leafy tree. During the Jewish holiday of Sukkot, people wave the Lulav in all directions to show they are thankful for the gifts they received during the year—the harvest, the sun, the rain, and the wind—coming from all directions. They also want to show that they hope for rain (and the other gifts) coming from all directions in the new year. Try it with me. Stand up and pretend you have a Lulav Bouquet in your two hands. Let's wave it to the east—in that direction."

Face east and begin the singing, as above; after two lines of the song, begin the movements as well, continuing until you've waved the Lulav in all four directions.

Repeat as desired. If you have a prop Lulav, give individuals a turn to wave the prop, while the others pretend along.

IMITATIVE MOVEMENTS

Some movements imitate a movement from real life. For example, if you hold your hands on an imaginary steering wheel, you are imitating the real-life movement of driving a car.

Other movements, however, do not imitate; they simply exist as abstract movements. Examples include touching your toes or tapping your hands on your shoulders.

When planning a music or movement program with children, it can be helpful to distinguish between songs that use imitative movements and ones that use abstract movements, if only to make sure that your movement activities aren't of only one kind. In addition, the distinction can help you if you're having trouble finding appropriate movements to go with a particular song; if you get stuck, ask yourself whether you've only tried imitative movements, for example, but haven't tried abstract ones.

The same movement, of course, could be imitative in one song and abstract in another. When you simply clap your hands, you are performing an abstract movement; but if you performed the same clapping movement to pantomime catching a mosquito, it would be imitative. The difference is not actually in the movement, but in your intention in performing it.

Like many of the activities described earlier, the next three activities use imitative movements.

MOVEMENT ACTIVITY 12—SO HE PLANTED GINGER (PLAYERS PERFORM MOVEMENTS THAT SUGGEST EACH LINE OF THE SONG)

SONG—"So He Planted Ginger" (page 132).

Sing the song with the words given on page 132, adding appropriate movements for selected phrases. Each movement will be repeated four times. For example, the first hand-movement, a side-to-side cutting motion, will occur once at each "x":

x   x   x   x

Gin-ger grows so quick-ly

Here are the other phrases, with a suggested movement for each one:

Nanny will not graze on ginger: cross and uncross both arms in front of you, as though saying, "No way!"

Magpie will not talk to Nanny: Flap "wings" by raising and lowering both your arms at your sides.

Beech tree won't give nut to Magpie: Wave "branches" by holding your arms outstretched in front of you, waving them up and down together.

River gave a drink to Beech Tree: Show the river "flowing," by holding your arms waist high, moving them from right to left and alternately raising one while lowering the other.

For the lines of the song not mentioned above, pat hands on thighs as you sing. During the final verse, use the same movements given above, even though the words are changed slightly (for example, "Beech tree won't give nut to Magpie" is replaced by "Beech tree gave a nut to Magpie," but you can use the same "branches" movement. On "Nanny went and grazed on ginger," move your arms vertically to represent hungry jaws opening and closing).

MOVEMENT ACTIVITY 13—RIDING WITH THE FROG (PLAYERS PERFORM MOVEMENTS THAT SUGGEST EACH VERSE OF THE SONG)

SONG—"There Was A Little Frog" (page 159).

Sing the song, adding appropriate movements for each verse. Each movement will be repeated several times. For example, the first movement in verse one (patting your hands on your thighs with your elbows rotated out to the sides, as though your arms were the front legs of a jumping frog) will occur six times, once at each "x":

x   x   x   x

1. There was a little frog who lived on a hill, uh-huh, uh-huh,

x   x
There was a little frog who lived on a hill,

The second movement for each verse, on the other hand, will occur only four times. For example, the second movement in verse one (swaying your upper body to one side—alternately right and left) will occur at each "y":

y   y   y   y
Who rustled and tussled like Buff-alo Bill, uh-huh, uh-huh.

Don't hesitate to perform some movements twice as fast, if that's more natural.

Here are the important phrases from other verses, with a suggested movement for each one:

2. *The frog took Mousie on one knee* (pantomime holding and bouncing a small creature on one knee)

   And said, "Oh, Mouse, will you marry me?" (pretend to hold the small creature up in front of your face, above eye level; bounce slightly at each "y")

3. *"Yes, but where will the wedding be?"* (hold hands, palms up at side; bounce your arms to produce a shrug)

   "Down in the swamp in a hollow tree" (point)

4. *The first to come was Mrs. Goose* (fold arms as wings)

   She took her fiddle and she cut loose (pantomime playing the fiddle)

5. *The next to come was Dr. Flea* (bounce two fingers of one hand along one leg)

   And danced a jig with the bumblebee. (use both hands, extending two fingers from each, to pantomime dancing along your leg)

6. *The last to come was Captain Snake* (move one arm side to side in a slithering fashion)

   And wrapped its tail around the cake (adding your other hand as the Cake, pantomime wrapping your snake arm around it)

7. *For a honeymoon they went to France* (use one hand as the frog, the other as the mouse; pantomime them bouncing off to one side)

   And that's the story of their romance. (wave good-bye in the direction in which the "frog" and "mouse" just left).

Change any motion that's too difficult for your group or doesn't make sense to them. If you can't think of a better movement, ask for their suggestions.

Repeat as desired.

Variation—taking roles. Choose players to take the roles of each character mentioned (frog, mouse, goose, flea, bumblebee, snake, cake), and have them act out the song as all sing it. Repeat with another group of seven players.

MOVEMENT ACTIVITY 14—I WENT DOWN TO OLD JOE'S HOUSE (FINGERPLAY)

This activity uses movements that are small, imitative, unchanging (the players don't change them from one singing to the next), and that don't repeat for very many beats. A song or rhyme accompanied by small, imitative, set movements is generally referred to as a "fingerplay."

SONG—"Old Joe Clark" (page 141).

If possible, don't give a spoken introduction to this activity; just begin to sing and perform the movements. At any desired moment, encourage the group to join in by saying, "You can do it, too!"

Sing the indented stanzas to the tune of the refrain; sing all the other stanzas to the tune of the verse.

Line of Song	Movement
My alarm went off this morning,	Hold index finger of right hand pointing away from you (palm up, to denote lying down); shake it rapidly (alarm going off).
I kicked off the sheet,	Flick index finger repeatedly.
I did my morning exercise	Index finger does "calisthenics."
Then fell right back asleep.	Index finger "lies down."
Round and around to Old Joe Clark's, *Round and around, I say,* *Round and around to Old Joe Clark's,* *I ain't got long to stay.*	Index finger "walks around" in circles.
I went down to Old Joe's house,	Index finger of right hand "walks" to fist of left hand.
I knocked on the door,	Index finger of right hand knocks on right side of left fist.
I tried the side, I tried the back,	Index finger knocks on far side (away from you) of left fist, then on left side.
Until my fist got sore.	Index finger shakes as though hurting.
Knock and knock at Old Joe Clark's, *Knock and knock, I say,* *Knock and knock at Old Joe Clark's,* *I ain't got long to stay.*	Index finger "knocks" on thin air.
Old Joe told me to come in,	Index finger of right hand "walks" to fist of left hand.

I did not know the route,	Index finger circles left fist.
He put me in his coffeepot,	Index finger pokes down into left fist.
And poured me out the spout.	Left fist tightens around right index finger; the joined hands rotate 180°, turning "upside down."
Let me out, Old Joe Clark,	Right index finger, still held in left fist, "tries
Let me out, I say,	to get out."
Let me out, Old Joe Clark,	
I ain't got long to stay.	
I went down to Old Joe Clark's,	Index finger of right hand "walks" to fist of left hand.
He finally let me in,	Left fist opens, palm up.
I sat on the red-hot stove,	Right index finger "lands" in center of left palm.
But got right up again.	Right index finger recoils up into the air.
Ouch, ouch, Old Joe Clark,	Right index finger wiggles rapidly, as though in pain.
Ouch, ouch, I say,	
Ouch, ouch, Old Joe Clark,	
I ain't got long to stay.	
I came back from Old Joe Clark's,	Index finger of right hand "walks" back to right side.
I got back in bed,	Index finger "lies down."
I threw my pillow in the air,	Index finger flicks imaginary pillow into the air.
It landed on my head.	Left fist grabs right index finger.
Stay in bed, Old Joe Clark,	Left fist and right index finger, still "attached," bounce softly.
Stay in bed, I say,	
Stay in bed, Old Joe Clark,	
Get up another day.	

If desired, repeat the final refrain to give a greater sense of finality—and to calm down after all the excitement!

If this fingerplay is too long for your group, omit one or more of the verses.

ABSTRACT MOVEMENTS

Some movements do not imitate movements from real life, but just exist on their own. Moving your arm in a circle *could* represent cleaning a window, but it can also be an abstract movement, enjoyable in its own right.

The following activities, like many of the "repeated pulse movements" described earlier, use abstract movements.

MOVEMENT ACTIVITY 15—CATCH MY CLAPPING
(PLAYERS ECHO A SERIES OF ABSTRACT MOVEMENTS)

SONG—"Charlie over the Ocean" (page 133).

Say, "Be my echo—I do it first, then you do what I did!" Sing, clapping your hands over your head at each "x":

x   x   x x

Char-lie, ov-er the o-cean ,

All should now repeat the song while clapping four times above the head. Next, without pausing, continue singing, while clapping your hands on your shoulders four times in the same steady rhythm:

x   x   x x

Char-lie, ov-er the sea,

Continue singing, this time clapping your hands in front of you, continuing the same steady rhythm for the four claps:

Charlie caught a blackbird,

After the group echoes your singing and movements, continue immediately, clapping your hands on your knees:

Can't catch me.

Once the group has echoed the singing and movements, begin again.

If desired, change the sequence of four movements. For example, clap on your head, your stomach, your legs, and your toes.

Alternatively, repeat the same sequence (e.g., over head, shoulders, in front, knees) many times. Then ask a player to become the leader, performing the four actions four times each as a "solo." After each line of the song, the other players will echo the singing and the movements. If desired, encourage the new leader to create four new movements, one for each phrase of the song.

MOVEMENT ACTIVITY 16—CHE CHE EXERCISES
(PLAYERS ECHO A SEQUENCE OF ABSTRACT MOVEMENTS)

The previous activities changed the movement after four or more beats; this activity changes the movement more quickly (with each beat).

SONG—"Che Che Ku Le" (page 138).

Say, "Be my echo–I do it first, then you do what I did!" Sing, performing the indicated action at each syllable:

Here are the actions that the letters stand for:

> "s"–tap your hands once on your shoulders;
>
> "f"–stretch both arms forward;
>
> "s"–tap your hands once on your shoulders (again);

"u"–lift both hands high over your head.

<pre>
  s   f   s   u
Che che ku le
</pre>

All should now repeat the song while performing the four actions. Next, without pausing, continue singing, while performing the same four actions:

<pre>
  s   f   s   u
Che che   ku - fi sa
</pre>

The players should echo your singing and movements.

Continue singing, performing the same four actions with each successive line of the song, and then waiting for the group to echo each line:

> Kofi sa langa
> Ka ta chi langa
> Kum a de de.

Once the group has echoed the singing and movements, begin again.

If desired, change the sequence of four movements. Here's an example:

> tap your hands on your shoulders;
> stretch your hands out to your sides;
> tap your hands on your shoulders;
> reach your hands down toward the ground.

Here's another example:

> stand straight, holding your waist;
> bend forward;
> come back to standing straight;
> bend your knees in a partial squat.

Some movement sequences, such as the previous one, will require you to sing the song quite slowly.

Instead of changing the sequence, you can repeat the same sequence many times. Then ask a player to become the leader, performing the same four actions five times each as a "solo." After each line of the song, the other players will echo the song and the movements. If desired, encourage each new leader to create a new sequence of four movements.

MOVEMENT ACTIVITY 17—NEVER DO WHAT I DO (PLAYERS PERFORM MOVEMENTS THAT ARE THE OPPOSITE OF THE LEADER'S MOVEMENTS)

This activity makes more cognitive demands on the players, because they have to decide what the opposite of the given movement is and perform it without a pause. Abstract movements can lend themselves to concepts like "opposites" in a way that imitative movements usually do not.

SONG—"Hill and Gully Rider" (page 150).

Sing the song once, clapping along:

Never do what I do,
   Hill & gully,
Never do what I do,
   Hill & gully,
If I go one way,
   Hill & gully,
You go the other way,
   Hill & gully,
No matter what the people say,
   Hill & gully.

Say, "In this song, you *never do what I do!* You do the opposite! So if I clap high (demonstrate), you don't clap high—you clap low. Your part is always on 'Hill and gully.' Let's try it; I'll clap high on my part, then you clap low on 'Hill and gully.'" Sing, as you clap four times above your head:

Never do what I do

Sing along as the players sing, while they clap four times near the floor:

Hill & gully.

Say, "Good!" If your group seems totally confused, consider teaching another activity, instead. Alternatively, simplify by having them always clap normally, even as you clap in different positions; when they're used to this method, they may be able to add the concept of opposites. If your group seems to mostly get it, repeat your "practice" lines. When they can do a couple lines with prompting, say, "Okay, let's try the whole song"; then sing the entire song. During each line of "your part," you'll clap four times above your head; during each "Hill & gully," the players will clap four times near the floor.

When the players are ready for more challenge, say, "Now, if I clap low, where will you clap?" Try the song once that way, with your clapping low and their clapping high. When this way is clear, try clapping high during one line of your part, and low during the next. The players, of course, will have to respond by clapping in the opposite way.

When the players are ready for still more challenge, say, "If I clap in front of me, where do you think the opposite place to clap will be?" Try the song once with you clapping in front of your body; the players will sing back while clapping behind their bodies.

Gradually, increase the repertoire of ways to clap, along with their opposites. Try each one by itself for a while before mixing it with previously learned ways.

Try clapping on one side (players will respond on the other side), with loud claps (soft), with a large movement (small), with a jerky movement (smooth), or even with a movement that's close to your body (far).

NONPULSE RHYTHMS

So far, all our movements have been in time with the pulse, or basic beat, of the song. They've been as steady as marching feet in a parade. The rhythms of movements, of course, can also be as varied as the rhythms of song words or of musical instruments.

In the next activity, the movement occurs only twice, on strongly accented beats.

MOVEMENT ACTIVITY 18—PULL ON THE ROPE
(PLAYERS PANTOMIME PULLING THE ROPES ON A SAILING SHIP)

SONG—"Round the Corner" (page 137).

Say, "Sailors used to have to pull up the sails on their ship. A long rope went up over a pulley, then down to the deck, and through another pulley. The sailors would stand in a line and pull the rope along the deck. To know when to pull together, they'd sing a song. See if you can tell when the sailors would pull." Sing the song, emphasizing the syllables in boldface type:

Oh, around the corner we will go,
***Round** the corner, **Sal**-ly.*

Say, "Did you hear the words that made you want to pull?" If your group doesn't answer or gives miscellaneous answers, sing it again. If they still don't seem to understand, say, "Let me show you how the sailors did it," and demonstrate pretending to pull a rope on the two underlined syllables. Then say, "Let's try it together!" Sing again, as all sing and pretend to pull a rope.

Repeat, singing as many of the verses from page 137 as you like.

Variation—vertical ropes. Some ropes were pulled as they came straight down from the mast. Have your group pretend to pull on a vertical rope.

Variation—pull with different body parts. Say, "If you couldn't pull the rope with your hands, how else could you pull it?" Suggestions might include feet, teeth, etc. Choose a suggestion, and say, "Good! This isn't how sailors really did it, but let's pretend to pull with our feet."

MOVEMENT ACTIVITY 19—CHE CHE CLAPPING
(PLAYERS ECHO CLAPPING IN RHYTHM)

In this activity, the movements occur in the rhythm of the sung words.

SONG—"Che Che Ku Le" (page 138).

Say, "Be my echo—I do it first, then you do what I did!" Sing, clapping at each syllable (marked by an "x"):

x   x   x   x
Che che ku le

Pause while the group echoes and claps. As soon as they finish, begin the next line of the song, again clapping at each "x":

x   x   x   x   x
Che che ku - fi sa

Pause while the group echoes and claps. Continue in this fashion for the remaining three lines of the song, clapping once for each syllable, and pausing after each line while the group echoes:

Ko - fi sa lan - ga
Ka ta chi lan - ga
Kum a de de.

Repeat. If desired, change leaders, change the movement, or change the character of the clapping and singing (fast or slow; smooth or jerky; angry, sleepy, or scared).

MOVEMENTS FOR STANDING, LYING, AND MOVING AROUND

The movement activities in the previous sections have been designed for players who are sitting down in a circle or group. The next activities require more space, preferably unobstructed by furniture. The following activities can save the day when children have been cooped up, by allowing them to meet their need for energetic activity.

GETTING PLAYERS TO STOP MOVING

As soon as you get your players out of their seats, you have a problem: how do you get them back? As a new teacher, my nightmare was a room full of children with whom I had lost contact. Avoiding that nightmare is simple: before you start them moving out of their seats, make sure you have established a signal for returning—a signal that will make it as attractive to stop moving as it is to continue.

The next two activities establish interesting ways to stop moving.

MOVEMENT ACTIVITY 20—GRAB THE CABBAGE (PLAYERS END THE SONG BY PANTOMIMING GRABBING A CABBAGE ON THE GROUND; OPTIONALLY, THEY JUMP LIKE RABBITS DURING THE REST OF THE SONG)

SONG—"Old Mr. Rabbit" (page 153).

Sing the song:

> *Old Mister Rabbit,*
> *You got a mighty habit,*
> *Of jumping in my garden*
> *And eating all my cabbage.*

Say, "Did you hear what the rabbit ate up?" (If no one did, sing the song again.) "That's right, cabbage. Where does cabbage grow? Does it grow up high or down near the ground? That's right; it grows right on the ground. When you hear the word 'cabbage,' grab the cabbage on the ground and freeze. Let's try it: 'cabbage.'" All should grab imaginary cabbage.

Say, "Okay, let me try to fool you. I'll just be talking along, and I won't tell you when I'm going to say . . . 'cabbage.'" Pause as all bend down and freeze again.

Say, "You're good at this! This time, I'll fool you by singing the word in the song. Ready?" Sing the song again; at the last word, all should bend down and grab imaginary cabbages.

At this point you can add the large-body movement activity. Say, "Now I'll make it even trickier. Can you jump up and down like a rabbit while I sing?" Repeat the song as all jump around, ending with bending and freezing, as before. Praise the group for being so hard to fool. If some forget to stop, exult: "Ah, ha! I think I fooled some of you. I'll give you another chance. Ready?"

Repeat as desired. If you like, substitute a different large-body movement.

Variation—ways to jump. Say, "Who has a different way to jump?" Choose a player whose hand is raised, and say, "Show us your way, Diane. Great! Let's all try Diane's way." Repeat as desired.

MOVEMENT ACTIVITY 21—WON'T YOU SIT DOWN? (PLAYERS PERFORM A SERIES OF STANDING MOVEMENTS IN WHICH THEY SIT DOWN AND STAND BACK UP, ALTERNATING WITH ANIMAL MOVEMENTS THAT MAY TAKE THEM AROUND THE ROOM)

This activity is similar to the previous one but provides a series of actions (not just a single action) once players stop moving.

SONG—"Sit Down" (page 121).

Sing the refrain of the song, performing the indicated movements:

line of song	action
Oh, won't you sit down?	Crouch, with palms up, arms at sides as though saying, "I don't know!"
No, I won't sit down.	Stand up, defiantly extending arms down at sides with clenched fists.
Oh, won't you sit down?	Crouch, as above.
No, I won't sit down.	Stand up, as above.
Oh, won't you sit down?	Crouch, as above.
No, I won't sit down,	Stand up, as above.
'Cause I just got here, I got to look around.	Turn around once, in place.

Say, "Try it with me!" Sing and move again, as all join in.

Once the players have practiced the refrain, you can add improvisational movements on the verse. For example, say, "Can you pretend to be a bird flying?" Sing the verse,

> *What's that yonder in the sky?*
> *Looks like a bird just flying by.*

End with the refrain, which will bring everyone to a stop. Continue with more verses. You can ask for variations on "flying," or for names of different kinds of birds to imitate (*Looks like a vulture flying through the sky*), or you can go on to different kinds of land-based animals:

> *What's that yonder on the ground?*
> *Looks like elephants walking around.*

If at any point you need to give instructions during the verse, you can sing whatever you need to say, without trying to rhyme:

> *Be careful not to hurt someone,*
> *Make sure those birds aren't having a crash.*
> *Thank you, Jason, that's much better,*
> *Now all the birds have room to fly.*

Repeat any verse as many times as desired. Come back to the refrain whenever you need "crowd control."

To end the song for the day, sing the last refrain this way, interchanging crouching and standing as appropriate to the words:

> *Oh, won't you stand up?*
> *No, I won't stand up!*
> *Oh, won't you stand up?*
> *No, I won't stand up!*
> *Oh, won't you stand up?*
> *No, I won't stand up,*
> *'Cause I'm out of breath, I gotta sit back down.*

For the final line, sit all the way down. Now your group is ready for another activity.

MOVEMENTS WHILE STANDING IN PLACE

The next two activities can be done even where space prevents walking, running, or crawling—in the aisles between rows of desks, for example.

MOVEMENT ACTIVITY 22—RALLY MOVEMENTS
(PLAYERS ALTERNATE JUMPING WITH OTHER MOVEMENTS THEY SUGGEST)

SONG—"Weldon" (page 129).

Sing the refrain:

> *Rally, rally, rally,*
> *I think I heard them say,*
> *Rally, rally, rally,*
> *I think I heard them say.*

Say, "Do you know what 'rally' means? It means to all come together to do something. But to do what? Let's jump. Ready?" Sing the refrain again as all jump up and down.

Say, "Who has a movement we can do while we're standing up?" Choose a player who has raised a hand, and say, "Maelinda, show us your way to move. Spinning around! Let's try spinning around, like Maelinda. Ready?" Sing the verse as all spin:

> *It's time to spin in Weldon,*
> *I think I heard them say,*

It's time to spin in Weldon,
I think I heard them say.

Say, "Do you remember what to do on 'rally'? Let's jump." Sing the refrain again as all jump.

Take another suggested movement from another player. Repeat as desired, always alternating a movement suggested by a player with a refrain of jumping. If you prefer, replace jumping with a more sedate movement for the refrain.

MOVEMENT ACTIVITY 23—HOLD AND JUMP (PLAYERS SUGGEST PARTS OF THE BODY TO HOLD WHILE JUMPING)

SONG—"Hold My Mule" (page 143).

Sing:

Hold my mule while I dance Josey,
Hold my mule while I dance Josey,
Hold my mule while I dance Josey,
Hello, Susan Brown-ie-o.

Say, "What did I say to hold? That's right, a mule. A mule is a little like a horse and a little like a donkey. Can you hold out your hands like you're holding a mule's reins? Good! Now all we have to do is to 'dance Josey.' Do you know what that means? I don't either! It might mean jumping, though. Let's try it. Keep holding your mule while you jump." Sing the song again, as all jump, holding arms out and forward.

Say, "Can you hold some part of your body while you jump? Who can think of a part of your body you can hold? Wow! Jacqueline is holding her feet. That's hard! Let's try it." Sing the song again, as all hold toes with hands, and try to jump up and down:

Hold my toes while I dance Josey . . .

Repeat as desired, having additional players make up other parts of the body to hold.

Variation—holding a partner. Say, "Can you hold someone else's hand? Find someone to hold hands with, while you jump." Sing as all hold a partner's hand and jump up and down:

Hold my hand while I dance Josey . . .

Repeat as desired, saying, "What other part of your partner's body could you hold?"

MOVING AROUND THE ROOM

Movements that take a person from one place to another are called locomotor movements. Any of the previous four activities can be used for locomotor movements, by alternating an around-the-room movement with the standing "refrain." The alternation helps players stop their locomotor movements and gives you a chance to make suggestions about "traffic management," such as, "I noticed last time there was almost a 'traffic accident.' When cars drive, they don't touch each other. I think we'd better leave some space, too, for safety."

Once players have mastered the art of stopping and have some traffic management skills, you can introduce activities such as the following, where one locomotor movement leads quickly to another.

MOVEMENT ACTIVITY 24—WAYS TO WALK
(PLAYERS SUGGEST WAYS TO PERFORM THE MOVEMENT NAMED IN THE SONG)

SONG—"Old Joe Clark" (page 141).

Sing the following refrain:

> Walked and walked to Old Joe Clark,
> Goodbye Betsy Brown,
> Walked and walked to Old Joe Clark,
> I'm a-going away from town.

Have players make up ways to walk (humorous, if you like). If desired, choose one player's variation and have all try it. To give more time for each variation, sing, whistle or hum the verse (your choice of words from pages 101 and 141) in between refrains.

Variations—other movements. Try making variations on other movements, as suggested by one of these refrains:

> Walk the chalk, Old Joe Clark,
> Goodbye, I'm gone,
> Walk the chalk, Old Joe Clark,
> With the golden slippers on.

> Row around, Old Joe Clark,
> Sail away and gone,
> Row around, Old Joe Clark,
> With the golden slippers on.

> Roll, roll, Old Joe Clark,
> Roll, roll, I say,
> Roll, roll, Old Joe Clark,
> You'd better be getting away.

MOVEMENT ACTIVITY 25—WE ALL STOP TOGETHER
(PLAYERS IMITATE THE LEADER'S WAY OF MOVING;
A NEW LEADER'S NAME IS CALLED OUT EACH TIME)

SONG—"Windy Weather" (page 136).

Say, "This is a game where you do what the leader does. I'm the leader now, so you do what I do, and stop when I stop. You can go in any direction, but walk like I'm walking. Ready?" Walk around the room, as all imitate you, singing,

> Windy weather, frosty weather,
> When the wind stops, we all stop together.

At the end of the song, stop for a moment. (If desired, freeze in a comical pose.) All should stop, too, in the same pose as you.

Repeat a few times, doing a different movement each time, until the group has mastered the idea.

When the group is ready for more challenge, say, "I'm going to let someone be the leader for one time—but I'm not going to tell you who. I'll just shout out the name when we stop. Ready?" Perform a movement as all imitate you, singing the song again. When all have stopped, shout out the name of another player and begin to sing again. If necessary, remind the player you named to begin moving in a new way, and remind the others whom they should imitate. At the end, remind the new leader to call out the name of another player who has not yet had a turn to be leader.

Variation—line game. Play this as a line game. All imitate the movement of the player at the head of the line. At the end of one time through the song, the leader goes to the end of the line, and the next player leads with a new movement.

Since the song is so short, the old leader has scarcely enough time to get to the end of the line before yet another leader begins. The effect can be exhilarating or confusing, depending on the abilities of your group.

MOVEMENTS WHILE LYING DOWN

Lying down movements require enough space for every player to lie down, but they don't require the players to be able to navigate around the space. It's possible to do the following two activities between rows of desks, or on cots or sleeping pads.

MOVEMENT ACTIVITY 26—FLOATING UP ARIRANG HILL (GUIDED RELAXATION FANTASY: PLAYERS LIE DOWN AND PERFORM MOVEMENTS AS SUGGESTED BY THE LEADER)

SONG—"Arirang" (page 139).

Say, "They say that if you know how to relax and you think of Arirang Hill, you can float right up it! Find a place to lie down where you have enough room to feel comfortable. Close your eyes, if it helps you feel relaxed and imagine better. Now lift one leg about a foot off the ground, and stretch it out toward Arirang Hill. Just think about stretching that leg for hundreds of miles." Sing the first half of the song with these words:

> *Arirang, Arirang, arariyo,*
> *You are leaving me to go past Arirang hill;*

Say, "Now lower that leg and lift and stretch the other one." Sing the second half of the song with these words:

> *Is that Arirang under a spell?*
> *The higher I am climbing, the higher it seems.*

Say, "Lower your leg. Now lift one arm and stretch it toward Arirang Hill." Sing the first half of the song again, with the previous words.

Say, "Let that arm drop and raise your other arm." Sing the second half again, with the previous words.

Say, "Now stretch your neck by turning your head from side to side." Sing the first half of the song with these words:

Arirang, Arirang, arariyo,
Arirang Valley, how well you grow;

Say, "Now take some deep breaths." Sing the second half of the song with these words:

In our village the harvest is good;
All through the land there will be plenty of food.

Say, "Do you feel relaxed? Do you feel as if you're floating over Arirang Hill?" Allow players to remain relaxed for a while or to comment on their sensations.

MOVEMENT ACTIVITY 27—STIFF AND FLOPPY (RELAXATION EXERCISE: LEADER CHECKS THAT PLAYERS' BODIES ARE STIFF, THEN FLOPPY)

SONG—"Good-bye, Old Paint" (page 140).

Say, "Lie down on the floor; find yourself enough room to be comfortable. Can you imagine you're the ground in the Old West—and there hasn't been any rain for months. Make your whole body as stiff and hard as soil that's dried out and needs rain."

Go from player to player, "testing" their arms and legs to see that they are stiff, singing as you go:

The ground's dry and dusty all over this land,
Good-bye, old Paint, I'm leaving Cheyenne.

If your strength allows, try raising the players' whole bodies off the ground. To do so, stand with one foot next to each ear of the lying player, place one of your hands under each of the player's shoulders, and lift the player to standing position. If the player isn't stiff enough, you may have to touch the part of the player's body that's bending, and say, "Make yourself stiff here." Once the player is upright, lower the player to the floor again.

If you wish, you can sing this verse, too:

The grass is a-dying all over this land,
Good-bye, old Paint, I'm leaving Cheyenne.

When you've checked each player for stiffness, go on to say, "Now the rain is falling! Feel yourself get softer and more moist. Little by little, you're getting as floppy and soft as mud. If I lift your hand now, it should fall back easily." Go around again, testing arms, legs, and/or heads for floppiness. Sing as you go:

The rain is a-falling all over this land,
Good-bye, old Paint, I'm leaving Cheyenne.

If you wish, you can add some of these verses:

The grass is a-rising all over this land,
Good-bye, old Paint, I'm leaving Cheyenne.

We spread down the blanket on the green, grassy ground,
Good-bye, old Paint, I'm leaving Cheyenne.

The horses and cattle were a-grazing all around,
Good-bye, old Paint, I'm leaving Cheyenne.

Continue until everyone is relaxed!

MOVEMENTS WITH OTHERS

As rewarding as individual movements can be, there is a special joy to moving in concert with others. Even though the movements in this section make demands on the players' social abilities, they also promise unmatched rewards in aesthetic pleasure and group unity.

Many of the previous activities involved moving in time with others, but the following activities involve movement while touching one or more other players. For some hints about dealing with peer-pressure and partner-choosing, see the section Play Party Games under the sub-heading About the Two Roles. For activities that help players learn to choose partners, see the section Games for Choosing.

For other activities that involve moving with others, consult the variations given with Movements 13—Riding with the Frog, and with Movements 23—Hold and Jump, above.

STATIC MOVEMENTS

Throughout this book, I've encouraged movements that are rhythmic—continuous movements that relate to the rhythm of the songs. Such movements help players develop a sense of rhythm, and a sense of purpose and shape in their movements. When movements aren't made with a sense of rhythm, they tend to become tense and mechanical. Many preschool fingerplay sessions attest to this problem.

Static movements have a place, however. If simply getting into a position is challenging, moving while in it might be impossibly difficult. In particular, when players are first learning to move with another person, almost any rhythmic coordination is too demanding. The next two activities, therefore, involve creating static shapes with a partner or group.

MOVEMENT ACTIVITY 28—I DON'T HAVE A TRIANGLE (PARTNERS OR SMALL GROUPS CREATE GEOMETRIC SHAPES TOGETHER)

SONG—"Poor Lonesome Cowhand" (page 156).

Sing:

> *I'm a poor, lonesome cowhand,*
> *I'm a poor, lonesome cowhand,*
> *I'm a poor, lonesome cowhand,*
> *A long way from home.*

Say, "Can you imagine the poor lonesome cowhand—out in the cattle country—who doesn't even have a plate to eat from? We can give the cowhand a round plate. Get a partner. Find a way to make a round plate-shape together." Sing, as all form circular shapes with arms, legs, and so on:

I don't have a plate,
I don't have a plate,
I don't have a plate,
To eat my dinner on.

Comment on the circles you see, calling attention to the variety of ways to make round shapes. You might say, "Look at all those round plates! I see that some people made circles with their fingers. Some people made a circle close to the ground. Get a new partner and find another way to make a round plate for the cowhand together." Repeat as desired.

When your players are ready to try forming other shapes, sing different verses, requiring different shapes:

I don't have a dollar . . .
To buy myself some clothes. (dollar bill—rectangle)

I don't have a rope . . .
To tie around a calf. (rope—straight line)

I don't have a triangle . . .
To call the cowhands in. (metal bell—triangle)

At any point, you can increase the challenge by saying, "This time, make groups of three. Find a way for all three of you to make a circle together." Change the size of the groups as desired. It's fun to end this activity by having your entire group form one final shape. If the shape is a circle, you have a formation for another activity. If the shape is a line, you're ready to leave the room!

MOVEMENT ACTIVITY 29—MAKING LETTER SHAPES (PARTNERS OR SMALL GROUPS CREATE SHAPES OF LETTERS TOGETHER)

SONG—"It's A Shame" (page 126).

Sing (clapping along, if you wish):

There's a letter we must make on our homework,
There's a letter we must make on our homework;
It's an A, B, C, D, E,
That's the letter we must make on our homework.

Say, "Find a partner. When you find one, hold your partner's hand and walk around together." Sing the song again, but extend the third line:

There's a letter we must make on our homework,
There's a letter we must make on our homework;
It's an A, B, C, D, E, F, G, H, I, J, K, L!

Stop singing suddenly. Say, "L! Find a way to make a letter 'L' with your partner!" Finish singing the song:

That's the letter we must make on our homework.

After partners have formed the shape of the letter "L," comment on the shapes you see, emphasizing their variety. For example, you might say, "Look at all those different ways to make an 'L'! Some people did it lying down; some did it standing up. Some are small, and some are big."

Repeat, with different partners, if you wish. Sing the entire song, extending the third line as long as desired. The last letter you sing is the one that the players should form.

For more challenge, increase the size of the groups, by saying, "This time, find groups of three." It's fun to end by having the entire group make an "O" or an "I."

RHYTHMIC MOVEMENTS

Compared to the previous two static movement activities, rhythmic movement activities demand more: not only must players get themselves into a position together, they must coordinate moving in time to the music. Since some of them also require players to create their own movements, it's important for the leader to give praise for all honest efforts. A few ill-timed criticisms can cause some players to stop participating and even to divert their efforts to disruption.

For other activities that require rhythm motions in a group, see the chapters on Games—in particular, the section on Rhythm Games. For ways to form a circle (a circle of players is needed for some of the following activities), see the section on Line and Circle Games.

Since the Rhythm Games don't generally require players to make up movements, they can be less threatening than the group movement activities given here. By the same token, however, Rhythm Games give less opportunity for creativity and may seem less rewarding to certain players.

MOVEMENT ACTIVITY 30—STANDING HIGH AND STANDING LOW (PARTNERS OR GROUPS OF THREE FIND WAYS TO MOVE TOGETHER WHILE AT DIFFERENT LEVELS IN SPACE)

SONG—"Down Came a Lady" (page 123).

Sing:

> *Daniel and Matty*
> *How will they go?*
> *Lord Daniel standing high,*
> *Little Matty standing low.*

Say, "Find yourself a partner. Now one of you is Lord Daniel; you stand up. The other is Little Matty; you crouch or sit or lie down low. See if you can find a movement you can do together even though you're at different heights. Try it!" Sing the song again, as all move in time to it.

Comment on the movements you see, emphasizing their variety. For example, you might say, "Look! Some people found ways to use their arms together. Some of you used one person's foot with another person's hand. Now switch: the one who was Matty is now Daniel. Find another movement to do together!" Sing the song again, as all create new movements with their partners.

Repeat, switching partners as desired. If you wish, you can have groups of three find three different levels and create some movement together that all three can participate in. You can even specify whether the movements should be done standing still or moving around the room.

MOVEMENT ACTIVITY 31—RAISING THE SAIL
(PARTNERS OR GROUPS, SITTING BACK-TO-BACK, RISE TO A STANDING POSITION)

SONG—"Juley" (page 148).

Sing rhythmically, clapping to emphasize the syllables in boldface type:

> *The sail she's a rising,*
> ***Oo*-*oo, **oo**-*oo,*
> *Haul her up together,*
> ***Walk** along, Miss **Ju**-liana Brown!*

Say, "Sailors on a sailing ship had to pull up the sails with long ropes. The wind was pulling against them, and the sails were heavier than one person could lift, so several sailors had to pull together. Pretend you're pulling on a rope when I do." Sing again, as all mime the rope pulling at the underlined syllables.

When your players understand where in the song to pull, say, "Great! Now you can be the sails and the sailors at the same time. Get a partner. Sit on the floor, back to back, bend your knees, and link your elbows with your partner. The two of you are the sail, and you're going to push yourselves up with your legs. Just like sailors, you have to work together! Push against your partner when I clap; in between, get your balance and get ready to push again. Ready?" Sing the song again, clapping at the underlined syllables, as the partners try to push each other to a standing position. When pairs succeed, cheer!

Repeat with new partners. If desired, increase the size of the groups. Three or more people can sit on the ground in a tight circle, back to back, knees bent, and elbows linked. It helps to stay very close to each other. The more people in a circle, the more challenging it is. If you like, have players try to set records for the most people who can raise a sail together.

MOVEMENT ACTIVITY 32—PASS THE SHAKE
(PLAYERS PASS A HANDSHAKE OR HUG
FROM PERSON TO PERSON AROUND A CIRCLE)

SONG—"I'm Going Home On The Morning Train" (page 135).
SPACE/FORMATION NEEDED—a standing circle of players.

Sing:

> *Take this shake and pass it on,*
> *Take this shake and pass it on,*
> *Take this shake, take this shake,*
> *Take this shake and pass it on.*

Say, "This song passes a handshake all the way around the circle. I'll start it off." Shake hands with the player to your left in the circle as you sing,

> *Take this shake and pass it on,*

Say to that player, "Now you turn around and shake hands with the next person." Sing the second line as that player shakes hands with the third player:

Take this shake and pass it on,

Continue singing one line of the song for each handshake. Four handshakes will happen during one time through the song. Repeat until the handshake returns to you.

Variation—faster shaking. If desired, add some rhythmic challenge by "passing the shake" twice during the third line. Say, "The song passes the handshakes faster here. You have to make your shakes go quickly!" One handshake happens during the first part of the third line:

Take this shake, . . .

Then a second handshake happens during the second half of the third line:

. . . take this shake,

In this way, a total of five handshakes occur during one time through the song.

Variation—pass the hug. Instead of passing a handshake, pass a hug. You may wish to say, "If you don't want to be hugged, just hold out your hand, and get a handshake instead." Sing the song this way:

Take this hug and pass it on . . .

MOVEMENT ACTIVITY 33—HANDS, MY PARTNER, DEARIE (PARTNERS CLAP HANDS OR OTHER BODY PARTS AND THEN CHANGE PARTNERS)

SONG—"Dance A Baby Diddy" (page 151).

Sing:

> *Hands, my partner, dearie,*
> *Will you never grow weary?*
> *Frolic and play, now while you may,*
> *And hands, my partner, dearie.*

Say, "Everyone find a partner." If there is an odd number of players, become the last player's partner; if not, stand alone. "Clap hands with your partner while we sing." Sing the song again, as all clap with partners. At the end, say, "Now, clap elbows with your partner." As all clap elbows, sing,

> *Elbows, my partner, dearie,*
> *Will you never grow weary?*
> *Frolic and play, now while you may,*
> *And elbows, my partner, dearie.*

After the song, call out the name of another part of the body, such as "Knees!" Sing the song again, beginning, "Knees, my partner, dearie." Repeat as desired.

Say, "When I say 'change,' find a new partner. One person will be left out; I won't be the leader anymore, but that person will become the new leader and will call out what to clap. Ready?" After any singing of the song, call out "change."

When all have changed partners, the partnerless player becomes the new leader. (Use yourself to create an odd number of players. In other words, if you were alone before, get a partner now; if you had a partner before, drop out now.) The leader calls out parts of the body and after any verse yells, "Change!" Then all will scramble for new partners, and a new player will become the leader.

Variation—calling out in the song. As the leader, do not call out the name of a new part of the body between verses. Instead, sing the new part in the final line of the song:

> *Hands, my partner, dearie,*
> *Will you never grow weary?*
> *Frolic and play, now while you may,*
> *And **elbows**, my partner, dearie.*

In the same way, do not call out "Change!" but sing the final line this way:

> *. . . And **change**, my partner, dearie.*

NEW VERSES

Songs consist of words and melodies. When you play a game or make up movements to a song, you usually leave the song unchanged. In this section, however, you will have the fun of changing a song's words.

It's possible to make completely new verses for any of the songs in this collection. It's easier and more reliable, however, to model your new verses on existing ones. In fact, you can make new verses by simply suggesting a replacement for one or more of the words in an exiting verse. The fewer words you replace, the simpler it is!

In traditional music for group singing, it's common to replace a single word. In folk hymns sung at revival meetings, for example, many songs begin with a verse about fathers (e.g., "Come on, fathers, join in the band!") and continue through the list of family members ("Come on mothers," sisters, brothers, children, etc.). When the group or the leader is tired of making up new verses in this way, the song is over!

In more complicated replacements, two or more substitutions must be made at once. If the song says, for example,

> *Down came a person, down came two,*
> *Down came Doug, and he was dressed in blue,*

then, when you change the name from "Doug" to "Rebecca," you also need to change the pronoun from "he" to "she." If Rebecca is wearing red, you may want to change the word "blue," as well.

In the most complicated replacements, you need to change a rhyming word, too. In our example, we might change "two" to a word that rhymes with "red." Then, to make sense, we have to change a whole phrase:

> *Down came a person, **eating some bread**,*
> *Down came **Rebecca**, and **she** was dressed in **red**.*

Follow the Words Set in Boldface Type

When the words to a song are given in the current section, the words to be replaced will be set in boldface type. This format lets you see at a glance what words to change.
Once you've learned a few techniques for eliciting suggestions from your group, you'll be able to understand the entire activity by just reading the verse with the changeable words set in boldface type.

ONE-PART SUGGESTIONS
ONE-WORD SUGGESTIONS: NAMES

Of all the possible substitutions, the simplest ones consist of a single word. Of these one-word suggestions, the easiest one for young children (or for those speaking an unfamiliar language) consists of suggesting the name of a person in the group.

The next two activities mention group members by name. The first is suited for starting a group time, the second for ending one.

NEW VERSES 1—I'M SO GLAD TO SEE YOU
(SING PLAYERS' NAMES IN THE SONG, ONE AT A TIME; STARTING GROUP-TIME)

SONG—"Juley" (page 148).

Sing the song, substituting your name for "Doug":

> **Doug** *is in the circle,*
> *Ya-ay! Ya-ay!*
> *I'm so glad to see you,*
> *Don't you know, I'm happy you are here.*

If desired, sing "classroom," instead of "circle."

Say (substituting your actual name), "My name is Doug. Sing the song to me." All sing the song.

Turn to the next person in the circle (or in the line, or to anyone in the group). If necessary, ask her to say her name. Say, "Let's sing the song for Jennifer." All sing:

> *Jennifer's in the circle,*
> *Ya-ay! Ya-ay!*
> *I'm so glad to see you,*
> *Don't you know, I'm happy you are here.*

Repeat with as many names as desired. If the group is not too large, welcome each player by singing his name.

Variation—several names at once. To include three names in a single verse, sing:

> *Jeremy, Marsha, and Linda,*
> *Ya-ay! Ya-ay! (etc.)*

If you wish, sing even more names:

> *Jeremy, Marsha, and Alina,*
> *Ya-ay! Ya-ay!*
> *Alex, Linda, and Lucy,*
> *Don't you know, I'm happy you are here.*

When you first introduce the song, it may make sense to sing one name at a time. On subsequent days, you can increase the pace of the activity by singing two or more names in each verse.

Variation—adding choices. Say, "Do I want the song loud or soft today? I think I'd like it soft. Sing the song softly to me." Sing the song softly, using your name, as all join in.

Ask the next person in the circle, "Jennifer, would you like the song loud or soft. Loud? Let's all sing it loudly for Jennifer." Sing the song loudly, using Jennifer's name, as all sing along. Repeat, as desired, singing one person's name each time, and letting that person choose "loud" or "soft."

Another day, vary the choice. Let each player choose "happy" or "sad"—or "fast" or "slow." Day by day, build a repertory of ways to sing the song. Eventually, just ask each player: "How would you like us to sing it today?"

NEW VERSES 2—OFF FOR MONTAN'.
(SING EACH PLAYER'S NAME, SENDING THEM ONE-BY-ONE TO ANOTHER LOCATION; ENDING GROUP-TIME)

SONG—"Good-bye, Old Paint" (page 140).

Say, "It's time to end our group time. Let's see who gets to leave first." "Count out" as you sing by pointing to one person at each "x":

x   x   x   x

I'm leav - ing Chey - enne, I'm off for Mon - tan',

x

Good - bye,

At this point, sing the name of the next person in the circle (or line), pointing to that person as you finish the song:

x

*. . . **Elisa**, I'm leaving Cheyenne.*

Say, "Elisa, it's your turn to leave the group and go out to your locker to get your coat." Substitute the actual place where you're sending people.

If desired, shake Elisa's hand and tell her something she did well during group time or during the day. Repeat for each group member.

Variation—multiple names. To send more players in a shorter time, sing two or more names in each verse:

***Elisa** and **Derek**, I'm leaving Cheyenne.*

ONE-WORD SUGGESTIONS: NOUNS AND VERBS

After names, the easiest one-word suggestions are usually common nouns and verbs. Other parts of speech (adjectives, adverbs, prepositions) may be slightly more difficult for players with limited language skills.

NEW VERSES 3—WHERE DID YOU GET HURT?
(PLAYERS SUGGEST PARTS OF THEIR BODIES
THAT HAVE BEEN HURT BUT HAVE HEALED)

SONG—"Old Joe Clark" (page 141).

Sing:

> *I went down to Old Joe Clark's,*
> *Thought I'd go a hunting,*
> *I fell down and hurt my **toe**,*
> *Came back home a-grunting.*

Say, "Did you hear what I hurt? That's right, my toe. Do you know that any part of our bodies can heal? Is there some part of your body that you hurt once that's all right now?" Call on a group member. If the group member says, "I hurt my leg," say, "Let's sing it in the song, 'I fell down and hurt my leg.' Ready?" Sing the song again, substituting "leg" for "toe."

Repeat as desired. To end, sing the "toe" verse again.

NEW VERSES 4—CHARLIE CAUGHT A BLACKBIRD
(PLAYERS SUGGEST ANIMALS TO BE CAUGHT)

SONG—"Charlie over the Ocean" (page 133).

Say, "Be my echo. I'll sing it first, then you sing it back to me." Sing, pausing to let the group echo each line:

> *Charlie, over the ocean,*
> *Charlie, over the sea,*
> *Charlie caught a **blackbird**,*
> *Can't catch me.*

Say, "Did you hear what Charlie caught? That's right, a blackbird. What else could Charlie catch?" If a player says, "a rabbit," say, "Great! A rabbit! Let's sing it!" Sing the song again, substituting "rabbit" for "blackbird."

Start again by asking "Who else can think of something that Charlie could catch?" Repeat as desired.

If you wish, have the player who suggested the verse sing the "lead" part with you, as all others echo what you two sing.

For the next activities, repeat the procedure given in the previous two. Begin by singing the model verse, then ask the first question given, pinpointing the words to be replaced. Next, ask group members to suggest replacement words, by asking the second question.

NEW VERSES 5—FILL YOUR HOUSE WITH PIE
(PLAYERS SUGGEST DIFFERENT TYPES OF PIE)

SONG—"Old Joe Clark" (page 141).

> *Old Joe Clark, he had a house,*
> *Fifteen stories high,*
> *And every story in that house*
> *Was filled with **chicken** pie.*

What was in Old Joe Clark's house?
What kind of pie would you like a whole house filled with?

Variation—substitute the player's name. If desired, also substitute the player's name. Thus, if Emily suggested pizza pie, you'll sing:

> *My friend **Emily** had a house,*
> *Fifteen stories high;*
> *And every story in that house*
> *Was filled with **pizza** pie.*

NEW VERSES 6—WHAT WOULD YOU MISS?
(PLAYERS SUGGEST WHAT THEY WOULD MISS)

SONG—"Poor Lonesome Cowhand" (page 156).

Say, "Can you imagine a poor, lonesome cowhand far from home, missing the things you have at home?"

> *I don't have a **dog**,*
> *I don't have a **dog**,*
> *I don't have a **dog**,*
> *O no, O no, O no.*

Did you hear what the cowhand misses?
What would you miss, if you were far away from home?

Variation—Spanish verses. Since this song was traditionally also sung in Spanish, it's a natural for making up verses in Spanish.

> *Yo no tengo **perro**,*
> *Yo no tengo **perro**,*
> *Yo no tengo **perro**,*
> *O no, O no, O no.*

Even if you don't speak Spanish yourself, use a group member or a dictionary to translate the English words that players suggest.

NEW VERSES 7—WHAT CAN A BABY DO WITH ME?
(PLAYERS SUGGEST DIFFERENT ACTION VERBS)

In this activity and the next one, players make up verses by suggesting a verb.

SONG—"Dance a Baby Diddy" (page 151).

> *Dancey, baby, dancey,*
> *How it shall gallop and prancey,*
> *Sit on my knee, now* **clap** *with me,*
> *And dancey, baby, dancey.*

Did you hear what the baby can do with me now?
What can a baby do *with* you?

NEW VERSES 8—WHAT WOULD YOU LIKE TO DO HERE?
(PLAYERS SUGGEST FAVORITE ACTIVITIES)

SONG—"Sit Down" (page 121).

Say, "One day, I came in this room all excited about painting. I couldn't wait to get to the easel and start to paint. But when I got to the easel, someone told me to sit down at my desk instead. But I said, 'No!'" Sing:

> *Oh, won't you sit down?*
> *No, I won't sit down!*

Say, "The voice went on saying it!" Sing:

> *Oh, won't you sit down?*
> *No, I won't sit down!*
> *Oh, won't you sit down?*
> *No, I won't sit down!*

Say, "So I told it why not." Sing:

> *Cause I just got to paint, and I won't sit down!*

Is there something you really wish you could do here?

Note: Some activities, like running, fit the refrain better this way:

> *Cause I just got here, I want to run around.*

NEW VERSES 9—WHAT HAVE YOU BEEN CALLED TO DO?
(PLAYERS SUGGEST THINGS THEY HAVE BEEN CALLED TO DO)

SONG—"Arirang" (page 139).

Sing:

> *Arirang, Arirang, arariyo,*
> *Over the hills of Arirang.*
> *Voices call me from far away.*
> *I must **follow**, I cannot stay.*

Did you hear what I was called to do?
What have you ever been called to do? (Did you ever feel that you had to do something or go some-where?)

If a group member says, "I once thought I should go home. Sure enough, when I got there, everyone was waiting for me, because I forgot we were going to my grandfather's that night," say, "Good! Can we sing, I must **go home**, I cannot stay?"

ONE-WORD SUGGESTIONS: ADJECTIVES, ADVERBS, PREPOSITIONS

Adjectives are almost as easy to come up with as nouns and verbs. Adverbs are a little more unusual, however. Prepositions, because there are so few of them in the language, are even more challenging.

Much of the fun in the following activities lies in imagining preposterous objects and actions. In New Verses 12—The Baby Who Could Sleep Anywhere, for example, the major difference between this enjoyable activity and a "preposition drill" is the fun of imagining the baby sleeping in unlikely relationships to the castle.

NEW VERSES 10—IMAGINARY FROG
(PLAYERS SUGGEST DIFFERENT ADJECTIVES TO DESCRIBE THE FROG)

SONG—"There Was a Little Frog" (page 159).

> *There was a **little** frog who lived on a hill, uh-huh, uh-huh,*
> *There was a **little** frog who lived on a hill,*
> *Who rustled and tussled like Buffalo Bill, uh-huh, uh-huh.*

Did you hear what kind of a frog was on the hill?
Can you imagine a frog in your own mind? What size is it? What color? What way does it act (e.g., wild, lazy, scary)? How does it feel (e.g., sad, angry)?

NEW VERSES 11—CRAZY GINGER
(PLAYERS SUGGEST DIFFERENT ADVERBS TO DESCRIBE HOW GINGER GROWS)

SONG—"So He Planted Ginger" (page 132).

> *The farmer planted ginger,*
> *Ginger grows so **quickly,***
> *The farmer got a nanny goat to graze on the ginger*

Nanny will not graze on ginger,
*Ginger grows so **quickly.***

Did you hear how ginger grows?
How else could ginger grow (e.g., slowly, weirdly, crookedly, sadly, suddenly)? Can you imagine a ginger plant growing? Make it a crazy ginger plant; how does it grow?

NEW VERSES 12—THE BABY WHO CAN SLEEP ANYWHERE (PLAYERS SUGGEST WHERE BABY CAN SLEEP WITH DIFFERENT PREPOSITIONS)

SONG— "Sloop, Bonnie Bairnie" (page 150).

*Sleep, bonnie bairnie, **behind** the castle,*
Bye, Bye, Bye, Bye.
You will have a golden apple,
Bye, Bye, Bye, Bye.

Did you hear where the baby is sleeping?
If the baby weren't *behind* the castle, where could it be (in front of, upon, below, inside, between the castles, around, through, above, etc.)?

ONE-PHRASE SUGGESTIONS

For most players, a group of words (a phrase) is almost as easy to suggest as a single word. In most cases, after all, a phrase represents just a single idea.

NEW VERSES 13—GOTTA DO IT IN THE MORNING (PLAYERS SUGGEST DIFFERENT THINGS THEY DO IN THE MORNING)

SONG—"Wake Me, Shake Me" (page 127).

Wake me, shake me,
Don't let me sleep too late,
*I gotta **get up early** in the morning,*
Swing on the garden gate.

Did you hear what I have to do in the morning?
What do you do in the morning?

NEW VERSES 14—WHAT CHORES DON'T YOU LIKE? (PLAYERS SUGGEST CHORES THEY DON'T LIKE TO DO)

SONG—"It's a Shame" (page 126).

*It's a shame to **wash the dishes** on a Sunday,*
*It's a shame to **wash the dishes** on a Sunday,*

When you got Monday, Tuesday, Wednesday, Thursday, Friday, Saturday,
*It's a shame to **wash the dishes** on a Sunday.*

Did you hear what I have to do that I don't like to do? (Wash the dishes)
What do you have to do that you don't like to do?

NEW VERSES 15—YES, I CAN!
(PLAYERS SUGGEST ACTIONS THEY WERE TOLD THEY COULD NOT DO)

SONG—"Hold My Mule" (page 143).

*Yes, I can and will **jump Josie**,*
*Yes, I can and will **jump Josie**,*
*Yes, I can and will **jump Josie**,*
Hello, Susan Brown-ie-o.

Did you hear what I'm going to do?
Was there ever something you were determined to do, no matter who told you that you couldn't?

MULTIPART SUGGESTIONS

The following activities require that two or more separate words or phrases be contributed.

Since the first of these activities uses the player's name as one of the items, it doesn't require an extra question by the leader. The other activities, however, may require you to ask an additional question to elicit the second item.

NEW VERSES 16—WHERE DO YOU LIVE?
(PLAYERS SUGGEST THEIR NAMES AND WHERE THEY LIVE)

SONG—"Weldon" (page 129).

***Brad** lives in **Weldon**,*
I think I heard them say,
***Brad** lives in **Weldon**,*
I think I heard them say.

Did you hear where Brad lives? (Weldon)
What is your name? Where do you live?

NEW VERSES 17—WHERE DO FOODS COME FROM?
(PLAYERS SUGGEST DIFFERENT FOODS AND WHERE THEY COME FROM)

SONG—"Old Mr. Rabbit" (page 153).

Old Mister Rabbit,
You've got a mighty habit,
*Of jumping in my **garden**,*
*And eating all my **cabbage**.*

Did you hear what the rabbit ate? (cabbage) Where was the cabbage? (in the garden)
What else could the rabbit eat?
Where does it come from?

If the player says, "The rabbit could eat cookies," say, "Where do cookies come from?" If the
answer is, "the oven," sing:

Old Mister Rabbit,
You've got a mighty habit,
*Of jumping in my **oven,***
*And eating all my **cookies**.*

NEW VERSES 18—WHEN YOUR FOOD COMES IN
(PLAYERS SUGGEST FAVORITE FOODS AND WHAT THEY LIKE WITH THEM)

SONG—"Back to Mexico" (page 125).

*What you gonna do when the **spaghetti** comes in, sugar babe,*
*What you gonna do when the **spaghetti** comes in, sugar babe,*
*What you gonna do when the **spaghetti** comes in,*
*Sit on the corner with **sauce** on your chin, sugar babe.*

Did you hear what food I'm waiting for? (spaghetti) Did you hear what was on my chin? (sauce)
What's your favorite food? What do you like on it?

NEW VERSES 19—EXCUSES
(PLAYERS MAKE UP EXCUSES)

SONG—"Hold My Mule" (page 143).

***Shoe's untied** and I can't **dance Josey**,*
***Shoe's untied** and I can't **dance Josey**,*
***Shoe's untied** and I can't **dance Josey**,*
Hello, Susan Brown-ie-o.

I'm so lazy, I'm too lazy to even dance. Did you hear why I can't dance? (My shoe's untied.)
Did you ever make an excuse why you couldn't do something? (Yes.) What couldn't you do? What was
your excuse?

NEW VERSES 20—WHAT KIND OF WEATHER?
(PLAYERS SUGGEST DIFFERENT TYPES OF WEATHER)

SONG—"Windy Weather" (page 136).

Windy weather,
Frosty weather,
When the wind blows,
We all blow together.

Did you hear what kind of weather I sang about? (Windy, frosty.) Did you hear what happens to us in it? (We all blow together.)
What other kind of weather can there be besides "windy" and "frosty"? What would happen to us in it?

If the kind of weather is "rainy," ask, "What can happen to us in the rain?" If the answer is "We'll get splashed," sing:

Rainy weather,
Rainy weather,
When the wind blows,
We get splashed together.

NEW VERSES 21—WHO LOVES YOU?
(PLAYERS SUGGEST WHO LOVES THEM AND WHY)

SONG—"Round the Corner" (page 137).

Oh, Tom loves me well, he loves me strong,
Round the corner, Sally,
He loves my singing, he loves me long,
Round the corner, Sally.

Did you hear who loves me? (Tom) Did you hear what he loves about me? (My singing)
Who is someone who loves you? What does that person love about you?

NEW VERSES 22—APPRECIATIONS
(LEADER SINGS TO EACH PLAYER WHAT HE LIKES ABOUT HER OR HIM)

SONG—"Juley" (page 148).

Maria, you are smart,
Oo - oo, oo - oo,
Maria, Maria, Maria,
Walk along, Miss Juliana Brown!

Say, "Did you hear what I like about Maria?" If the answer is, "She's smart," say, "Great! Let's all sing it to Maria!" Sing the song to her.

Say, "Who would like a turn to hear something I like about you?" If George raises his hand, say, "George! I'd be happy to tell you something I love about you. Ready?" Sing an appropriate appreciation to George, such as,

George, you are delightful,
Oo - oo, oo - oo,

George, George, George,
Walk along, Miss Juliana Brown!

In many parts of our society, it's unusual for people to say out loud what they like about each other. As a result, you may need to be especially sensitive to your group's needs and abilities when using this activity.

Some children may feel embarrassed to hear these appreciations out loud. They may giggle or do things to distract attention from the activity. I often explain to the group that it's okay to feel embarrassed, and that letting the giggles *out* may help to let the nice words *in*. At the same time, I won't let anyone insult another or distract from someone else's turn to be appreciated. I might say, "It's okay to feel embarrassed about this, but I can't let you take away from George's turn. Would you like your turn next?"

If it's too embarrassing for individuals to be appreciated in front of the group, you can pave the way by finding time in the course of other activities to whisper private appreciations into each child's ear.

NEW VERSES 23—EVERYBODY DOING IT
(PLAYERS SUGGEST THINGS THEY COULD ALL EAT OR DO AT ONCE)

SONG—"Hold My Mule" (page 143).

> *Big **wad of gum**, and everybody **chewing** it,*
> *Big **wad of gum**, and everybody **chewing** it,*
> *Big **wad of gum**, and everybody **chewing** it,*
> *Hello, Susan Brown-ie-o.*

Can you imagine a piece of gum so big that we could all chew on it at once?
What else could we all eat or drink at once?

If someone says, "A big chocolate milk shake," say something like, "Wow! Pretend you all have straws and this room is one big milk shake!"

> *Great big **milk shake**, and everybody **drinking** it . . .*

What else could we all do at once if we had something big enough?

If someone says, "take a bath," say, "Sure, let's sing":

> *Great big **tub**, and everybody **bathing in** it . . .*

NEW VERSES 24—WHAT JOB WOULD YOU LIKE?
(PLAYERS SUGGEST JOBS THEY WOULD LIKE)

SONG—"I Wish I Was A Cowpoke" (page 130).

> *I wish I was a **cowpoke**,*
> *In some **cowpoke** land,*
> *With **boots** on my feet,*
> *And a **lariat** in my hand.*
> > *Honor to your right,*
> > *Honor to your left,*

Swing your right-hand partner,
And promenade to the left.

Did you hear what I want to be? (a cowpoke)
If you could be anything in the world, what would you be?
What would you wear on your head? What would you be holding in your hand?

If someone says "a space man," say, "Great! Women can go into space, too. Can we say 'space explorer'? What would you wear on your head if you were a space explorer? What would you have in your hand?" If the answers are "helmet" and "laser gun," sing:

*I wish I was a **space explorer**,*
*In some **space explorer's** land,*
*With a **helmet** on my head,*
*And a **laser gun** in my hand . . .*

SOLO-SINGING OPPORTUNITIES

In all the Making Verses activities above, group members make their suggestions by speaking them to you. Next, you repeat their suggestion to the group. Finally, everyone sings the suggestion. This three-step process can become cumbersome, in time.

Once the making of new verses is a familiar activity, however, you can speed the process by having group members sing their suggestions directly. This structure requires the individual making a suggestion to sing a solo. Obviously, the solo could be for the entire verse. In this section, however, you'll learn techniques for helping individuals sing shorter, easier solos—thus making the whole process of making verses faster and more exciting.

To sing suggestions in this way, the members of your group will have to know the song well (to teach it, have them make up verses first in the conventional way, until—after enough days or weeks—they have learned the melody). In addition, they need to have developed their sense of rhythm and control of their speech. Inserting new words into a song on the fly is like loading a moving wagon: if you're not sure where to put your load or if you can't coordinate letting go with your hands, you'll miss!

The shortest solos consist of a single word, line, or phrase. The easiest short solos don't come at the beginning of a verse, but after the verse has "gotten rolling." In addition, some pieces of a melody are easier to sing than others, and some make it easier to insert an extra syllable or two to accommodate longer suggestions. Taking all these factors into account, the following activities are presented in their approximate order of difficulty.

TEACHING SOLO SINGING

To introduce a group to the technique of solo singing their suggestions, choose a song for which they've enjoyed making verses already. For example, suppose they've enjoyed New Verses 3—Where Did You Get Hurt? (page 101). One day, say, "I'm going to keep my idea a secret. I won't tell you what I'm going to sing. I'll put it right in the song. Are you ready? Sing it with me!" Sing:

I went down to Old Joe Clark's,
Thought I'd go a hunting,

At this point, say, "Just me!" Sing the next line by yourself:

*I fell down and hurt my **toe**,*

Motion for all to join again, or say, "Everybody!" Sing the final line together:

Came back home a-grunting.

Say, "Is there anyone who can do what I just did?" If a group member volunteers, say, "Great! Now, decide what part of you it is that you're going to say got hurt—but don't tell us! Keep it a secret! Did you decide? Good! We'll sing—but when we get to 'I fell down and hurt my ____,' you'll sing it all by yourself. Ready?"

Sing the song with the group, motioning them to be silent while the chosen person sings her solo line. Motion the group to join back in for the final line of the verse.

If this first child does not succeed, it may have been too soon to teach this technique. Don't tell anyone that they didn't do it right; just go back to the familiar way, without comment. Try again in a few weeks.

If this first child succeeds, say, "That was great! Does anyone else want to do what she did?" Repeat with another group member.

SPEEDING UP THE PROCESS EVEN MORE

Eventually, it will be easy for your group to make their suggestions through solo singing, avoiding the interruptions to the song required by speaking each suggestion before singing it.

In the form of solo singing described above, however, there are still interruptions. You call on a group member, have the group sing the song (with the soloist singing one phrase or line), then you stop the song to call on a new solo singer.

To eliminate stopping to identify the next singer, call on more than one solo singer at a time. Say, "Do you think we could have two secrets in a row? Raise your hand if you want to sing your secret in the song." Call on two group members, then tell one to go first, and the other to wait for the second time through the song. Sing the song twice through, pointing at the appropriate solo singer at the appropriate times. If two succeed, try even more. You might even try to set a group record!

For the ultimate in exciting, efficient, solo singing of suggestions, don't identify the solo singers before you start singing. Just say, "Raise your hand if you'd like a turn to sing your secret in the song, and keep it raised. I'll point to you when it's your turn to sing." Stand in front of each soloist in time to warn him that his turn is coming, then point to him when he should sing his solo phrase. Since no one knows who the next solo singer will be, the group will be on the edge of their chairs, ready to join in at a moment's notice. Mastery of this format is a splendid achievement in group cooperation and listening!

NEW VERSES 25—WHAT GROWS IN THE GARDEN?
(SOLO SINGING—PLAYER SUGGESTS WHAT GROWS)

This activity and the next two activities are similar to previous ones (#17, #4, and #5, respectively), except that they are adapted for solo singing.

SONG—"Old Mr. Rabbit" (page 153).

> *Old Mister Rabbit,*
> *You've got a mighty habit,*
> *Of jumping in my garden,*
> *And eating all my **cabbage**.*

Did you hear what the rabbit ate? (cabbage) Where was the cabbage? (in the garden)
What else grows in a garden, that a rabbit could eat?

Have the solo singer sing just the last word. Alternatively, have her sing the last line, or even the last two lines.

NEW VERSES 26—WHAT DID CHARLIE CATCH?
(SOLO SINGING—PLAYER SUGGESTS WHAT CAN BE CAUGHT)

SONG—"Charlie over the Ocean" (page 133).

> *Charlie, over the ocean,* (the group echoes each line)
> *Charlie, over the sea,*
> *Charlie caught a **blackbird**,*
> *Can't catch me.*

Did you hear what Charlie caught? (a blackbird)
What else could Charlie catch?

Since "Charlie over the Ocean" is an echo song, the solo singer can sing the "lead" part, and be echoed by the group. Alternatively, you can sing the lead part for the first, second, and fourth lines, allowing the solo singer to sing the lead on the third line only.

NEW VERSES 27—WHAT KIND OF PIE?
(SOLO SINGING—PLAYER SUGGESTS TYPE OF PIE)

SONG—"Old Joe Clark" (page 141).

> *Old Joe Clark, he had a house,*
> *Fifteen stories high,*
> *And every story in that house*
> *Was filled with **chicken** pie.*

What was in Old Joe Clark's house? (chicken pie)
What kind of pie would you like a whole house filled with?

Variation—substitute the player's name. If desired, also substitute the player's name. Thus, if Hsueh-tze suggested scallion pie, the group will sing:

> *My friend **Hsueh-tze** had a house,*
> *Fifteen stories high,*
> *And every story in that house*

Then Hsueh-tze can sing the end of the song by herself:

> *Was filled with **scallion** pie.*

Alternatively, let the solo singer sing the last two lines.

NEW VERSES 28—WHAT KIND OF ANIMAL DO I SEE? (SOLO SINGING—PLAYER SUGGESTS ANIMALS)

SONG—"Sit Down" (page 121).

> *What's that yonder that I see?*
> *Looks just like some **birds** to me.*
> *What's that yonder that I spy?*
> *Looks like **birds** a-passing by.*

What do I see? (birds)
What animal could you pretend to see?

This song has a question-and-answer form: lines one and three are questions, and the other two lines are answers. Have the solo singer sing the second line. Additionally, the solo singer can also sing the fourth line.

Variation—other things passing by. In place of animals, choose any category: forms of transportation, scary creatures, types of airplanes, movie stars, or things that it would be silly to see passing by.

NEW VERSES 29—WHAT DECORATES OUR SUKKAH? (SOLO SINGING—PLAYERS SUGGEST DECORATIONS FOR THE SUKKAH)

SONG—"HaSukkah" (page 154).

> *Our Sukkah, made of wood,*
> *With our **flowers** it is good,*
> *Our Sukkah, made of wood,*
> *With our **flowers** it is good.*

A Sukkah is a special booth made for the Jewish harvest festival, Sukkot. People eat in it and sometimes even sleep in it during the holiday. Sukkah's are traditionally decorated with flowers, fruits, and sometimes tablets with the names of seven Jewish patriarchs. Other decorations may include drawings, vegetables, and sewn or knitted objects.

What is in our Sukkah? (flowers)
What else could we use to decorate it?

Have the solo singer sing the second line. Then the whole group can repeat the suggestion in the fourth line.

NEW VERSES 30—WHAT WOULD YOU HAVE BET? (SOLO SINGING—PLAYERS SUGGEST WHAT THEY WOULD BET)

SONG—"Stewball" (page 144).

It was a big day (uh-huh)
In Dallas (uh-huh)
Oh, don't you wish you (uh-huh)
Was there (was there),

Oh, you'd-a bet your (uh-huh)
*Last **dollar** (uh-huh)*
On that iron (uh-huh)
Gray mare (gray mare).

Refrain:

Bet on Stewball, and you might win, win, win,
Bet on Stewball, and you might win.

What did I think you'd bet? (my last dollar)
What would you bet?

Since this song has a call-and-response form, the solo singer can sing the call (It was a big day), and the group can sing the response (uh-huh). Everyone can sing together on the refrain.

Let the solo singer sing all the "call" lines, or just one or two.

Variation—where was the race. If desired, have the solo singer make two suggestions: what you'd bet, and where the race was (i.e., for "Dallas" sing the name of another place).

As an added challenge, have two singers make solo suggestions in each verse: one sings the name of the place, the other what to bet.

For even more difficulty, require that the item to be bet have some connection to the place named. For instance, if the place is Paris, the thing to be bet might be "your last beret"; if Boston, "your last bean." If your group has a knowledge of world geography, make the place a country and the item bet its currency (or else it's chief export product). This variation makes a great geography quiz!

NEW VERSES 31—WHAT'S YOUR FAVORITE FOOD?
(SOLO SINGING—PLAYER SUGGESTS FOODS)

This activity is similar to #18, but it is adapted for solo singing.

SONG—"Back to Mexico" (page 125).

*What you gonna do when the **cake** comes in, sugar babe,*
*What you gonna do when the **cake** comes in, sugar babe,*
*What you gonna do when the **cake** comes in,*
*Sit on the corner with **crumbs** on your chin, sugar babe.*

Did you hear what food I'm waiting for? (cake) Did you hear what was on my chin? (crumbs)
What's your favorite food? What do you like on it?

One solo singer can sing both suggestions (e.g., when the **chips** come in, sit on the corner with **salt** on your chin). In this case, the solo singer would begin the verse. The group can sing the second line and "Sugar Babe."

Alternatively, two singers can each sing one of the suggestions. The second singer has to think fast!

RHYMING VERSES

Up to now, we have carefully avoided any changes that affect the rhyming words in a verse. To be sure, in Making Verses 17—Where Do Foods Come From? we changed the word "cabbage" (which originally was a near-rhyme for "habit"), but we didn't try to preserve the rhyme by also changing "habit."

Making up rhyming verses requires an additional set of skills. First, the group members must think of a suggestion, as usual. But then they need to find another word that rhymes with their suggestion. Next, they must put that new rhyming word back in the verse, making any required changes to the other words in the verse.

To teach this complex process to a group, break it down. First, use nonrhyming suggestions, as in the previous activities. Then, use the next activity below, which teaches how to create rhyming nonwords. When you introduce the use of actual rhyming words, do so with songs that don't require much rearranging of words to make them work.

At all times, ask the group to make one decision at a time. For example, if a child suggests "beets," for what Old Mr. Rabbit might eat, don't begin by saying, "Who can make a line that rhymes with 'and eating all my beets'?" Instead, structure the activities for them by asking a series of questions that each require only one step to answer. You might say first, "What's a word that rhymes with 'beets'?" If they suggest, "sweets," say, "Good! Now what could "sweets" have to do with a rabbit?" As in Making Verses activities #33–37, continue one step at a time until the group has completed the verse. Once the process is familiar, then you can begin to leave out some of the steps.

ARBITRARY RHYMES

Here's a step-by-step description of the process of finding a word that rhymes with a given word. First, we create nonwords that rhyme with the given word, by substituting various sounds for the word's first sound. If we are trying to find a word that rhymes with "bird," for example, we fit various initial sounds onto "ird." This process might get us "dird," "curd," "mird," "lird," and "word." Then, we filter out those sound combinations that are not actually words. In this case, that leaves us with "curd" and "word." Of course, some people may use a different—but equivalent—mental process. Still, there are two different kinds of mental operations: generating possible sound combinations and choosing among the possibilities.

In the activity that follows, it's not necessary to filter out the nonwords! The song uses nonsense syllables beginning with the letter "k," so we can practice creating nonwords without having to discard those syllables that aren't words.

NEW VERSES 32—GREEN AND YELLOW ANIMALS (RHYMING WITH NONWORDS)

SONG—"Kitty Kasket" (page 134).

Say, "This is a pretend story. Are you ready to hear it? Well, I'm in big trouble. I lost my handkerchief yesterday. Do you know why I lost it? I saw a very strange dog, and the dog surprised me so much, I just threw my handkerchief away. The strange thing about the dog was the color of its fur." Sing,

> *Kitty, kitty **kog**,*
> *Green and yellow **dog**,*
> *Lost my handkerchief yesterday,*
> *It's all full of mud, so I tossed it away.*

Say, "Did you hear the color of its fur? That's right, green and yellow! Then I found my handkerchief again—but I saw another strange animal." Sing,

> *Kitty, kitty **kabbit**,*
> *Green and yellow **rabbit**,*
> *Lost my handkerchief yesterday,*
> *It's all full of mud, so I tossed it away.*

Say, "Did you hear what animal it was? That's right, a rabbit. What animal do you think I saw next?" Choose a group member. If the group member said, "Skunk," say, "A skunk! Yes! Now, let me see. Dog—kog. Rabbit—kabbit. Skunk—_____ what should it be? Yes, 'Skunk—kunk'! Let's sing,

> *Kitty, kitty **kunk**,*
> *Green and yellow **skunk**,*
> *Lost my handkerchief yesterday,*
> *It's all full of mud, so I tossed it away.*

Continue asking for other animals. Each time, repeat the entire list of rhyming pairs (e.g., "Dog—kog, Rabbit—kabbit, Skunk—kunk") before asking for the nonword that rhymes with the new animal.

ONE-SYLLABLE RHYMES

All the following activities require finding an actual word that rhymes with a suggested word.

In the first activity, a group can use a single list of rhyming words. The subsequent activities require generating a new list of rhyming words for each suggestion.

NEW VERSES 33—DOWN CAME A CREATURE (RHYMING WITH "TWO")

SONG—"Down Came A Lady" (page 123).

Say, "This is a song about pretend (imaginary) creatures. I'm going to pretend I saw some. Ready?" Sing,

> *Down came a creature,*
> *Down came two,*
> *Down came another one,*
> *With a **stomach painted blue**.*

Say, "Did you hear how those creatures looked? That's right, their stomachs were painted blue! What are some other words that rhyme with 'two'?"

With the group, make a list—orally, in pictures, or in writing—of words that rhyme with "two." Your list might be something like this one:

blue

flew

goo

moo

shoe

stew

you

Say, "What could one of those words have to do with a different kind of creature?" If Nekima says, "Goo!" say, "What part of the creature was made of goo?" If she says, "It's hair," say, "Great! Let's put it in the song." Sing:

Down came a creature,
Down came two;
Down came another one,
And its hair was made of goo.

Repeat, using a different word from the same list or a different idea using the same word, "goo." For each word that someone picks from the list, ask an appropriate question, such as "what part of the creature made the sound, 'moo'?"

NEW VERSES 34—WHAT ANIMAL CAME IN? (RHYMING WITH ANIMAL NAMES)

SONG—"There Was a Little Frog" (page 159).

Sing all the verses of the song, or just these three:

The first to come was Mrs. Goose, uh-huh, uh-huh,
The first to come was Mrs. Goose,
Took her fiddle and she cut loose, uh-huh, uh-huh.

The next to come was Doctor Flea, uh-huh, uh-huh, . . .
And danced a jig with the bumblebee . . .

The last to come was Captain Snake, uh-huh, uh-huh . . .
And wrapped its tail around the cake . . .

Say, "Did you hear what animals came in to the wedding? Yes, a goose, a flea, and a snake. What other animal can you imagine coming in?" If someone says, "A hen," say, "What are some words that rhyme with hen. The group members might say, "Den. Again. Men. Pen. Ten. Then. When."

Say, "What could one of those words have to do with what the hen did at the wedding?" If some-one says, "She used a pen to make signs," say, "Great! How can we arrange the words so that 'pen' comes at the end?" If someone says, "She made the signs with her pen," say, "Great! Let's sing it in the song." Sing:

The next to come was Mrs. Hen, uh-huh, uh-huh,
The next to come was Mrs. Hen,
She made the signs with her pen, uh-huh, uh-huh.

NEW VERSES 35—WHO'S THAT YONDER IN HISTORY?
(RHYMING COLORS AND ACTIVITIES OF HISTORICAL FIGURES)

SONG—"Sit Down" (page 121).

Say, "Can you imagine being in a place where you could see everyone who ever lived through all of history? Here's what some people sang about singing." Sing

Who's that yonder dressed in red?
Must be the children that Moses led.
Who's that yonder dressed in blue?
Must be the children who are coming through.

Say, "What colors were the children dressed in? That's right, red and blue. Instead of red, what's another color someone could wear?" If someone says, "brown," say, "Great! What are some words that rhyme with brown?" The group will suggest several words, such as "clown, crown, down, drown, frown, gown."

Say, "If you could see everyone who ever lived in history, who would you want to see?" If someone says, "Neil Armstrong," say, "Good! What could one of our words have to do with Neil Armstrong?" If someone says, "He came down from the moon," say, "Excellent! How do we get the word 'down' at the end of the line?" If someone says, "Looks like Armstrong flying down," sing

*Who's that yonder dressed in **brown**?*
***Looks like Armstrong flying down**.*
Who's that yonder dressed in blue?
Must be the children who are coming through.

If desired, sing the refrain, too—with or without movements (see Movement Activity #21—Won't You Sit Down?).

Hints—giving more help to beginning rhymers. In the Neil Armstrong example just given, your group may need even more help than described. For example, they may not find a connection between "down" and "Neil Armstrong." To help in this case, ask the group to talk about Neil Armstrong: "What do you know about Neil Armstrong?" Then repeat the list of rhyming words. If necessary, talk about each one separately: "Let's see. 'Clown'—what could that have to do with Neil Armstrong. Was he a clown? No? Well, we could say, 'Neil Armstrong was no clown.' How about 'crown'? Can't think of any connection? Okay, let's go on to 'down.' What could you say about the moon and 'down'? Do you think Neil Armstrong deserves to be 'put down'?"

Once your group has come up with an idea that connects Neil Armstrong and one of the rhyming words, they may still need more help in shaping their idea into a line of the song. If they say, "He came down from the moon," your response will be "Excellent! How do we get the word 'down' at the end of the line?" But their next try might be something like, "He was up on the moon, but then later he came down." This doesn't name Neil Armstrong or fit the rhythm of the song too well. At this point, you can sing:

Who's that yonder dressed in brown?
Neil Armstrong dut dut down.

"Dut dut" is what you sing to fill out the missing syllables in the song. Now say, "What could we say instead of 'dut dut' to make it fit in the song?" Sing it again, if needed. Responses might include "flying," "landing," or "he came." If someone says, "bringing his landing module down," say, "Great! We need to make that shorter, to fit in 'dut dut.' How about "Neil Armstrong touching down"?

Variation—any categories. Instead of choosing a person from history, choose from any category of people: people from TV sitcoms, from the Bible, from Dickens's novels, etc. Alternatively, choose a vantage point from a microscope inside a plant or animal:

What's that yonder dressed in green?
The strangest cytoplasm ever seen.

Choose any other real or imaginary vantage point to see things from, e.g., high above the city, under a meadow, or in the future.

NEW VERSES 36—WHAT WOULD YOUR HOUSE BE FULL OF? (RHYMING THINGS YOU LOVE WITH CHARACTERISTICS OF HOUSES)

SONG—"Old Joe Clark" (page 141).

Sing:

> **Old Joe Clark**, he had a house,
> **Fifteen stories high**,
> And every story in that house
> Was filled with **chicken pie**.

Say, "What was in Old Joe Clark's house? That's right, chicken pie. If you could have a whole house full of one thing, what would it be?" If a group member says, "money," say, "Good! What's your favorite kind of money?" If Aaron says, "Hundred-dollar bills," say, "Great! Let's think of words that rhyme with 'bills.'" Answers may include: "fills, hills, kills, mills, pills, thrills." Say, "What could one of those words have to do with a house?" If the group gives several answers, such as "in the hills," "by the mills," or "made of pills," say, "Aaron, this is your verse. Which do you want us to sing?" If Aaron says, "in the hills," sing

> **If my friend Aaron** had a house,
> **He'd build it in the hills**,
> And every story would be full
> Of **hundred-dollar bills**.

TWO-SYLLABLE RHYMES

As difficult as it may be for some children to rhyme "bat" and "cat," it can be even more demanding to find rhymes for two-syllable words, such as "rabbit" and "habit." For the more sophisticated child, however, such rhymes provide a new challenge and delight.

The following activity assumes that children already understand syllables and accented syllables.

NEW VERSES 37—TWO-SYLLABLE ADVENTURES
(RHYMING TWO-SYLLABLE WORDS)

SONG—"Hill and Gully Rider" (page 150).

Sing:

Hill and gully rider, hill and gully,
Hill and gully rider, hill and gully,
***Oh I went to the mountain**, hill and gully,*
***And I drank from the fountain**, hill and gully,*
***When I went to the mountain**, hill and gully.*

Say, "Did you hear where I went? That's right, to the mountain. How many syllables in 'mountain'? That's right, two. Which syllable was accented? Yes, the first syllable, 'moun-.' In this song we can make up verses about any word, as long as it has two syllables and the accent is on the first syllable. Can anyone think of a word like that?" If someone says, "rocket," say, "Great! Does 'rocket' have two syllables? Yes, you're right. Is the accent on the first syllable? Good, it is. That means we can use 'rocket' in this song. What are some words that rhyme with 'rocket'?"

Your group will suggest a list of words, such as "pocket, socket, sock it, walk it, sprocket." Say, "That's very interesting! Some of those words are two-syllable words, and some of them are really two words, each with one syllable. Either will work! Which of our words could have to do with a rocket?" If someone says, "it didn't work, so we had to walk it," say, "Great! let's try it this way." Sing:

Hill and gully rider, hill and gully,
Hill and gully rider, hill and gully,
***I got in a rocket**, hill and gully,*
***But I had to walk it**, hill and gully,*
***When I got in a rocket**, hill and gully.*

Variation—three rhyming words. Say, "We used two words to rhyme together: 'rocket' and 'walk it.' Is there another one that rhymes with them that could have to do with our broken rocket?" If someone says, "it broke a sprocket," say, "Good! Let's make a verse this way." Sing:

Hill and gully rider, hill and gully,
Hill and gully rider, hill and gully,
***I got in a rocket**, hill and gully,*
***But it broke a sprocket**, hill and gully.*
***So I had to walk it**, hill and gully.*

THE SONGS

SONG #1

SIT DOWN

REFRAIN:

Oh, won't you sit down? Lord, I can't sit down.
Oh, won't you sit down? Lord, I can't sit down.
Oh, won't you sit down? Lord, I can't sit down,
'Cause I just got here, I gotta look around.

    1. *What's that yonder that I see?*
        Looks just like some birds to me.
        There go the birds a flying by,
        Look at all those birds, way up in the sky.

(REFRAIN)

    2. *What's that yonder that I spy?*
        Looks like monsters, crawling by.
        Look at all the monsters on the ground,
        Look at all those monsters crawling around.

FINAL REFRAIN:

Oh, won't you stand up? Lord, I can't stand up.
Oh, won't you stand up? Lord, I can't stand up.
Oh, won't you stand up? Lord, I can't stand up,
'Cause I'm out of breath, I gotta sit back down.

BACKGROUND

Originally an African-American spiritual, this song had verses describing what you could see in heaven.

For detailed background, resources and curricular tie-ins, see page 173.

For sources, see page 197.

GAMES

#16—Games for Choosing. *What's Your Choice?*, page 12.

MOVEMENTS

#21—Movements for Standing, Lying, and Moving Around. *Won't You Sit Down?*, page 86.

NEW VERSES

#8—One-Part Suggestions. *What Would You Like To Do Here?*, page 103.

#28—Solo Singing Opportunities. *What Kind of Animal Do I See?*, page 113.
#35—Rhyming Verses. *Who's That Yonder in History?*, page 118.

SONG #2

DOWN CAME A LADY

> 1. Down came a lady,
>   Down came two,
>   Down came old Daniel's wife,
>   And she was dressed in blue.
>
> 2. Down came a lady,
>   Down came two,
>   Down came Lucy,
>   And she was dressed in brown.

BACKGROUND

Originally the first verse of a mountain ballad known widely in the English-speaking world, this version comes from Virginia.

For detailed background, resources, and curricular tie-ins, see page 193.

For sources, see page 198.

GAMES

#3—Games for Choosing. *Colored Dinosaurs*, page 4.

#25—Chasing and Racing. *Down Came a Monster*, page 20.

#55—Lines and Circles. *The Great Turn-Around*, page 42.

MOVEMENTS

#30—Movements with Others. *Standing High and Standing Low*, page 94.

NEW VERSES

#33—Rhyming Verses. *Down Came a Creature*, page 116.

SONG #3:

AL CITRON

> *Al citron de un fandango sango, sango, sabaré,*
> *Sabaré de la randela con su triki triki tron.*

BACKGROUND

This song was for a children's stone-passing game in Mexico. Although several of the individual words have meanings, taken together the words are nonsense.

For detailed background, resources, and curricular tie-ins, see page 189.

For sources, see page 198.

GAMES

#34—Guessing and Hiding. *Who Has the Lemon?*, page 27.
#62—Rhythm Games. *Triki*, page 48.

MOVEMENTS

#2—Repeated Pulse Movements. *What to Clap With*, page 69.

ABOUT THE MUSIC

Most songs have lines (or phrases) that are four or eight beats long. "Al Citron" may feel uncomfortable to sing at first, because its phrases are 10 beats long.

BACK TO MEXICO

1. I'm going back to Mexico, sugar babe,
   I'm going back to Mexico, sugar babe,
   I'm going back to Mexico,
   Say goodbye before I go, sugar babe.

2. Never seen the likes since I've been born, sugar babe,
   Never seen the likes since I've been born, sugar babe,
   Never seen the likes since I've been born,
   Picking up sticks and parching corn, sugar babe.

3. What you gonna do when the meat comes in, sugar babe,
   What you gonna do when the meat comes in, sugar babe,
   What you gonna do when the meat comes in,
   Sit on the corner with grease on your chin, sugar babe.

BACKGROUND

This string-band song is a tune played at dances and other social events in the rural south. A more widely circulated version begins, "You get a line and I'll get a pole . . . we'll go fishing in the crawdad hole."

For detailed background, resources, and curricular tie-ins, see page 179.

For sources, see page 198.

GAMES

#4—Games for Choosing. *Who's Been Here Since I've Been Gone?*, page 4.

#12—Games for Choosing. *Steal a Partner Before I Go*, page 9.

#28—Chasing and Racing. *Parch*, page 21.

#75—Play-party Games. *Double-L Swing*, page 63.

MOVEMENTS

#7—Repeated Pulse Movements. *Ways to Say Goodbye*, page 72.

NEW VERSES

#18—Multi-Part Suggestions. *When Your Food Comes In*, page 107.

#31—Solo-Singing Opportunities. *What's Your Favorite Food?*, page 114.

ABOUT THE MUSIC

You may expect the first, second and fourth phrases of this melody to have another measure! Most songs we know (including this song's cousin, "Crawdad") have four (or two) measures in each line of melody, not three. Think of this as a clever surprise in each line!

I'm go-ing back to Mex-i-co, su-gar babe,

I'm go-ing back to Mex-i-co, su-gar babe,

I'm go-ing back to Mex-i-co,

Say good-bye be-fore I go, su-gar babe.

SONG # 5:

IT'S A SHAME

1. It's a shame to make your bed on a Sunday,
   It's a shame to make your bed on a Sunday,
   When you got Monday, Tuesday, Wednesday,
   Thursday, Friday, Saturday,
   It's a shame to make your bed on a Sunday.

2. It's a shame to empty the garbage on a Sunday,
   It's a shame to empty the garbage on a Sunday,
   When you got Monday, Tuesday, Wednesday,
   Thursday, Friday, Saturday,
   It's a shame to empty the garbage on a Sunday.

3. It's a shame to wash the dishes on a Sunday,
   It's a shame to wash the dishes on a Sunday,
   When you got Monday, Tuesday, Wednesday,
   Thursday, Friday, Saturday,
   It's a shame to wash the dishes on a Sunday.

BACKGROUND

Adapted from an Appalachian string-band song, this humorous song seems to have descended from a children's rhyme about activities that were prohibited on Sunday.

For detailed background, resources and curricular tie-ins, see page 180.

For sources, see page 198.

GAMES

#42—Guessing and Hiding. *Hot and Cold Singing*, page 33.

MOVEMENTS

#29—Movements with Others. *Making Letter Shapes*, page 93.

NEW VERSES

#14—One-Part Suggestions. *What Chores Don't You Like?*, page 105.

SONG #6:

WAKE ME, SHAKE ME

1. Wake me, shake me,
   Don't let me sleep too late,
   I gotta get up early in the morning,
   Swing on the garden gate.

> 2. I say it's wake me, shake me,
>   Don't let me sleep too late,
>   I gotta put on my clothes in the morning,
>   Swing on the garden gate.
>
> 3. Wake me, shake me,
>   Don't let me sleep too late,
>   I gotta walk in the woods in the morning,
>   Swing on the garden gate.
>
> *(Repeat first verse.)*

BACKGROUND

Originally an African-American spiritual about getting to heaven, this song has led to several adaptations and parodies.

For detailed background, resources, and curricular tie-ins, see page 174.

For sources, see page 198.

GAMES

#41—Guessing and Hiding. *Walking My Lost Dog*, page 32.

#60—Rhythm Games. *Passing the Oatmeal*, page 46.

MOVEMENTS

#3—Repeated Pulse Movements. *Wake My Body in the Morning*, page 69.

NEW VERSES

#13—One-Part Suggestions. *Gotta Do It in the Morning*, page 105.

WELDON

REFRAIN:

1. Let's go down to Weldon,
    I think I heard them say,
    Let's go down to Weldon,
    I think I heard them say.

    Rally, rally, rally
    I think I heard them say,
    Rally, rally, rally,
    I think I heard them say.

(REFRAIN)

2. Jesse lives in Weldon,
    I think I heard them say. (2x)

3. Cory lives in Weldon,
    I think I heard them say. (2x)

(REFRAIN)

4. Fare thee well in Weldon,
    I think I heard them say. (2x)

(REFRAIN)

BACKGROUND

This song is a play-party game from Texas, with versions known in many other states. Players used it to provide music and directions for their own "dances," which varied from very simple circle games to complex series of square-dance figures.

For detailed background, resources, and curricular tie-ins, see page 183.

For sources, see page 198.

GAMES

#6—Games for Choosing. *Take Me Down to Weldon*, page 5.

#9—Games for Choosing. *Get Yourself a Partner*, page 7.

#51—Lines and Circles. *Circle Two in Weldon*, page 40.

#69—Play-party Games. *Double Swing*, page 56.

#76—Play-party Games. *Let's Go Down to Weldon*, page 64.

MOVEMENTS

#22—Movements for Standing, Lying, and Moving Around. *Rally Movements*, page 87.

NEW VERSES

#16—Multi-Part Suggestions. *Where Do You Live?*, page 106.

Verse:

Let's go down to Wel-don, I think I heard them say,

Let's go down to Wel-don, I think I heard them say.

Refrain:

Ral-ly, ral-ly, ral-ly, I think I heard them say,

Ral-ly, ral-ly, ral-ly, I think I heard them say.

SONG #8:

I WISH I WAS A COWPOKE

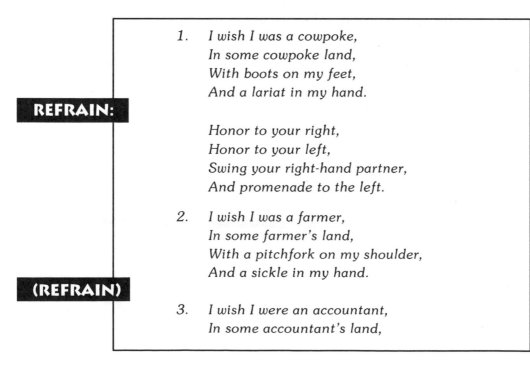

1. I wish I was a cowpoke,
   In some cowpoke land,
   With boots on my feet,
   And a lariat in my hand.

REFRAIN:

Honor to your right,
Honor to your left,
Swing your right-hand partner,
And promenade to the left.

2. I wish I was a farmer,
   In some farmer's land,
   With a pitchfork on my shoulder,
   And a sickle in my hand.

(REFRAIN)

3. I wish I were an accountant,
   In some accountant's land,

With a checkbook in my pocket,
And a pencil in my hand.

(REFRAIN)

BACKGROUND

This play-party song was probably based on a cowhand song, which was in turn based on a hymn! For detailed background, resources, and curricular tie-ins, see page 183.

For sources, see page 199.

GAMES

#5—Games for Choosing. *Walk Around the Prairie*, page 5.

#70—Play-party Games. *Honor to Your Corner*, page 57.

#71—Play-party Games. *Haystack On My Shoulder*, page 58.

NEW VERSES

#24—Multipart Suggestions. *What Job Would You Like?*, page 109.

SO HE PLANTED GINGER

1. *So he planted ginger, ginger grows so quickly.*
   So he got a nanny goat to graze on the ginger.
   > *Nanny will not graze on ginger,*
   > *Ginger grows so quickly.*

2. *So he got a magpie, to stay and talk to Nanny,*
   So he got a magpie, to stay and talk to Nanny:
   > *Magpie will not talk to Nanny,*
   > *Nanny will not graze on ginger,*
   > *Ginger grows so quickly.*

3. *So he went to Beech Tree, to give a nut to Magpie,*
   So he went to Beech Tree, to give a nut to Magpie:
   > *Beech Tree won't give nut to Magpie*
   > *Magpie will not talk to Nanny,*
   > *Nanny will not graze on ginger*
   > *Ginger grows so quickly.*

4. *So he went to River, to give a drink to Beech Tree.*
   So he went to River, to give a drink to Beech Tree:
   > *River gave a drink to Beech Tree,*
   > *Beech tree gave a nut to Magpie,*
   > *Magpie stayed and talked to Nanny,*
   > *Nanny went and grazed on ginger,*
   > *Ginger grows so quickly.*

BACKGROUND

This song is adapted from a Bulgarian children's song, a distant relative of the English nursery rhyme, "The Old Woman and Her Pig."

For detailed background, resources, and curricular tie-ins, see page 194.

For sources, see page 199.

GAMES

#46—Lines and Circles. *The Ginger Game*, page 36.

MOVEMENTS

#12—Sequential Pulse Movements. *So He Planted Ginger*, page 77.

NEW VERSES

#11—One-Part Suggestions. *Crazy Ginger*, page 104.

So he plant-ed gin - ger, gin-ger grows so quick-ly.

So he got a nan-ny goat to graze on the gin - ger.

(Repeat as needed in verses 2,3,4 only:)

Nan-ny will not graze on gin-ger, gin-ger grows so quick-ly.

SONG #10:

CHARLIE OVER THE OCEAN

The leader sings each line, then the group repeats it:

> 1.   *Charlie, over the ocean,*
>   *Charlie, over the sea,*
>   *Charlie caught a blackbird,*
>   *Can't catch me.*
>
> 2.   *Charlie, over the ocean,*
>   *Charlie, over the sea,*
>   *Charlie caught a black cat,*
>   *Can't catch me.*
>
> 3.   *Charlie, over the ocean,*
>   *Charlie, over the sea,*
>   *Charlie caught a black fish,*
>   *Can't catch me.*

BACKGROUND

A descendant of a Scottish political song, this African-American game song comes from Alabama.
For detailed background, resources, and curricular tie-ins, see page 186.
For sources, see page 199.

GAMES

#10—Games for Choosing. *Charlie Had a Partner*, page 8.
#20—Chasing and Racing. *Can't Catch Me*, page 16.
#26—Chasing and Racing. *Color Tag*, page 20.
#64—Rhythm Games. *Charlie over the Jump Rope*, page 49.

MOVEMENTS

#15—Sequential Pulse Movements. *Catch My Clapping*, page 81.

NEW VERSES

#4—One-Part Suggestions. *Charlie Caught A Blackbird*, page 101.

#26—Solo-Singing Opportunities. *What Did Charlie Catch?*, page 112.

Char-lie, o-ver the o-cean,

Char-lie, o-ver the sea,

Char-lie caught a black bird,

Can't catch me.

SONG #11:

KITTY KASKET

> *Kitty, kitty kasket,*
> *Green and yellow basket,*
> *Lost my handkerchief yesterday,*
> *It's all full of mud, so I tossed it away.*

BACKGROUND

This song is a version of "Drop the Handkerchief" gathered from African-American children in Alabama.

For detailed background, resources, and curricular tie-ins, see page 187.

For sources, see page 199.

GAMES

#17—Chasing and Racing. *Lost My Handkerchief*, page 14.

MOVEMENTS

NEW VERSES

SONG #12:

I'M GOING HOME ON THE MORNING TRAIN

1. I'm going home on the morning train,
   I'm going home on the morning train,
   Well, it's I'm going home, you know that I'm going
       home,
   I'm going home on the morning train.

2. The evening train might be too late,
   The evening train might be too late,
   Well, that evening train, I say that evening train,
   I'm talking 'bout, evening train might be too late.

3. Get right on and let's go home,
   Get right on and let's go home,
   Well, it's get right on, I tell you, get right on,
   I'm saying, get right on and let's go home.

BACKGROUND

Originally an African-American spiritual, this song used the train metaphor to speak of eagerness for heaven.

For detailed background, resources, and curricular tie-ins, see page 174.

For sources, see page 199.

GAMES
#2—Games for Choosing. *The Royal Throne*, page 3.
#18—Chasing and Racing. *Catching the Morning Train*, page 15.

MOVEMENTS
#32—Movements with Others. *Pass the Shake*, page 95.

SONG #13:

WINDY WEATHER

Windy weather,
Frosty weather,
When the wind blows,
We all go together.

BACKGROUND
This is a game from the children in a Dublin, Ireland, housing project.
For detailed background, resources, and curricular tie-ins, see page 189.
For sources, see page 200.

GAMES
#11—Games for Choosing. *The Leaves Blow Together*, page 8.

MOVEMENTS

NEW VERSES

Wind-y weath-er, frost-y weath-er,

When the wind blows, we all go to-geth-er.

SONG #14:

ROUND THE CORNER

1. Oh, around the corner we will go,
      (chorus:)   Round the corner, Sally.
    Oh, around the corner we will go,
      (chorus:)   Round the corner, Sally.

2. Oh, I wish I was in Mobile Bay . . .
3. Oh, around the corner we will go . . .
4. Oh, to Callyo we're bound to go . . .
5. Oh, around the corner we will go . . .
6. Oh, I think that now we've hauled enough . . .
7. Oh, around the corner we will go . . .

BACKGROUND

This song is a sea shanty that, like many, has also been used for other kinds of work—including corn shucking.

For detailed background, resources, and curricular tie-ins, see page 163.

For sources, see page 200.

GAMES

MOVEMENTS

NEW VERSES

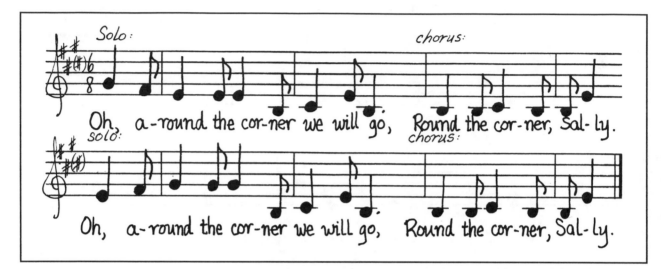

SONG #15:

CHE CHE KU LE

The leader sings each line, then the group repeats it:

> *Che che ku le,*
> *Che che kufi sa,*
> *Kofi sa langa,*
> *Ka ta chi langa,*
> *Kum a de de.*

BACKGROUND

This children's game song is from Ghana, Africa. The words are nonsense.
For detailed background, resources, and curricular tie-ins, see page 190.
For sources, see page 200.

GAMES

MOVEMENTS

Che che ku le

Che che ku - fi sa

Ko - fi sa lan - ga

Ka ta chi lan - ga

Kum a - de - de

SONG #16:

ARIRANG

Arirang, Arirang, arariyo,
Arirang Valley, how well you grow.
In our village the harvest is good,
All through the land there will be plenty of food.

BACKGROUND

"Arirang" is often described as the unofficial national song of Korea.
For detailed background, resources, and curricular tie-ins, see page 194.
For sources, see page 200.

GAMES

#39—Guessing and Hiding. *How's the Harvest?*, page 31.

MOVEMENTS

#26—Movements for Standing, Lying, and Moving Around. *Floating Up Arirang Hill*, page 90.

NEW VERSES

#9—One-Part Suggestions. *What Have You Been Called to Do?*, page 103.

A - ri-rang, A - ri-rang, a - ra-ri - yo,

A - ri-rang Val - ley, how well you grow.

In our vil - lage the har - vest is good,

All through the land there will be plen - ty of food.

SONG #17:

GOOD-BYE, OLD PAINT

1. *Old Paint's a good pony, he paces when he can,*
    Good-bye, old Paint, I'm leaving Cheyenne.

2. *I'm leaving Cheyenne, I'm off for Montan',*
    Good-bye, old Paint, I'm leaving Cheyenne.

3. *My foot's in the stirrup, my bridle's in my hand,*
    Good-bye, old Paint, I'm leaving Cheyenne.

4. *Good-bye, Little Annie, I'm off for Montan',*
    Good-bye, old Paint, I'm leaving Cheyenne.

BACKGROUND

A cowhand song about a spotted horse, this tune became the traditional ending waltz for cowhand dances.

For detailed background, resources, and curricular tie-ins, see page 165.

For sources, see page 200.

GAMES

#45—Lines and Circles. *Leaving Cheyenne*, page 35.

MOVEMENTS

#27—Movements for Standing, Lying, or Moving Around. *Stiff and Floppy*, page 91.

NEW VERSES

#2—One-Part Suggestions. *Off For Montan'*, page 200.

Old Paint's a good po-ny, he pa-ces when he can,
Good-bye, old Paint, I'm leav-ing Chey-enne.

SONG #18:

OLD JOE CLARK

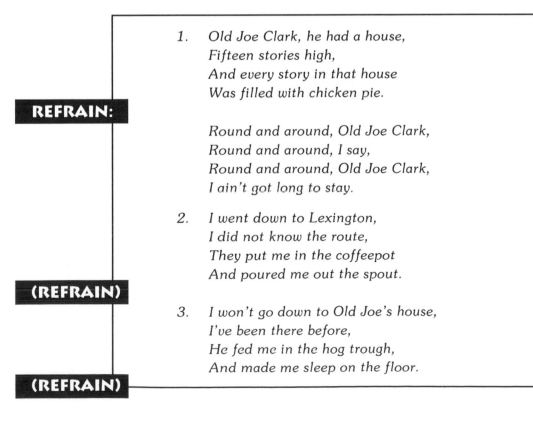

1. Old Joe Clark, he had a house,
Fifteen stories high,
And every story in that house
Was filled with chicken pie.

REFRAIN:
Round and around, Old Joe Clark,
Round and around, I say,
Round and around, Old Joe Clark,
I ain't got long to stay.

2. I went down to Lexington,
I did not know the route,
They put me in the coffeepot
And poured me out the spout.

(REFRAIN)

3. I won't go down to Old Joe's house,
I've been there before,
He fed me in the hog trough,
And made me sleep on the floor.

(REFRAIN)

BACKGROUND

One of the best-known string-band songs, "Old Joe Clark" has also seen extensive use as a play-party song.

For detailed background, resources, and curricular tie-ins, see page 180.

For sources, see page 201.

GAMES

#52—Lines and Circles. *Believe I'm Falling Down*, page 41.

#68—Play-party Games. *Promenade the Corner*, page 54.

#72—Play-party Games. *Double Allemande*, page 60.

#77—Play-party Games. *Euchre Ring*, page 66.

MOVEMENTS

#1—Repeated Pulse Movements. *What Goes Around?*, page 68.

#14—Sequential Pulse Movements. *I Went Down to Old Joe's House*, page 79.

#24—Movements for Standing, Lying, and Moving Around. *Ways to Walk*, page 89.

NEW VERSES

#3—One-Part Suggestions. *Where Did You Get Hurt?*, page 101.

#5—One-Part Suggestions. *Fill Your House With Pie*, page 102.

#27—Solo-Singing Opportunities. *What Kind of Pie?*, page 112.

#36—Rhyming Verses. *What Would Your House Be Full Of?*, page 119.

HOLD MY MULE

> 1. Hold my mule while I dance Josey,
>   Hold my mule while I dance Josey,
>   Hold my mule while I dance Josey,
>   Hello, Susie Brown-ie-o.
>
> 2. Had a glass of buttermilk and I danced Josey . . .
>   Hello, Susie Brown-ie-o.
>
> 3. Wouldn't give a nickle if I couldn't dance Josey . . .
>   Hello, Susie Brown-ie-o.
>
>   *(Repeat first verse.)*

BACKGROUND

This play-party song—known to both African Americans and whites—was so popular in parts of Texas that the events were known as "Josey parties."

For detailed background, resources, and curricular tie-ins, see page 184.

For sources, see page 201.

GAMES

#14—Games for Choosing. *Lost My Partner and I Can't Dance Josey*, page 11.

#32—Chasing and Racing. *Circle Hopping*, page 24.

#65—Play-party Games. *Two in the Middle*, page 51.

#73—Play-party Games. *Rights and Lefts*, page 61.

MOVEMENTS

#23—Movements for Standing, Lying, and Moving Around. *Hold and Jump*, page 88.

NEW VERSES

#15—One-Part Suggestions. *Yes, I Can!*, page 106.

#19—Multipart Suggestions. *Excuses*, page 107.

#23—Multipart Suggestions. *Everybody Doing It*, page 109.

Hold my mule while I dance Jo-sey,

Hold my mule while I dance Jo-sey,

Hold my mule while I dance Jo-sey,

Hel-lo, Su-sie Brown-ie-o.

SONG #20:

STEWBALL

After every line, the group responds with the words in parentheses:

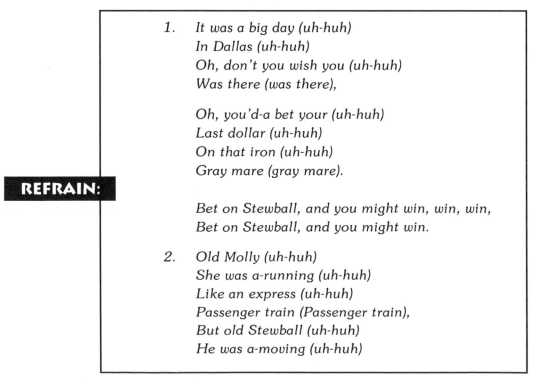

1. It was a big day (uh-huh)
    In Dallas (uh-huh)
    Oh, don't you wish you (uh-huh)
    Was there (was there),

    Oh, you'd-a bet your (uh-huh)
    Last dollar (uh-huh)
    On that iron (uh-huh)
    Gray mare (gray mare).

    REFRAIN:

    Bet on Stewball, and you might win, win, win,
    Bet on Stewball, and you might win.

2. Old Molly (uh-huh)
    She was a-running (uh-huh)
    Like an express (uh-huh)
    Passenger train (Passenger train),
    But old Stewball (uh-huh)
    He was a-moving (uh-huh)

Like a midnight (uh-huh)
Shower of rain (shower of rain)

3. Oh, the old folks (uh-huh)
    Did holler (uh-huh)
    And the young folks (uh-huh)
    Did bawl (did bawl),
    But the children (uh-huh)
    Just said, "A-look at (uh-huh)
    That noble (uh-huh)
    Stewball (stewball)."

BACKGROUND

Originally an Irish ballad about a spotted horse, this song has become an African-American prison work song.

For detailed background, resources, and curricular tie-ins, see page 170.

For sources, see page 201.

GAMES

#15—Games for Choosing. *Grandstand Partners*, page 11.

#21—Chasing and Racing. *Racing Round the Track*, page 17.

#29—Chasing and Racing. *Race with the Dollar*, page 22.

#66—Play-party Games. *Move It Round*, page 52.

MOVEMENTS

#8—Repeated Pulse Movements. *Hoeing on a Prison Gang*, page 72.

NEW VERSES

#30—Solo-Singing Opportunities. *What Would You Have Bet?*, page 113.

SONG #21:

ATSE ZETIM OMDIM

Atse zetim omdim,
Atse zetim omdim.
La, la,
La, la, la, la, la,
La, la, la, la, la, la, la, la, la, la.

Atse zetim omdim,
Atse zetim omdim.

La, la, la, la, la, la, la, la
Atse zetim omdim,
La, la, la, la, la, la, la, la
Atse zetim omdim.

BACKGROUND

This Jewish children's song is for *Tu B'shvat*, the ancient "New Year's Day of Trees," which has become a "Jewish Arbor Day" of tree planting in Israel. It falls in our January or February.

"Atse zetim omdim" means "Olive trees are standing," which may be sung in place of the Hebrew words.

"Zetim" is pronounced "zay-team." (On the recording that accompanies this book, "zetim" is mis-pronounced.)

For detailed background, resources, and curricular tie-ins, see page 177.

For sources, see page 201.

GAMES

#43—Guessing and Hiding. *Finding Your Part*, page 34.

#47—Lines and Circles. *Winding the Olive Tree*, page 37.

MOVEMENTS

#6—Repeated Pulse Movements. *Planting a Tree*, page 72.

A-tse ze-tim om-dim, a-tse ze-tim om-dim.

La, la, la la la la la,

La la la la la la la la, la, la.

A-tse ze-tim om-dim, a-tse ze-tim om-dim.

La la, la la la la la la, a-tse ze-tim om-dim,

La la, la la la la la la, a-tse ze-tim om-dim.

SONG #22:

JULEY

1. Juley, you're a lady,
   Oo-oo, oo-oo,
   Juley, Juley, Juley,
   Walk along, Miss Juliana Brown!

2. Peter, I like your smile,
   Oo-oo, oo-oo,
   Peter, Peter, Peter,
   Walk along, Miss Juliana Brown!

3.   Linda, you are strong,
     Oo-oo, oo-oo,
     Linda, Linda, Linda,
     Walk along, Miss Juliana Brown!

BACKGROUND

Originally an African-American sea shanty, this song was used to coordinate a group of sailors pulling on the ropes that raise the sails.

For detailed background, resources, and curricular tie-ins, see page 164.

For sources, see page 202.

GAMES

#1—Games for Choosing. *Juley, You're Amazing*, page 3.

#8—Games for Choosing. *Getting to Know You*, page 6.

MOVEMENTS

#31—Movements with Others. *Raising the Sail*, page 95.

NEW VERSES

#1—One-Part Suggestions. *I'm So Glad to See You*, page 99.

#22—Multipart Suggestions. *Appreciations*, page 108.

HILL AND GULLY RIDER

1. *Hill and gully rider, hill and gully,*
   Hill and gully rider, hill and gully,
   Got my horse and come down, hill and gully,
   But my horse done stumble down, hill and gully,
   And the night-time come a-tumbling down, hill and gully.

2. *Hill and gully rider, hill and gully,*
   Hill and gully rider, hill and gully,
   And a-bend down, low down, hill and gully,
   And a-low down, bessie down, hill and gully,
   And you better mind you stumble down, hill and gully.

BACKGROUND

Originally a Jamaican game song, "Hill and Gully Rider" has more recently become a Calypso song.

"Bessie down" means to crouch. As a dance step, it means to bend the knees and slowly move down.

For detailed background, resources, and curricular tie-ins, see page 190.

For sources, see page 202.

GAMES

#13—Games for Choosing. *Getting New Horses*, page 10.
#48—Lines and Circles. *Bessie Down*, page 38.

MOVEMENTS

#17—Sequential Pulse Movements. *Never Do What I Do*, page 82.

NEW VERSES

#37—Rhyming Verses. *Two-Syllable Adventures*, page 120.

Hill and gul-ly rid-er, hill and gul-ly,

Hill and gul-ly rid-er, hill and gul-ly,

Got my horse and come down, hill and gul-ly,

But my horse done stum-ble down, hill and gul-ly,

And the night-time come a tum-bling down, hill and gul-ly.

SONG #24:

DANCE A BABY DIDDY

1. *Dance a baby diddy,*
   What can mammy do wid'e?
   Sit on her lap, give it some pap,
   And dance a baby diddy.

2. *Dancy, baby, dancey,*
   How it shall gallop and prancey,
   Sit on my knee, now kissy me,
   And dancy, baby, dancey.

3. *Dance a baby diddy,*
   What can daddy do wid'e?
   Sit on my lap, give it some pap,
   And dance a baby diddy.

BACKGROUND

This English nursery ditty was probably used for "dandling" a baby—bouncing it up and down on an adult's lap.

"Pap" is any soft food for babies.

For detailed background, resources, and curricular tie-ins, see page 167.

For sources, see page 202.

GAMES

#35—Guessing and Hiding. *Who Cried?*, page 27.
#56—Lines and Circles. *Sit In Our Laps*, page 43.

MOVEMENTS

#33—Movements with Others. *Hands, My Partner, Dearie*, page 96.

NEW VERSES

#7—One-Part Suggestions. *What Can A Baby Do with Me?*, page 103.

Dance a ba - by did - dy,

What can mam-my do wid-'e?

Sit on her lap, give it some pap,

And dance a ba - by did-dy.

OLD MR. RABBIT

> 1. Old Mister Rabbit,
>   You've got a mighty habit,
>   Of jumping in my garden
>   And eating all my cabbage.
>
> 2. Old Mister Rabbit,
>   You've got a mighty habit,
>   Of jumping in my garden
>   And eating all my tomatoes.
>
> 3. Old Mister Rabbit,
>   You've got a mighty habit,
>   Of jumping in my garden
>   And eating all my broccoli.
>
> 4. Old Mister Rabbit,
>   You've got a mighty habit,
>   Of jumping in my freezer
>   And eating all my ice cream.
>
> *(Repeat first verse.)*

BACKGROUND

Alone or as part of longer songs, this animal verse has been used frequently by both African-American and white rural singers—as a game song, a work song, an instrumental tour-de-force, and a play-party song.

For detailed background, resources, and curricular tie-ins, see page 187.

For sources, see page 202.

GAMES

#23—Chasing and Racing. *Catching the Rabbit*, page 18.

#27—Chasing and Racing. *Cabbage Tag*, page 21.

#61—Rhythm Games. *Hot Cabbage*, page 47.

MOVEMENTS

#20—Movements for Standing, Lying, and Moving Around. *Grab the Cabbage*, page 85.

NEW VERSES

#17—Multipart Suggestions. *Where Do Foods Come From?*, page 106.

#25—Solo-Singing Opportunities. *What Grows in the Garden?*, page 111.

Old Mis-ter Rab-bit, you've got a might-y hab - it,

Of jump-ing in my gar-den and eat-ing all my cab-bage.

SONG #26

HASUKKAH

> HaSukkah, mah yafah,
> Umah tov lashevet bah,
> HaSukkah, mah yafah,
> Umah tov lashevet bah.

BACKGROUND

"HaSukkah" is a children's song for the Jewish autumn festival of Sukkot, when temporary booths or "Sukkot" (plural of "Sukkah") are built. The Hebrew words say, "The Sukkah, how beautiful; how good it is to sit in it."

For detailed background, resources, and curricular tie-ins, see page 177.

For sources, see page 203.

GAMES

#38—Guessing and Hiding. *What Will We Eat in the Sukkah?*, page 30.

#58—Rhythm Games. *Sukkah Pounding*, page 45.

MOVEMENTS

#4—Repeated Pulse Movements. *How to Build a Sukkah*, page 71.

#11—Sequential Pulse Movements. *Waving the Lulav*, page 75.

NEW VERSES

#29—Solo-Singing Opportunities. *What Decorates Our Sukkah?*, page 113.

Ha -Suk -kah, mah ya-fah, u-mah tov la-she-vet bah,

Ha -Suk -kah, mah ya-fah, u-mah tov la -she-vet bah.

SONG #27

TRAIN IS A-COMING

1. *Train is a-coming, oh, yeh,*
   Train is a-coming, oh, yeh,
   Train is a-coming, train is a-coming,
   Train is a-coming, oh, yeh.

2. *You better get your ticket, oh, yeh . . .*
3. *Whistle is a-blowing, oh, yeh . . .*
4. *Train going home now, oh, yeh . . .*

BACKGROUND

Originally an African-American spiritual, this song had verses eagerly anticipating the journey to heaven on a figurative railroad.

For detailed background, resources, and curricular tie-ins, see page 175.

For sources, *see* page 203.

GAMES

#31—Chasing and Racing. *Trains Race to a Tie*, page 24.

#44—Lines and Circles. *Make a Train*, page 35.

#57—Lines and Circles. *The Train Leaves the Roundhouse*, page 44.

MOVEMENTS

#10—Repeated Pulse Movements. *Jobs On a Train*, page 74.

Train is a-com-ing, oh, yeh,

Train is a-com-ing, oh, yeh,

Train is a-com-ing, train is a-com-ing,

Train is a-com-ing, oh, yeh.

SONG #28:

POOR LONESOME COWHAND

1. *I'm a poor, lonesome cowhand,*
   I'm a poor, lonesome cowhand,
   I'm a poor, lonesome cowhand,
   A long way from home.

2. *Soy un pobre vaquero,*
   Soy un pobre vaquero,
   Soy un pobre vaquero,
   O no, O no, O no.

3. *Yo no tengo madre,*
   Yo no tengo madre,
   Yo no tengo madre,
   O no, o no, O no.

4. *I don't have a mother,*
   I don't have a mother
   I don't have a mother,
   O no, O no, O no.

(Repeat first verse.)

BACKGROUND

This song was sung in both English and Spanish by English-speaking cowhands and their Spanish-speaking equivalents, vaqueros and vaqueras. Verse two translates verse one approximately, and verse three translates verse four.

For detailed background, resources, and curricular tie-ins, see page 165.

For sources, see page 203.

GAMES

#37—Guessing and Hiding. *Whose Face is This?*, page 29.

#40—Guessing and Hiding. *Finding the Cowhands*, page 32.

MOVEMENTS

#28—Movements with Others. *I Don't Have A Triangle*, page 92.

NEW VERSES

#6—One-Part Suggestions. *What Would You Miss?*, page 102.

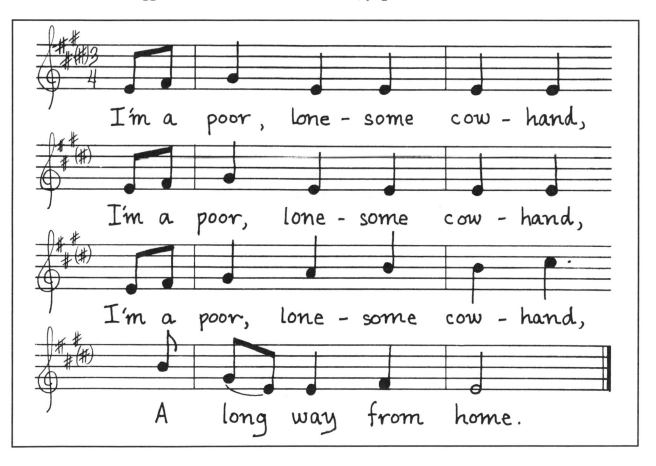

SONG #29:

SLEEP, BONNIE BAIRNIE

Sleep, bonnie bairnie, behind the castle,
Bye, bye, bye, bye.
Thou shalt have a golden apple,
Bye, bye, bye, bye.

BACKGROUND

This lullaby comes from Newcastle, in the north of England. "Bairnie" means "little child"; "bonnie" means "dear."

For detailed background, resources, and curricular tie-ins, see page 167.

For sources, see page 203.

GAMES

#33—Guessing and Hiding. *Where's the Golden Apple?*, page 26.

MOVEMENTS

#5—Repeated Pulse Movements. *How to Soothe a Baby*, page 71.

NEW VERSES

#12—One-Part Suggestions. *The Baby Who Can Sleep Anywhere*, page 105.

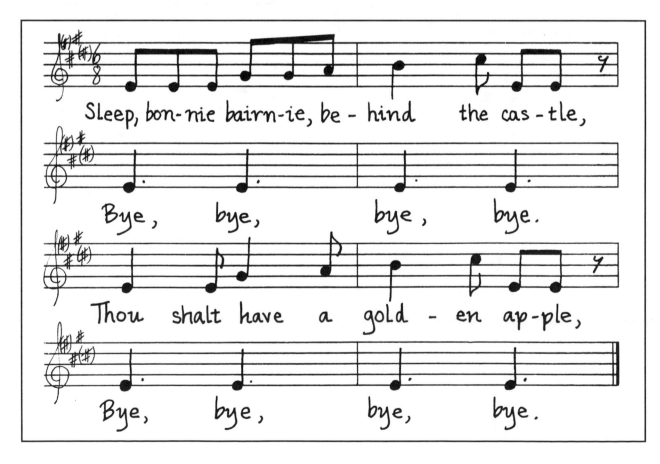

THERE WAS A LITTLE FROG

1. There was a little frog who lived on a hill, uh-huh, uh-huh,
   There was a little frog who lived on a hill,
   Who rustled and tussled like Buffalo Bill, uh-huh, uh-huh.

2. The frog took Mousie on one knee, uh-huh, uh-huh, . . .
   And said "Oh, Mouse, will you marry me?" . . .

3. "Yes, but where will the wedding be . . .
   "Down in the swamp in a hollow tree," . . .

4. "What will we have for the wedding supper" . . .
   "A black-eyed pea and a pound of butter" . . .

5. The first to come was Mrs. Goose . . .
   Took her fiddle and she cut loose . . .

6. The next to come was Doctor Flea . . .
   And danced a jig with the bumblebee . . .

7. The last to come was Captain Snake . . .
   And wrapped its tail around the cake . . .

8. For a honeymoon they went to France . . .
   And that's the story of their romance . . . .

BACKGROUND

This song is a U.S. variant of the best-known nursery song in the English language—with written versions going back to 1611!

For detailed background, resources, and curricular tie-ins, see page 167.

For sources, see page 204.

GAMES

#7—Games for Choosing. *The Animal Party*, page 6.

#36—Guessing and Hiding. *Who's the Mousie?*, page 28.

#74—Play-party Games. *The Grand Right-and-Left*, page 62.

MOVEMENTS

#13—Sequential Pulse Movements. *Riding With the Frog*, page 77.

NEW VERSES

#10—One-Part Suggestions. *Imaginary Frog*, page 104.

#34—Rhyming Verses. *What Animal Came In?*, page 117.

BACKGROUND, CURRICULAR TIE-INS, AND FOLLOW-UP RESOURCES

You can use and enjoy the folksongs in this book without knowing anything further about them. But if you want to explore the songs in more depth, you'll have several needs, which this chapter is designed to meet.

To maximize the teaching potential and satisfaction of using folksongs with children, you need to know where the songs came from, how they were used while in oral tradition, and what they meant to those who sang them.

The most powerful way to connect to the traditional cultures and singers of these songs is to listen to traditional recordings. You may wish to listen for your own preparation and sense of style, or you may want to play these recordings for children after they've learned the songs in their own way. In either case, you need a discography of traditional recordings, which follows in this chapter.

To use these folksongs in your presentation of various subjects or to use them as a starting point for further exploration, you need information about related books and recordings and an index of related subjects that might appear in your curriculum.

WHAT'S IN THIS CHAPTER

This chapter discusses the background of the 30 songs in this collection, in five main sections: work songs, religious songs, dance songs, game songs, and ballads and other songs. Most of the sections are divided into subsections (for ex-

ample, "dance songs" includes subsections about string-band songs and play-party songs).

Within each section, general information about the category of song is given first, followed by a discussion of each song. Each section or subsection also includes a bibliography/discography of traditional recordings and of further resources for extending the study of the song by exploring other musical and cultural examples.

At the end of each section, there's a list of topics for potential curricular tie-ins. (These lists are assembled into a Subject Index in the back of the book).

FINDING BOOKS AND RECORDINGS

Books go in and out of print. Recordings become unavailable, then are reissued—often in new formats. I have tried to cite references of lasting value, in the hopes they will remain available.

If you find that a book listed in this chapter is out of print, please try your library. If your library does not have the title, don't give up! Ask your reference librarian to try interlibrary loan. In my town, this costs a small fee per title, but it gives me access to library collections across the country.

Many of the recordings recommended in this chapter were originally published by Folkways Records, which has been purchased by the Smithsonian Institution. To buy Folkways recordings that have been reissued on LP, cassette, or CD by the Smithsonian (or for a catalog of other folk music recordings) contact:

Round-Up Records, P.O. Box 154, N. Cambridge MA 02140; (617) 661-6308; order line, (800) 443-4272.

For cassette reproductions of any other Folkways recordings, contact:

Smithsonian/Folkways Recording, Office of Folklife Programs, 955 L'Enfant Plaza, Suite 2600, Smithsonian Institution, Washington DC 20560; (202) 287-3262.

WORK SONGS

In our postindustrial society, music and work don't seem to belong together. But for most of the world and for most of the world's history, singing and working have been natural companions.

Especially in European-derived cultures, there is often a strong division between work and art, between accomplishment and pleasure. But work songs bridge that division and remind us that work can be esthetic and music can be productive.

Most of the work songs in this collection accompanied the work of men in occupations that are now obsolete. But childcare is traditionally the work of women, and its work songs (lullabies and nursery rhymes) are alive and well.

Work songs are a natural point of entry for the study of occupations, history, and geography. But they also tell us a lot about social organization, including cooperation, job hierarchies, and work roles (such as prisoner versus supervisor, officer versus sailor, and who does child care within a family and for the families of others).

This collection contains four categories of work songs: sea shanties, cowhand songs, lullabies and nursery rhymes, and prison songs. It's worth noting, though, that in past centuries many work songs passed freely from one category to another. Sea songs were put to use felling timber, and cowhand songs found their way out to sea. The docks, in particular, became a place where songs were transmitted across race and vocation by the cosmopolitan dock workers. As a result, each category describes a kind of work better than it describes a kind of song.

SEA SHANTIES

Sea shanties are work songs sung at sea. In the days when commercial vessels travelled by wind power, large crews were required to raise, lower, and maintain a ship's sails and rigging. Sailors sang for their own entertainment, of course, but most shanties served to coordinate the efforts of the crew. When pulling a sail tight against the wind, everyone had to pull together, or the wind would win!

Most shanties used a shanty leader who led the song. The shanty leader needed a loud, clear voice to be heard above the wind in the rigging and the rattling of pulleys and chain cables. Moreover, the shanty leader paced the song, therefore pacing the work. If the song was too slow, the work was inefficient and took too long. If the song was too fast, on the other hand, the work was too tiring.

The shanty leader also chose what words to sing. Most shanties alternate a solo line (sung by the shanty leader) with a chorus line (sung by the rest of the crew). The shanty leader chose his lines from stock verses that appeared in many songs, but he often added original verses about the situation at hand or even about gossip on board the ship. Such verses could inspire the sailors to work harder. In fact, a good shanty was said to be worth 10 sailors on the rope.

Halliard Shanties

Both "Round the Corner" and "Juley" are "halliard shanties," used for pulling particular parts of the ship's rigging.

The typical sailing ship had three masts, each supporting several cross-pieces, known as yardarms. Each yardarm supported the top (or the bottom) of a sail. The ropes used to raise the moveable yardarms were known as haul-yards or halliards (also spelled "halyards"). To unfurl a sail attached to a moveable yardarm, the halliard was pulled, raising the yardarm. (See diagram on next page.)

No shanty was needed until the wind caught the sail and began pulling the rope in the opposite direction. At that point, the shanty leader would begin a halliard shanty, to coordinate the sailors in this sustained and difficult work.

ROUND THE CORNER

As a sea shanty, "Round the Corner" was used as a halliard shanty. The shanty leader sang a line of the verse, then the crew responded with "Round the corner, Sally." While the leader sang, the crew got ready, re-adjusting their grip on the rope as necessary. At the syllables "round" and "Sal," the sailors gave a pull. If the wind was very strong in the sails or the sailors were tired, they might omit one pull from each line.

To sailors, the phrase "round the corner" often meant "around Cape Horn." "Round the corner Sallies," however, were prostitutes. Many of the traditional verses to this song (not included here) refer to women in stereotypical ways—reflecting, evidently, the sex-role stereotypes prevalent among sailors of the age of sail.

Another traditional verse mentioned a destination:

> To Callyo we're bound to go,
> Round the corner, Sally,
> Around that corner where there's ice and snow,
> Round the corner, Sally.

The final verse said, in sailor's jargon, to pull the sail taut:

> So round 'er up an' stretch 'er luff (etc.)
> I think by Gawd we've hauled enough (etc.).

Like a number of sea shanties, "Round the Corner" has also been used for other kinds of

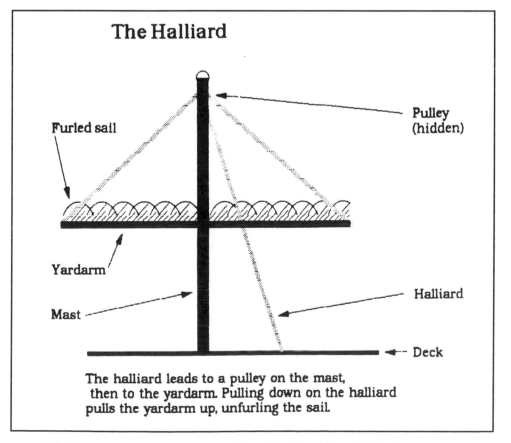

The Halliard

Furled sail

Pulley (hidden)

Yardarm

Mast

Halliard

Deck

The halliard leads to a pulley on the mast, then to the yardarm. Pulling down on the halliard pulls the yardarm up, unfurling the sail.

work. In particular, it was used for corn shuckings, where two teams in friendly competition often shucked large mounds of corn. The teamwork at these events required the same sort of "call and response" work songs required for raising sails. Other sea shanties (such as "Whiskey Johnny") were used at corn shuckings, too, with changes to some of the words. It was easy to change "Round the Corner, Sally" to "Round the Corn, Sally!" (Of course, we don't know for sure which form came first.)

JULEY

"Juley" is a shanty from African-American sailors, possibly from the Gulf of Mexico. Since many songs about a "Julie" or "Julia" came from the West Indies, our song may have, too. Like many shanties, "Juley" shows influences from several cultures.

Before it was sung at sea, "Juley" may have been a cotton-loading song. Stevedores (many of them African Americans) would load bales of cotton into the hold of a ship. Once the hold was filled, more cotton would be added by compressing the cargo with "jackscrews," large jacks with a screw-like mechanism. The whole job became known as "screwing cotton." The stevedores sang songs borrowed from other forms of work, including river-boat and *voyageur* songs. (*Voyageurs* were the fur trappers and guides who paddled the waterways of Canada and the nothern United States.) They learned songs from the ocean-going sailors, too, making the cotton ports into what one shanty expert calls "shanty marts," where a good song could pass easily from one culture and vocation to another.

As a halliard shanty, "Juley" would be sung with pulls on the syllables in boldface type:

> *Juley, you're a lady,*
> ***Oo*** *- oo,* ***oo*** *- oo,*
> *Juley, Juley, Juley,*
> ***Walk*** *along, Miss* ***Ju****-liana Brown.*

When the sail was finally taut enough, the officer of the watch would holler "Belay!" or "Well enough," bringing the shanty to an abrupt halt.

TIE-INS AND RESOURCES
Curricular Tie-ins

African Americans: History
Clothing: Sources and Production
Cooperation
Cross-Cultural Transmissions
Food: Sources and Production
Music: Occupational Uses
Science: Ropes and Pulleys
Seas and Oceans
Sex-Role Stereotypes
Transportation
U.S. History: Trade
West Indies

Traditional Recordings

You can hear traditional performances of sea songs on these two records:

Emrich, Duncan, ed. *American Sea Songs and Shanties (I).* Library of Congress AFS L26. LP.

Emrich, Duncan, ed. *American Sea Songs and Shanties (II).* Library of Congress AFS L27. LP.

Resources

For information about sailors and their songs, presented for children, see these two books:

Heaton, Peter, and Maria Bird. *Songs Under Sail: A Book of Sailor Shanties.* London: Burke, 1963.

Hurd, Michael. *Sailors' Songs and Shanties.* London: Oxford University Press, 1965.

The following illustrated book for children describes the construction of a wooden sailing ship, such as those on which our shanties might have been sung:

Adkins, Jan. *Wooden Ship: The Building of a Wooden Sailing Vessel in 1870.* Boston: Houghton-Mifflin, 1978.

Write to this address for an entire catalog and bibliography of sea records, books, and prints: Sea Heritage Foundation, 254-26 75th Avenue, Glen Oaks, NY 11004.

COWHAND SONGS

Part of the work of a cowhand (I use "cowhand" or "cowpoke" to avoid the gender-specific terms "cowboy" and "cowgirl") was singing to the cattle, especially at night.

Singing reassured the cattle of the cowhand's familiar presence, covering up unfamiliar and startling noises. The shake of a horse with its heavy saddle, the snap of a twig, howl of a coyote, or hoot of an owl—all might cause a dangerous stampede. Some cowhands insisted that singing to the cattle made the entire drive go better.

For a cowhand, singing was an important job skill—some say, an essential one. One cowpuncher wrote of keeping a job, in spite of being new on it, because he could sing. Another called singing "a necessary accomplishment of his trade." Still another claims that night herding so often involved singing that it was referred to as "singin' to 'em."

As important as a good relationship with the cattle was the cowhands' relationship to their horses. They spent more time with them than with any person and became understandably fond of them. A well-trained horse was vital to maneuvering or roping cattle. The cowhand's livelihood—and sometimes life—depended on this partnership with a reliable, intelligent horse. As a result, it's no surprise that both of our cowhand songs, like many others, refer to the practical and sentimental value of a good horse.

Unlike the cowhand story songs, or "ballads," both of the cowhand songs in this collection were often sung with improvised words. They could easily have humorous or even rough verses, but they had to be sung gently, omitting any startling sound or tone. All lullabies are work songs; these cowhand songs are work songs that had to be lullabies.

POOR, LONESOME COWHAND

Although the westerns have emphasized the contributions of white, male cowhands, the actual work was done by men and women of four ethnic groups: Anglo, Hispanic, African American, and Native American.

"Poor Lonesome Cowhand," reported to have been sung by gauchos of Argentina as well as cowhands of the U.S. Southwest, is one of the few sung in both Spanish and English to the same tune.

Cow herders travelled far from settlements, across hundreds of miles of great plains. Even on the same shift, they rode too far apart to talk. Far from the comforts of their former homes and families, they were thrown together with strangers. They expressed some of their feelings of longing and loss by singing songs like this one.

GOOD-BYE, OLD PAINT

The oldest known version of "Good-bye, Old Paint" was sung by a African-American cowpoke named Charlie Willis, who learned it on a trail drive from Texas to Wyoming, around 1885.

A paint horse, which can be of any breed, has more than one color, usually with large patches of a single color. Paints were also called pintos (after the Spanish *pintar,* which means "to paint," or possibly from *pintado,* which means "spotted"). Other names included circus horses, calico horses, and skewballs. (See Stewball, page 170.)

In some remote places, "Good-bye, Old Paint" was sung for dancing until a fiddle player arrived. In parts of Texas and Oklahoma, it became traditional to end *every* evening of dancing by waltzing to the unaccompanied singing of "Good-bye, Old Paint." In New Mexico, it was *even* said that as long as anyone could remember or improvise a new verse, the dance would continue. No wonder there are dozens of verses!

Aaron Copeland used the best-known variant of this tune in his ballet *Billy the Kid.*

TIE-INS AND RESOURCES
Curricular Tie-ins

Animals: Cattle
Animals: Horses
African Americans: History
Families: People without Families

Food: Sources and Production
Hispanic Americans: History
Music: Occupational Uses
Native Americans: History
U.S. History: Frontier
U.S.: Southwest Region.

Traditional Recordings

You can hear traditional cowhand songs (in most cases, sung by actual cowhands) on these recordings:

Emrich, Duncan, ed. *Cowboy Songs, Ballads, and Cattle Calls from Texas.* Library of Congress AFS L28. LP.

Jackson, Harry. *The Cowboy: His Songs, Ballads & Brag Talk.* Folkways Records FH 5723. LP.

In the 1920s, a number of authentic cowhands made commercial recordings. Several have been reissued, including these:

Allen, Jules. *The Texas Cowboy.* Bear Family Records FU 12502. LP.

Authentic Cowboys and Their Western Folksongs. RCA Victor LPV-522. LP.

When I Was a Cowboy. Morning Star Records 45008. LP.

The following four traditional recordings of "Good-bye Old Paint" (all with tunes different from the one given here) show interesting variation in tune, text, form, and use of the fiddle. For a fiddle version learned from Charlie Willis, as well as another unaccompanied version, see:

Emrich, Duncan, ed. *Cowboy Songs, Ballads, and Cattle Calls from Texas.* Library of Congress AFS L28. LP.

Dick Duvall sings the related song, "My Sweetheart's a Cowboy," on:

Emrich, Duncan, ed. *Anglo-American Songs and Ballads.* Library of Congress AFS L20. LP.

Harry McClintock sings a slicker version with fiddle and guitar accompaniment on:

McClintock, Harry. *Hallelujah! I'm a Bum.* Rounder Records 1009. LP.

Resources

You'll get a general description of the cowpoke's life, complete with excellent photographs and a collection of songs, in:

Sackett, S. J. *Cowboys and the Songs They Sang.* New York: William R. Scott, 1967.

A sense of cowpoke life as it continues in present-day Nevada is well portrayed in:

Marshall, Howard W., and Richard E. Ahlborn. *Buckaroos in Paradise: Cowboy Life in Northern Nevada.* Washington, DC: Library of Congress, 1980.

For marvelously detailed information about what cowhands actually did, how and why they did and still do it, and what equipment they used, see this book (the skills of a cow horse are described on pages 149–53):

Ward, Fay E. *The Cowboy At Work.* New York: Hastings House, 1958.

To learn more about cowhand dances, see:

Larkin, Margaret. *Singing Cowboy: A Book of Western Songs.* New York: Oak Publications, 1963. Page 169.

Lomax, John A., and Alan Lomax. *American Ballads and Folksongs.* New York: Macmillan, 1934. Page 383.

To learn more about night herding, see:

White, John I. *Git Along, Little Dogies: Songs and Songmakers of the American West.* Urbana, IL: University of Illinois Press, 1975. Pages 46–53.

To learn more about paint horses, see:

Tinsley, Jim Bob. *He Was Singin' This Song.* Orlando, FL: University of Central Florida, 1981. Pages 122–29.

Watts, Peter. *Dictionary of the Old West, 1850–1900.* New York: Alfred A. Knopf, 1977. Page 236.

African-American cowhands are given long-overdue recognition in this book:

Durham, Philip, and Everett L. Jones. *Adventures of the Negro Cowboys.* New York: Bantam, 1966.

You can discover more about Hispanic cowhands (vaqueros) in:

Gonzalez, Jovita. "Folk-Lore of the Texas-Mexican Vaquero." In *Texas and Southwestern Lore,* edited by J. Frank Dobie, Pages 7–22. Dallas, TX: Southern Methodist Press, 1967. First printed 1927.

If you need more information about any particular aspect of cowhand life or history, try this bibliography (e.g., for more sources about vaqueros, look at pages 38–43):

Dobie, J. Frank. *Guide to the Life and Literature of the Southwest.* Dallas, TX: Southern Methodist Press, 1974. First printed 1942.

For references about cowhand poetry, see the Resources section under Play-Party Songs, page 186.

LULLABIES AND NURSERY SONGS

Lullabies are sung to children to help them sleep. Nursery rhymes and songs are sung to children to entertain them. Even though many cultures seem to put little value on the work of caring for and educating children, the songs used with such work are nonetheless work songs.

Some nursery songs (like "There Was a Little Frog") entertain children with their lyrics and sprightly tunes. Others (such as "Dance a Baby Diddy") traditionally occupy young children with physical horse-play with an adult.

DANCE A BABY DIDDY

This English nursery ditty appears to be a "dandling song"—a song an adult sings while bouncing an infant up and down in the adult's arms or lap. The word "dandle," by the way, seems related to an Italian word, *dandolare,* which means to dandle or to swing.

The oldest reference to "Dance a Baby Diddy" is contained in the description of a performance by "an old Italian way-faring puppet-showman of the name of Piccini," whose Punch and Judy shows in England date back to about 1780. By 1828, "Dance a Baby Diddy" was already referred to as "the common nursery ditty."

Like many lullabies, "Dance a Baby Diddy" has verses that refer to the child's future, not always in the most cheerful way:

> *Smile, my baby bonny,*
> *What will time bring on 'e?*
> *Sorrow and care, frowns and grey hair,*
> *So smile, my baby bonny.*
>
> *Laugh, my baby beauty,*
> *What will time do to ye?*
> *Furrow your cheek, wrinkle your neck,*
> *So laugh, my baby beauty.*

SLEEP, BONNIE BAIRNIE

This lullaby hales from the town of Newcastle, in the northern part of England. Only one version of it is known to me.

Newcastle-upon-Tyne is the county seat of Northumberland, which borders on Scotland. It's northern dialect shares some words with Scotish dialect, such as "bairnie," which means "little child." ("Bairn" is the Scottish word for "child.") "Bonnie" or "bonny" means "pretty" or "pleasing to the sight." Sometimes, as in this song, "bonnie" is a term of endearment, meaning "dear."

"Sleep, Bonnie Bairnie" was sung to a turn-of-the-century British folklorist by a Miss Harrison, who in turn learned it from an "old family nurse." Miss Harrison described how the nurse had accented each of the "Bye's," loudly clapping her hand onto her leg and tapping her feet. Many traditional lullabies have soothing melodies but violent words (think of "on a tree top, the bough will break, the cradle will fall")—but this one has the reverse: soothing words and a knee-slapping tune!

THERE WAS A LITTLE FROG

This song is an uncommon version of an all-time favorite, more widely known as "The Frog's Courtship" or "Froggie Went A-Courting." As such, it is one of the best-known and longest-documented songs in the English language. It has been used as a dandling song and a lullaby, too.

The earliest surviving version of the song—published by Thomas Ravenscroft in 1611—begins like this:

> *It was the Frogge in the well,*
> *Humble-dum, humble-dum,*
> *And the merrie Mouse in the Mill,*
> *Tweedle, tweedle, twine.*

Over the centuries, dozens of nonsense refrains have evolved, from "humble-dum" to "Sing, song, kitty, can't you kie me O," to our matter-of-fact "uh-huh." At the same time, hundreds of narrative verses have described nearly every facet of the courtship, wedding, and further adventures of the animal bride and groom. In versions from the United States, in particular, singers seem to delight in listing animal after animal as wedding guest, finding clever ways to fit the animal into the rhyme:

> *Next came in were two little ants . . .*
> *Fixing around to have a dance. . . .*
>
> *Next came in was a butterfly . . .*
> *She fanned the company as she went by. . . .*
>
> *The next one came was a little moth . . .*
>
> *And she spread out the tablecloth. . . .*
>
> *The next that came was Misses Skeeter . . .*
> *My, but she could dance and teeter. . . .*

A Texas variant uses the song for dandling a child. (See "Sleep, Bonnie Bairnie," above.) The adult holds the child on the adult's knees, swaying them back and forth until the words "uh-huh," at which point the adult stops suddenly, causing the child to fall off.

A number of white adults have recalled childhood experiences in which African-American women took care of them, using versions of this song as lullabies, sometimes accompanied by dramatic gestures and sounds.

TIE-INS AND RESOURCES
Curricular Tie-ins

African Americans: History
Animals: Amphibians
Animals: Fantasies and Fictions
Animals: Insects
Child Care: History and Lore
Cross-Cultural Transmissions
England
Families: Child Raising
Italy: Language
Music: Occupational Uses
Romance and Courtship
Scotland: Language
U.S.: Texas
Weddings
Women: Traditional Occupations of

Traditional Recordings

For traditional recordings of lullabies from around the world, sung in many languages by ordinary people, you will want to hear this collection:

Mendelssohn, Lillian, ed. *Lullabies of the World.* Ethnic Folkways Library FE 4511. 2 LP's, plus booklet.

To hear the folk music of Northumberland (home of "Sleep, Bonnie Bairnie") along with songs from the other regions of England, listen to:

Kennedy, Peter, and Alan Lomax, eds. *English Folk Songs. (Columbia World Library of Folk and Primitive Music, Volume III).* Columbia AKL 4943. LP.

Northumberland's distinctive, quiet bagpipes, the Northumbrian smallpipes, can be heard on:

Billy Pigg: The Border Minstrel. Leader LEA 4006. LP.

For a sampling of music north of the Scots-Northumbrian border, including a lullaby and some game songs, listen to:

Lomax, Alan, ed. *Folk Songs from Scotland. (Columbia World Library of Folk and Primitive Music, Volume VI).* Columbia AKL 4946. LP.

Of the many traditional recordings of variants of "There Was A Little Frog," the following exhibit a variety of musical traditions. Four different partial recordings by traditional English singers are given on:

Kennedy, Peter, and Alan Lomax, eds. *Animal Songs (The Folksongs of Britain Volume X)*. Caedmon TC 1225. LP.

A sprightly Irish version, sung by the Clancy grandchildren, appears on:

Hamilton, Diane, ed. *So Early in the Morning*. Tradition Records TLP 1034. LP.

Across the sea in the United States, variants from the Adirondack, Ozark, and Appalachian mountains, respectively, are sung on:

Lawrence Older. Folk-Legacy Records FSA-15. LP.

Lomax, Alan, ed. *American Folk Songs for Children*. Atlantic SD-1350. LP. (sung by Almeda Riddle).

Ritchie, Jean. *Children's Songs and Games from the Southern Mountains*. Folkways Records FC 7054. LP.

An African-American relative, "Hambone," is recorded on:

Jones, Bessie. *Step It Down*. Rounder Records 8004.

Resources

Three good printed collections of lullabies are:

Cass-Beggs, Barbara, and Michael Cass-Beggs. *Folk Lullabies*. New York: Oak Publications, 1969.

Commins, Dorothy Berliner. *Lullabies of the World*. New York: Random House, 1967.

Miller, Carl S. *Rockabye Baby: Lullabies of Many Lands and Peoples*. New York: Chappell Music, 1975.

For other dandling rhymes and knee-riding rhymes, see:

Opie, Iona, and Peter Opie, eds. *The Oxford Nursery Rhyme Book*. London: Oxford University Press, 1975.

I would love to hear from readers who know dandling rhymes from other cultures.

"Dance a Baby Diddy" deals with the nature of babies. For titles and synopses of many books for children about dealing with a new sibling, see pages 375–78 of the index of this reference book:

Dreyer, Sharon Spredemann. *The Bookfinder: A Guide to Children's Literature about the Needs and Problems of Youth Aged 2–15*. Circle Pines, MN: American Guidance Service, 1977.

On the recording that accompanies this book, "Sleep, Bonnie Bairnie" is sung as a round. For an attractive collection of rounds that includes a history and how-to of round singing, see:

Yolen, Jane, ed. *Rounds About Rounds*. New York: Franklin Watts, 1977.

An inexpensive source of rounds from many countries is:

101 Rounds For Singing. Delaware, OH: Informal Music Service, n.d.

For references to folktales about frogs (or other animals), see:

MacDonald, Margaret Read. *The Storyteller's Sourcebook: A Subject, Title, and Motif Index to Folklore Collections for Children*. Detroit, MI: Gale Research Company, 1982. (The subject references for "frog" are on pages 625–26.)

PRISON SONGS

In the United States, prison work songs have been sung almost entirely by African-American prisoners from Southern prisons. Like sea shanties (see above), prison work songs are used to coordinate the efforts of a group, whose singing usually alternates with the solo singing of a leader. Unlike sea chanties, however, prison songs accompany jobs that may last for hours at a time. Since the song leader controls the pace of the work, the song leader is essentially the leader of the work crew. As a result, the position of song leader traditionally carries prestige.

Just as different kinds of jobs at sea call for different kinds of songs, prison songs are used in different ways for varied jobs: chopping down trees, chopping fallen logs into sections, hoeing, and harvesting cane or cotton. Some jobs, such as felling a tree by a team of choppers, require precise coordination to avoid injury and therefore require particular kinds of songs. (In fact, white prison crews, who traditionally do not sing work songs together, are unable to do the kinds of axe-work that require the most precise teamwork.) For other jobs, such as cutting cane or cotton-picking, coordination is less important than raising morale. For these jobs, then, almost any song will do, if it can be sung at an appropriate tempo for the work at hand.

Since prison inmates work against their will in a highly regulated environment, their opportunities for self-expression are exceedingly limited. By an unspoken agreement with their supervisors, prisoners are allowed to *sing* complaints and other forms of protest that they would not be allowed to speak.

STEWBALL

Although the earliest record we have of "Stewball" as a work song dates from 1906 in Mississippi, "Stewball" is a descendant of an Irish ballad. (See the section on ballads, below.) Many details of the story appear in both Anglo-American ballad forms and African-American work song forms.

First printed in 1822, the oldest known ballad version tells of a race in Kildare, Ireland, between "Skew Ball" and "Miss Sportly," a mare owned by Sir Ralph Gore. (A "skewball" or "skewbald" horse, by the way, has a white coat with reddish-brown blotches, like a paint horse—see "Goodbye, Old Paint," discussed on page 165.) Versions of this ballad had already travelled to the United States at least by 1829 and have been collected from Vermont to Texas. On a broader commercial scale, an Anglo-American ballad version was adapted and popularized in the 1960s by the group Peter, Paul and Mary.

The song circulated in African-American tradition, as well. By the 1930s, "Stewball" was the most widely known prison chain-gang song in Louisiana, Texas, Mississippi, and Tennessee.

Pioneering folklorists John and Alan Lomax toured the southern United States many times collecting folksongs. In 1933 they met Huddie Ledbetter, known as "Leadbelly," who was then a prisoner at the Louisiana State Penitentiary at Angola. They were so taken with him as a performer and person that they carried his recorded plea for pardon to the governor of Louisiana. When the pardon was granted, they devoted themselves for a year to Leadbelly's musical career. Among the priceless legacy of recordings by Leadbelly are at least two renditions of "Stewball."

For hoeing or chopping wood to "Stewball," the Lomaxes found the entire work group hoeing or chopping at the words in boldface type:

> It was a **big** day (uh-**huh**)
> In **Dal**-las (uh-**huh**)
> Don't you **wish** you (uh-**huh**)
> Was **there** (was **there**).

For picking cotton or cutting stalks of sugar cane, however, each worker decided on an individual way to work in time to the song.

TIE-INS AND RESOURCES
Curricular Tie-ins

African Americans: History
Animals: Horses
Clothing: Sources and Production
Cooperation
Cross-Cultural Transmissions
Food: Sources and Production
Ireland: History
Music: Occupational Uses
Sports: Horse Racing
U.S. History: Penal System
U.S.: South

Traditional Recordings

Two different versions of "Stewball" by Leadbelly (Huddie Ledbetter) are available on:

Leadbelly's Last Sessions, Volume One. Folkways Records FA 2941. LP.

Leadbelly Sings Folk Songs. Folkways Records FA 2488. LP.

A 1959 recording of "Stewball," along with other authentic prison songs from Louisiana, can be heard on:

Oster, Harry, ed. *Prison Worksongs: Recorded at Angola.* Arhoolie Records 2012. LP.

For other recordings of prison songs recorded "in the field," listen to:

Jackson, Bruce, ed. *Wake Up, Dead Man: Black Convict Work Songs from Texas Prisons.* Rounder Records 2013. LP.

Seeger, Toshi, et al., eds. *Negro Prison Camp Worksongs.* Folkways Records FE 4475. LP.

Resources

For a variety of U.S. work songs presented for children, see:

Siegmeister, Elie. *Work and Sing: A Collection of Songs That Helped Build America.* New York: Edward B. Marks Music Corporation, 1953.

An accessible essay on African-American work songs appears on pages 89–122 of:

Courlander, Harold. *Negro Folk Music, U.S.A.* New York: Columbia University Press, 1963.

For a scholarly treatment of prison songs, complete with bibliography and discography, refer to the following, which also discusses the relation of music to movement for the various jobs (pages 31–33):

Jackson, Bruce. *Wake Up, Dead Man: Afro-American Worksongs from Texas Prisons.* Cambridge, MA: Harvard University Press, 1972.

For more about Leadbelly, see the introductions to:

Asch, Moses, and Alan Lomax. *The Leadbelly Songbook.* New York: Oak Publications, 1962.

Lomax, John A., and Alan Lomax. *The Leadbelly Legend.* New York: Folkways Music Publishers, 1959.

There's also a novelized biography of Leadbelly (which later gave rise to a movie):

Garvin, Richard M., and Edmond G. Addeo. *The Midnight Special.* New York: Bernard Geis Associates, 1971.

You can hear some of Leadbelly's songs for children on:

Leadbelly Sings Play-Party Songs, Volumes I & II. Stinson Records SLPX 39. LP.

Leadbelly. *Negro Songs for Young People.* Folkways Records FC 7533. LP.

The 1822 Irish ballad about "Skew Ball" has been recorded on:

Lloyd, A. L. *Champions and Sporting Blades.* Riverside Records RLP 12-652. LP.

One traditional U.S. melody for "Stewball" has even been arranged for concert band:

Kubik, Gail. *Stewball: Variations on an American Folk Tune.* New York: Southern Music Publishing Co., Inc. n.d.

RELIGIOUS SONGS

The cultures of the world have given rise to hundreds of traditions of religious music. Only two such traditions are represented in this collection: African-American religious folksongs (black spirituals) and Jewish holiday songs. (Of the other traditions that might have been included, I happened to be ignorant of songs that met the specific requirements for inclusion in this collection: playable with only the E-major chord and adaptable for a general audience.)

SPIRITUALS

Black spirituals are the Christian religious folk music of African Americans. They have their own history, merging aspects of European-American and African cultures. Because of the social controversies faced by African Americans throughout the centuries, these beautiful songs have been the subject of controversy, too.

The first spirituals were sung by slaves who had been converted to Christianity. Not all slave owners welcomed the spirituals, however. The slave masters were always fearful of organized rebellion. As a result, many feared all forms of education for slaves, including religious education. They feared the development of slave leaders (including preachers) and assemblies of slaves (including religious services). They feared, too, that if the slaves were allowed to make music in "non-Christian" (meaning non-European) styles, they might be moved to defiance and mass action.

The efforts of ministers and missionaries eventually overcame the slave owners' reluctance. By the second quarter of the nineteenth century, it became common practice to Christianize slaves and even to allow them their own services. Given the masters' fears and the long history of prohibition of slave services, though, it's not surprising that many black spirituals were sung in secret meetings, in hushed voices (for fear of discovery by the patrols or "patterollers"). It's also not surprising that slave composers learned to hint at ideas or to cast them in metaphor, rather than state them outright.

"Discovery" of the Spirituals

Until about 1860, the only form of African-American music to be widely known outside the plantation world was the minstrel song. Presented by white performers in "black face," these songs often consisted of a refrain with religious content alternating with a series of more secular, humorous verses. Sometimes based on authentic African-American folksongs, they were usually adapted to foster the stereotype of the slave as ignorant and happy-go-lucky.

Imagine the surprise, then, of the Northerners who first heard the spirituals during the Civil War (the War between the States). Letters and articles came back North describing this original, deeply felt, and often mournful music. At this early stage in the development of white consciousness about African Americans, the spirituals were considered proof that African Americans could create musical works of art.

Years later, the wider world discovered *white* religious folk music in certain rural sections of the United States. Some critics claimed that these "white spirituals" were, in fact, the real sources of the songs previously thought to have been created by the slaves. This musicological debate took on the tenor of a moralistic war between the proponents of slave creativity and their detractors.

This debate was only possible because of a series of divisions in the world. First, European imperialism divided Europeans from native peoples everywhere, making it difficult for Europeans to conceive of culture and religion in any terms but their own. Second, racism divided white people from African Americans, making it possible for some whites to lose sight of the humanness of African Americans. Third, the industrial revolution had divided city people from rural people, allowing city people to lose touch with oral tradition; this division led to the "discovery" of folk music (first African American, then white) by the city world. It also meant that the debate relied on written versions of the songs, which lacked the more African musical contributions.

In the absence of these divisions, it would have been obvious that:

♪ African-American slaves were like other people, creating a unique culture from the materials at hand;

♪ both African American and white religious folk musics are beautiful artistic achievements;

♪ the two folk traditions co-existed, influencing and feeding each other.

It also appears now that the European contribution to the spirituals included Christianity (including the Bible and the tradition of English-language hymns) and the division of the world into secular and religious domains. The African contributions included the incorporation of movement into religious worship, the use of improvisational lyrics, and certain musical elements such as short, repeating rhythmic elements; the "blues" scales; and the use of overlapping antiphonal singing. (In antiphonal singing, two voices or groups of voices sing back and forth to each other; for an example, listen to "I'm Going Home on the Morning Train" on the accompanying recording.)

Spirituals in Changing Contexts

The spirituals have not only survived the attempt to deny African-American authorship, but they have also survived the trivializing effect of the minstrel stage and its successors that have held up parodies of African-American religious songs for the amusement of white audiences. Some of these parodies, like "Dese Bones Gwine Rise Again" and "One More River to Cross," are now used as children's songs, acted out with gestures in schools and summer camps.

In the light of this history of using spirituals in nonreligious contexts for the ridicule of African Americans, a question arises: is it demeaning to African Americans to sing the songs in this book as nonreligious children's songs?

On the one hand, using these songs without awareness of their origin or significance can perpetuate the idea that the products of African-American culture do not require respect. European Americans have alternately treated black spirituals as quaint examples of "primitive" culture and as raw material to be formed into "real" compositions. Since we have few so examples of respectful treatment to imitate, we need to approach spirituals with extra sensitivity.

On the other hand, there are reasons that using these songs in a music-session context might not necessarily be disrespectful, if done with care. First, the spirituals have always been fluid rather than fixed, changing from one singing to the next, responding to the needs of the moment. Second, the use of movements in children's versions of spirituals goes against the *European* standards of respect for religious songs, but not against African standards. Movement in most African cultures is an essential part of religions observance. Third, spirituals have always been adapted to the situation at hand, whether religious or secular. They were used as

work songs for rowing and harvesting, and even changed to reflect emancipation and, later, the civil rights movement

Be cautious about "minstrelizing" these songs. Listen to traditional recordings of spirituals (see the listings below). Treat them as cultural treasures. Before using them, ask yourself, "What was the noble impulse behind this song in its original context?" Then teach them with respect and with enjoyment. With your help, these songs can live in and enrich a new environment: your classroom or your home.

SIT DOWN

"Sit Down" is a spiritual that has been used to express hope of heaven. Some versions just expect a place to "sit down and rest a little while"; others elaborate on what will be seen there (the "children that Moses led," etc.)

In other versions, the hope of entering heaven has been combined with demands for rewards. In one related spiritual, the soul entering heaven says:

> *My Lord, you know that you promise me,*
> *Promise me a long white robe and a pair of shoes.*

In response, the Lord says:

> *Go yonder, angel, fetch me a pair of shoes*
> *Place them on my servant's feet.*
> *Now, servant, please set down.*

The servant refuses, asking in subsequent verses for a starry crown, a golden waistband, and angel wings. If we imagine a slave singing such a song, we must admire the proud spirit of the singer who says, in effect, "I want everything I'm entitled to, or no reward at all!"

Camp-Meeting Song. Camp meetings were enormous religious revival meetings, often lasting for several days or longer and involving thousands of people (often both African American and white), many of whom travelled for days to participate. Songs from African-American and white traditions were able to pass back and forth during such events.

Two characteristics of "Sit Down" mark it as a likely camp-meeting song. First, the verses are meant to be learned quickly. The ones that begin "who's that yonder that I see . . ." appear in many songs; folklorists call these "floating verses." Such verses would be already familiar to people singing the song for the first time. Some versions of "Sit Down" just substitute a single word in each refrain to make additional verses: "Sit down, sister" becomes "Sit down, brother," etc. Second, the refrain and verses of "Sit Down" both feature a series of questions and answers, which may have been sung by leader and group. These characteristics would help a huge group learn a new song and join in immediately.

Easter Rock. A version of "Sit Down" features prominently in an all-night Easter ceremony from Louisiana. Beginning with a procession of 12 women—dressed in white, carrying kerosene lanterns, and preceded by a man carrying a banner—the ceremony continues with a ritual meal in front of the congregation, eaten by the 12 women with partners they choose to join them.

After the meal, the 12 women march around the table as the congregation sings spirituals, including a "Sit Down" variant sung as a dialogue between the banner-carrier and the 12 women. This ceremony continues through dawn, when a sunrise service begins. After the service, the 12 women march out singing, followed by the rest of the congregation in single or double file.

In this ceremony, we can glimpse some of the religious significance of the invitation to "sit down," and of the reply "I can't sit down." The person who can't sit down is simply too joyful and curious about heaven to keep from investigating its wonders. This song is an example of exuberant joy, with all the depth of feeling associated with Easter itself.

WAKE ME, SHAKE ME

Like "Sit Down" (above), "Wake Me, Shake Me" began as an African-American religious song and has found its way from the church into the classroom and summer camp.

As a spiritual, the words always refer to swinging on the Golden Gate (not the "garden gate" as in our version). The singer wishes to wake up on time on Judgment Day, fearing to miss the chance to get into heaven "before the heaven doors close."

Both white and African-American parodies of this song exist, describing the desire to wake up on an ordinary day (not the day of judgment). As in minstrel songs, these secular verses are often combined with a religious refrain about heaven.

The song gave rise to a "floating verse" that shows up in unrelated songs. One hobo song even turns it into a description of catching a freight train:

> Wake me, shake me, don't let me sleep too late.
> I want to catch the Golden Steps as she comes out that gate.

I'M GOING HOME ON THE MORNING TRAIN

Like "Train Is A-Coming" (below), this song uses train imagery to convey a religious message. The Morning Train becomes a metaphor for a variety of feelings about life.

When the first railroads appeared in the United States, some religious leaders denounced them as inventions of the devil. Within 50 years or so, however, the Gospel Train had become nearly as familiar—in both African-American and white religious music—as the Chariot or the Ark.

Some songs use the train as a metaphor for impending Judgment, warning us to repent before the train comes. Some even portray the train as a vehicle of punishment: sinners will have to ride the Hell-Bound Train. Still others, like the two train songs in this book, seem to view the train as the means of transportation to heaven. They imagine the joyful trip as the whistle blows and the other "saints" climb on board.

"I'm Going Home," in particular, focuses on the hopefulness of a journey to heaven, with a minimum of moralizing. The oldest printed version (1899) emphasizes the good news of taking the train to heaven:

> Gwine to get on the evening train, train . . . (etc.)
>
> U, how do you know, know . . . (etc.)
>
> My Lord told-a me so, so . . . (etc.)
>
> Let God's people get 'board, 'board . . . (etc.)

Other similar versions elaborate the happy details of the journey ("She's stopping at every station as she goes"). Some spell out the joys awaiting the riders when they get to heaven ("I know my crown is going to fit me well" or "Well, Jesus gonna meet me over there . . .").

This song expresses an attitude toward dying, too. It looks forward to death, as leading to release and freedom ("Well, you back back hearse and get your load . . ."). If there is any sadness associated with dying, it's just the farewells ("Oh, goodbye, brother, I'm going away"). Rather than postpone death, the singer yearns for it ("Feel like I want to take a ride . . ."), and even feels urgency to end this life ("Get ready, chillun, let's go home").

All in all, "I'm Going Home on the Morning Train" uses a simple metaphor to create a rich emotional texture. Even as you sing it with a game or other activity, you can be aware of its tender mix of present pain and hope for the future.

TRAIN IS A-COMING

The verses to "Train Is A-Coming"—like those of the previous song—use a simple one-line form to express a train metaphor.

The simplicity of this song's verses may stem from a camp-meeting origin (see "Sit Down," above). On the other hand, it may have been that simple songs like this one were the easiest to give new verses, and so were the first to evolve from older songs about other forms of transportation. Indeed, at least two spirituals collected in 1901 begin with several verses about walking or just "going" to heaven and conclude with verses similar to this song's verses about taking the train.

Whatever its origin, this piece is clearly a euphoric song about the prospect of going to heaven. Unlike "I'm Going Home on the Morning Train" (above), the various versions of this song don't seem to express any personal longing or weariness, just jubilation at the approach of Judgment Day:

> There's a great day a-coming . . . (etc.)
>
> I am sure God is ready . . . (etc.)
>
> I'm on my way to heaven . . . (etc.)
>
> Bound for glory . . . (etc.)
>
> Judgment's coming . . . (etc.)

Even as a game or movement song, you can sing this song with an awareness of its tone of excitement—excitement about a train that's coming to take us to a better life.

TIE-INS AND RESOURCES
Curricular Tie-ins

African Americans: History
African Americans: Religion
Cross-Cultural Transmissions
Death: Attitudes Toward
Easter
Hope
Industrial Revolution
Metaphor
Minstrel Shows
Movements: Cultural Attitudes Toward
Racism
Social Gatherings
Transportation: Trains
U.S. History: Civil War
U.S. History: War between the States
U.S.: Louisiana

Traditional Recordings

The tradition of singing spirituals still exists in the coastal islands off Georgia and South Carolina. Three excellent traditional recordings from those islands are:

Been in the Storm So Long. Folkways Records FS 3842. LP.

Johns Island, South Carolina: Its People and Songs. Folkways Records FS 3840. LP.

Moving Star Hall Singers. *Sea Island Folk Festival.* Folkways Records FS 3841. LP.

For solo, duet, and group singing (respectively) of spirituals, listen to:

Courlander, Harold, ed. *Negro Folk Music of Alabama: Rich Amerson, II.* Folkways Records FE 4472. LP.

Courlander, Harold, ed. *Negro Folk Music of Alabama—Spirituals.* Folkways Records FE 4473. LP. (This recording features the singing of Doc Reed and Vera Hall Ward, most often in duet. It includes Doc Reed's solo recording of "I'm Going Home on the Morning Train.")

Lomax, Alan, ed. *Negro Church Music.* Atlantic SD-1351. LP. (Includes a recording of "I'm Going Home on the Morning Train.")

This recording contains several forms of spiritual singing:

Courlander, Harold, ed. *Negro Folk Music of Alabama: Religious.* Folkways Records FE 4418. LP.

The only semitraditional recording of "Sit Down" is of a distant variant:

The Staples Singers. *Swing Low.* Exodus Records. EX-63. LP. (Also includes a variant of "I'm Going Home on the Morning Train.")

A traditional variant of "Wake Me, Shake Me," titled, "Trying to Get to Heaven in Due Time," can be heard by an outstanding singer-guitarist:

Davis, Rev. Gary. *Say No to the Devil.* Prestige Bluesville 1049. LP.

For nonspirituals related to "Wake Me, Shake Me," listen to:

Carson, Fiddlin' John. *Old Hen Cackled and the Rooster's Gonna Crow.* Rounder Records 1003. LP.

Darby and Tarlton. Bear Family Records BF 12 504. ("New York Hobo")

Of the several traditional recordings of "I'm Going Home on the Morning Train" (in addition to those mentioned above), I recommend these (the first is closest to our version):

Davis, Rev. Gary. *Sun is Going Down.* Folkways Records FS 3542. LP. ("Morning Train")

Green, Archie, ed. *Railroad Songs and Ballads.* Library of Congress AFS L61. LP.

McDowell, Mississippi Fred. *Get Right Church.* Everest Archive of Folk and Jazz. FS-253. LP. ("Get Right Church")

Resources

An illustrated collection of spirituals for children is:

Bryan, Ashley. *Walk Together Children.* New York: Atheneum, 1974.

Several spirituals are collected in the following book, along with other genres of African-American folksongs:

Glass, Paul. *Songs and Stories of Afro-Americans.* New York: Grosset & Dunlap, 1971.

An excellent volume accompanies the Sea Island recordings described above, including photographs and the actual words and stories of the singers:

Carawan, Guy, and Candie Carawan. *Ain't You Got a Right to the Tree of Life?* New York: Simon and Schuster, 1966. (Other editions also exist; check *Books in Print* for which edition is currently available.)

An arrangement of "Sit Down" for Orff instruments (high-quality instruments easily playable by children) appears in:

McRae, Shirley W. *Glow Ree Bee: Traditional Black Spirituals, Arranged for Unchanged Voices and Orff Instruments.* Memphis, TN: Memphis Musicraft Publications, 1982. ("Oh, Won't You Sit Down?")

For an "Orff arrangement" of "Train Is A-Coming," see:

Nichols, Elizabeth. *Orff Instrument Source Book: Volume 1.* Morristown, NJ: Silver Burdett Co., 1971.

The following books contain folksongs and/or other folklore about trains:

Botkin, B. A., and Alvin F. Harlow, eds. *A Treasury of Railroad Folklore.* New York: Bonanza Books, 1953.

Cohen, Norm. *Long Steel Rail: The Railroad in American Folksong.* Urbana, IL: University of Illinois Press, 1981.

JEWISH HOLIDAY SONGS

In the same way that Christmas songs range from the tender and sacred ("Silent Night") to nonreligious songs about holiday symbols ("Oh, Christmas Tree," "Santa Claus is Coming to Town"), to children's songs with no overt religious feeling ("Rudolph the Red-Nosed Reindeer"), Jewish holiday songs vary in seriousness and sacred content. The following two songs describe holiday symbols with no doctrinal content. They are likely to be heard in religious and cultural schools or in the observance of families of all Jewish denominations.

Both the songs given here are originally in Hebrew, the ancient sacred tongue of Jews that has become the daily language of the modern state of Israel.

ATSE ZETIM OMDIM—OLIVE TREES ARE STANDING

"Atse Zetim Omdim" is a children's song for *Tu B'Shvat,* sometimes known as "the Jewish Arbor Day." In ancient days, it was an early spring holiday with legal significance. More recently, Tu B'Shvat has become associated with spiritual awakening, with tree planting, with the greening of the state of Israel, and with ecological awareness.

The fifteenth day of the month of Shvat (which corresponds to January or February), Tu B'Shvat is one of the four ancient "New Year's Days" in the Jewish calendar, each marking the new year for a different kind of activity. The religious year began in the fall; the governmental

year (which year of a king's reign is it?) began in the spring; the year for counting the age of animals (for tax purposes) began at the end of the summer; and the year for counting the age of a fruit tree began at the end of winter (January or February in Israel). Trees were tithed on the basis of their age; a tree's growth was felt to begin for the year on the day the sap started flowing below the ground, traditionally on Tu B'Shvat. Thus, Tu B'Shvat is the "new year's day of trees."

Since Tu B'Shvat is the day when life awakens in trees, it is also considered a milestone on the way to the awakening of spring in the world and in our spirits.

Arbor Day, the U.S. holiday for planting trees, began in Nebraska in 1872. In the following years the Jewish settlers in Palestine, who planted trees as a matter of survival and of reclaiming the desert, taught their children to plant trees on Tu B'Shvat. Perhaps the newer holiday influenced the older! Jews who do not live in Israel often raise money on Tu B'Shvat for trees to be planted in Israel and plant trees of the types that grow in Israel in their own synagogues.

In recent years, many Jews have made Tu B'Shvat a day for ecological awareness. By focusing on the miracle of trees returning to life after their winter dormancy, Tu B'Shvat can make us more aware of the fragile interrelationship of all life in our environment.

The olive tree is a special symbol of renewal since it sends up new shoots to continue the life of the dying older tree. The olive trees in the song may be the famous ones outside of Jerusalem.

HASUKKAH

"HaSukkah" is a children's song for the Jewish harvest holiday of Sukkot.

Sukkot is celebrated for eight (in some places, nine) days, starting on the first full moon of autumn. Once the greatest of Jewish festivals, it remains the most joyous. After the sense of rebirth at Rosh HaShannah (New Year) and the reconciliation with God at Yom Kippur (the Day of Atonement), Jews enjoy a sense of fulfillment with the harvest festival: the close of one agricultural year and a clean start for the next.

The holiday of Sukkot is named for the booths (singular, *Sukkah)* or "tabernacles," which all observant Jews are required to build and take meals in during the festival. The booths are required to be large enough to eat and perhaps even sleep in. Their roofs, made of materials in their natural form (e.g., branches, not boards) must shade the sun, but not be so permanent that they block the rain. They must be specially constructed and decorated each year. In Eastern Europe, the walls of the Sukkah were often hung with white sheets and decorated with various fruits and flowers. Sometimes tablets are hung on the walls, naming seven Jewish patriarchs of past centuries who are invited to attend in spirit. Other decorations may include drawings, vegetables, and sewn or knitted objects.

An ancient feature of Sukkot is the waving of the lulav (palm branch); see Movement Activity #11—Waving the Lulav, page 75.

Sukkot began as a harvest festival, giving thanks for crops of one year and asking for what is needed for the next. In the course of the centuries, it also became a participatory historical experience that connects current generations with the exile in the desert of the ancient Israelites (described in the Biblical Book of Exodus). The dwelling in booths is seen as a reminder of the temporary structures of wanderers, of the uncertainty of all life, and of misfortune, even at the most prosperous times. Above all, it reminds us that, even living in temporary structures in exile, we must not give up but must keep hope alive and continue to seek the earthly and the spiritual Promised Land.

TIE-INS AND RESOURCES
Curricular Tie-ins

Arbor Day
Bible: Exodus
Deserts
Ecology
Farming: Importance of Water
Food: Harvest
Fruit Trees
Home and Exile
Homes: Construction
Hope
Seasons: Spring
Seasons: Fall
Seasons: Winter
Trees
U.S.: Nebraska

Traditional Recordings

I am not aware of any traditional recordings of these songs or of any similar songs. A nontraditional recording of "HaSukkah" exists, however:

Bluestein, Gene. *Songs of the Holidays.* Folkways FC 7554. LP.

Other Jewish holiday songs, including five more for Sukkot, can be heard on:

Fifty-one Holiday Songs for Limor. Amirefrath Records SA 32039. LP.

Resources

To find recordings or books about Jewish holidays or customs, try the yellow pages of any good-sized city, looking for a Jewish bookstore or gift store (look under Judaica or Books— Judaica). A mail-order source of Jewish children's books and tapes is Tree of Life Book Club (P.O. Box 303, Newton Highlands, MA 02161-0004).

For a child's explanation of the holidays of Sukkot and Tu B'Shvat, complete with some activities and stories, see:

Margolis, Dr. Isidor, and Rabbi Sidney L. Markowitz. *Jewish Holidays and Festivals.* Secaucus, NJ: Citadel, 1962.

A number of similar compilations exist. Food activities for the holidays are given in:

Burstein, Chaya M. *A First Jewish Holiday Cookbook.* New York: Bonim Books, 1979.

For contemporary adult interpretations of the holidays, along with a calendar showing when they fall through the year 2009, see:

Waskow, Arthur. *Seasons of Our Joy: A New-Age Guide to the Jewish Holidays.* New York: Bantam, 1982.

Sukkot involves the construction of special booths. For another celebration requiring special booths, see the section in this chapter on "Hill and Gully Rider" (page 190), which refers to a Jamaican celebration called "tea meetings."

Tu B'Shvat is only one of a number of tree-planting holidays worldwide. For more about Arbor Day, read pages 107–11 of:

Krythe, Maymie R. *All About American Holidays.* New York: Harper and Brothers, 1962.

A Chinese tree-planting festival is mentioned in:

Gaer, Joseph. *Holidays Around the World.* Boston: Little, Brown and Company, 1953.

For an introduction to the folklore of trees, see:

Krappe, Alexander H. *The Science of Folk-Lore.* New York: Barnes and Noble, 1974. Reprint of 1930 edition.

For tales about trees from a variety of cultures, refer to pages 720–21 of *The Storyteller's Sourcebook* (see page 169).

Science materials about trees are too numerous and widely diversified to list here, but they have an obvious connection with "Atse Zetim Omdim."

Other Sukkot and Tu B'Shvat songs (as well as songs for other Jewish holidays) can be found in these books:

Coopersmith, Harry. *The New Jewish Song Book.* New York: Behrman House, 1965.

Eisenstein, Judith, and Frieda Prensky. *Songs of Childhood.* N.p.: United Synagogue Commission on Jewish Education, 1955.

Pasternak, Velvel. *The New Children's Songbook.* Cedarhurst, NY: Tara Publications, 1981. (Tara Publications is also a first-rate mail-order source for Jewish music books and recordings).

A simple piano arrangement of "Atse Zetim Omdim" can be found in:

Steiner, Eric. *Hebrew Songs for the Young Pianist, Book Two.* New York: Mills Music, 1952.

DANCE SONGS

In world folklore, dance songs are numerous and varied. This collection features dance songs from two U.S. traditions, the string band song and the play-party song.

STRING BAND SONGS

String bands perform music for dance and entertainment. Typically from the white, rural south (many African-American string bands have also existed), they can include a variety of stringed instruments, such as fiddle, guitar, banjo, and mandolin. They sometimes add nonstringed instruments, including harmonica, percussion, and even the gallon jug. Vocals may be included throughout a performance, included sporadically, or not included at all.

In the earliest days of the recording industry in the United States, only classical music was recorded. Later, record companies found they could record music in various local communities and sell the records to members of those communities. In the 1920s, record companies issued separate catalogs for "old-timey" music, "race" (African-American) music, and various "ethnic" specialities, including Polish, German, Jewish, Croatian, and other musicians.

When the star system was invented, recording companies found it more profitable to market a very few star performers nationwide, and the specialty catalogs fell into decline. Along the way, however, commercial companies documented folk styles in many parts of the country, including the string band music that was later superseded by bluegrass and country-and-western.

BACK TO MEXICO

"Back to Mexico" is adapted from several western North Carolina versions of a widely known song that probably dates back to the turn of the century. All of these versions are sung by musicians who have been associated with Tom (Clarence) Ashley, who first recorded in the 1920s.

This song is an member of a loosely related song family that's known throughout the South. It has been sung by both whites and African Americans, and has been used both as an entertainment and a dance song. It's typically composed of "floating verses"—verses that appear with many different melodies and in combination with a variety of other verses.

"Back to Mexico" is related to other songs with refrains like "sugar babe," "honey babe," or "sweet thing," including the well-known "Crawdad Song." Many verses to these songs continue the theme of "what you gonna do when . . . ," introduced in our third verse:

> *What you gonna do when your licker gives out,*
> *Stand around the corner, mouth parched out.*
>
> *What you gonna do when your man goes away,*
> *Get me a better one the very next day.*

During World War I, this became appropriate during rationing ("What you gonna do when your shoes give out").

The only parallel I know to our second verse comes from a minstrel song, "Clar de Track":

> *Ring dem bells and Jim Crack Corn,*
> *I never see de like since I been born.*

IT'S A SHAME

"It's A Shame" has a convoluted history. It almost certainly began as a warning rhyme about things prohibited to Christians on Sunday, similar to this English children's rhyme:

> *Yeow mussent sing a' Sunday,*
> *Becaze it is a sin,*
> *But yeow may sing a' Monday*
> *Till Sunday cums agin.*

A similar song from Texas was used as a lullaby, and—like our song—lists the days of the week. Several black spiritual versions exist, too.

The complexity of interracial borrowing becomes apparent as we see a parody of a similar spiritual—learned in St. Louis from African Americans and sung by whites in a vaudeville show in New York, 1922:

> *Ain't it a shame to steal on Sunday,*
> *Ain't it a shame to steal on Sunday,*
> *Ain't it a shame to steal on Sunday,*
> *Ain't it a shame,*
> *Ain't it a shame to steal on Sunday,*
> *When you got Monday, Tuesday,*
> *Wednesday, Thursday, Friday, Saturday, too,*
> *Ain't it a shame.*

Our version was adapted from similar parodies, for children to sing about chores they don't like.

So, the song that began as a religious warning became a humorous protest song in two different ways—first for those feeling restricted by Sunday taboos, and later for children whose chores seemed restrictive on *any* day.

OLD JOE CLARK

"Old Joe Clark" is the best known of all string band songs. Scores of versions have been collected from all over the South and Southwest, containing over a hundred distinct verses and dozens of different refrains.

No one knows for sure who "Old Joe Clark" was. Some claim "an old Negro banjo picker" from Clay County, Kentucky; others say the song began in Grayson County, Virginia; still others say the song refers to a veteran of the War of 1812, who was given, instead of back pay, land in the Blue Ridge mountains.

Typically, "Old Joe Clark" was played on fiddles and banjos for square dances and big-circle partner dances, with verses and refrains sung sporadically to add interest during the dance. In communities where dancing to instrumental music was frowned upon, "Old Joe

Clark" became a play-party song (see below), as well.

TIE-INS AND RESOURCES

Curricular Tie-ins

Cross-Cultural Transmissions
Days of the Week
England
Minstrel Shows
Musical Instruments
Parodies
Religion. Sabbath Prohibitions
Social Gatherings
U.S.: Blue Ridge Mountains
U.S.: Kentucky
U.S.: North Carolina
U.S.: South
U.S.: Southwest Region
U.S.: Texas
U.S.: Virginia
U.S. History: Recording Industry
U.S. History: War of 1812
U.S. History: World War I
Vaudeville

Traditional Recordings

The traditional recording closest to our version of "Back to Mexico" is:

Old Time Music at Clarence Ashley's, Volume 1. Folkways Records FA 2355. LP. ("I'm Going Back to Jericho")

Dozens of other members of the "Crawdad Hole" song family have been recorded. Here is a small sampling:

Carson, Fiddlin' John. Old Hen Cackled and the Rooster's Gonna Crow. Rounder Records 1003. LP. ("Watcha Gonna Do When Your Licker Gives Out?")

Graham, Addie. Been a Long Time Traveling. June Appal Records JA 020. LP. ("The Dummy")

Old Time Music at Clarence Ashley's, Part Two. Folkways Records FA 2359. LP. ("Crawdad")

The Poplin Family. Folkways Records FA 2306. LP. ("Crawdad")

Songs to Grow On, Volume 2. Folkways Records FC 7020. LP ("Crawdad Hole," sung by Cisco Houston)

"It's A Shame" is adapted from this recording:

Carson, Fiddlin' John. Old Hen Cackled and the Rooster's Gonna Crow. Rounder Records 1003. LP. ("It's a Shame to Whip Your Wife On a Sunday")

Two related African-American songs are:

Ledbetter, Huddie. Leadbelly's Last Sessions. Volume One. Folkways Records FA 2941. LP. ("Ain't It A Shame to Go Fishin' On Sunday")

McTell, Blind Willie. Atlanta Twelve String. Atlantic Records SD-7224. LP. ("Ain't It Grand to Live a Christian")

"Old Joe Clark" has been so widely recorded that a survey of traditional and country music could be based on it. Two archaic versions, one African American, one white, are recorded on:

Ain't Gonna Rain No More: An Historical Survey of Pre-Blues and Blues in Piedmont North Carolina. Rounder Records 2016. LP.

Traditional Music from Grayson and Carroll Counties. Folkways Records FS 3811. LP.

Oklahoma songster Woody Guthrie sings a simple version with guitar on:

Guthrie, Woody. Library of Congress Recordings. Elektra Records EKL-271-272. LP.

Among the many old-timey recordings with singing are these:

Ernest V. Stoneman and the Blue Ridge Corn Shuckers. Rounder Records 1008. LP.

Music from South Turkey Creek. Rounder Records 0065. LP.

Finally, here's a bluegrass version, also including singing:

Bluegrass from the Blue Ridge. Folkways Records FS 3832. LP.

Resources

For recordings of string band music in general, see the traditional recordings listed in the previous section by Clarence Ashley, Fiddlin' John Carson, J. E. Mainer, and Ernest V. Stoneman, as well as the anthology Bluegrass from the Blue Ridge, which contains a history of the string band.

For a folk-revivalist recording of songs suitable for children from the old-timey tradition, listen to:

> The New Lost City Ramblers. *Old Timey Songs for Children.* Folkways Records FC 7064. 10" LP.

"It's A Shame" probably parodies a religious song. Other well-known folksongs are also parodies of religious songs, such as "The Old Gray Mare Ain't What She Used to Be," which is descended from the spiritual "Old Gray Horse":

> *Birmingham Quartet Anthology: Jefferson County, Alabama (1926–1953).* Clanka Lanka Records (a division of Mr. R&B Record Sales). 2 LPs. ("I am leaning on the Lord"; also includes some religious songs whose parodies seem to have become part of the songs!)
>
> Sandburg, Carl. *The American Songbag.* New York: Harcourt, Brace, Jovanovich, 1955 (reprint of 1927). Page 102.

Another example is "She'll Be Coming Round the Mountain," which is based on "When the Chariot Comes." On the other hand, secular tunes such as "Captain Kidd" have been borrowed for religious songs such as "Wondrous Love." For these last two borrowings, see:

> Agay, Denes. *Best Loved Songs of the American People.* Garden City, NY: Doubleday & Company, 1975. Page 61 ("Wondrous Love") and page 302 ("She'll Be Comin' Round the Mountain").
>
> Katz, Bernard. *The Social Implications of Early Negro Music in the United States.* New York: Arno Press, 1969. Page 117 ("When the Chariot Comes").
>
> Lomax, Alan. *The Folk Songs of North America in the English Language.* Garden City, NY: Doubleday and Company, 1960. Pages 15–16 ("Captain Kidd").

"It's A Shame" lists the days of the week. Some stories about the days of the week are referenced on page 604 of *The Storyteller's Sourcebook* (see above, page 169). For superstitions and sayings about the days, see:

> Whitney, Annie Weton, and Caroline Canfield Bullock. *Folk-Lore from Maryland.* New York: Kraus Reprint Co., 1969 (reprint of 1925).

"Old Joe Clark" paints a picture of an American folk character, however inconsistently. Other U.S. folk characters in song and story are presented in:

> Coffin, Tristram Potter, and Hennig Cohen, eds. *The Parade of Heroes.* Garden City, NY: Doubleday, 1978.

In 1942, "Old Joe Clark" served as the model for a topical song, "Round and Round Hitler's Grave," which is given in:

> Lomax, John A., and Alan Lomax. *Folk Song U.S.A.* New York: New American Library, 1975.

PLAY-PARTY SONGS

Straddling the border between dance songs and game songs, play-parties have a history that is closely associated with the westward expansion of the United States.

As the frontier of the United States spread from Kentucky west to present-day Ohio, Missouri, Texas, Oklahoma, Idaho, and other states, a similar set of conditions were created again and again. Communities were established where people must rely on their own resources for amusement, where travel was somewhat difficult within the community, where large gathering places and musical instruments were scarce, and where—in many places—dancing was prohibited for church members.

What were people in such communities to do for social amusement? In addition to work-related events such as husking-bees, apple cuttings and carpet-tackings, and nonwork gatherings such as literary parties and plays, they also held dance-like events that avoided the elements frowned upon by the church. These events were called play-parties, frolics, bounce-arounds, or swinging plays—the exact name depending on local custom.

In some ways, play-parties represent limit-testing on a large scale. Dancing is prohibited? The church says, "Yes." The teens say, "Okay, exactly what movements to music are allowed?" The church says, "Just those innocent children's games." The teens say, "Okay, we'll do those! We'll just spice them up a bit." In time, the "dancers" and the local church developed clear guidelines for what was allowed.

In most locales, the two major differences between a play-party and a dance were the name of the event and the absence of instrumental music. The fiddle, in particular, was known as the devil's own instrument, and so the players had to dance to the music of their own voices. In most places, it was also forbidden to have a caller instructing the players, and so the words to the songs needed to give the instructions. In other places, various movements were also prohibited, such as the "waist swing." In some other places, play-parties were entirely forbidden; in still others, they were accepted and became identical to square dances, except for the absence of instrumental music.

Even though there was usually no caller, one person was often recognized as the leader, organizing the figures and serving as an informal master of ceremonies. In some communities, the leader was chosen for social abilities, such as drawing out any strangers, teasing the players, or telling jokes to make people comfortable. In others, the only requirements were a loud singing voice and a facility with adapting the words:

> *The typical leader is . . . loud-mouthed and funny. Every one can hear him. . . . He goes to all the parties—one a week during the winter. . . . He remembers all the verses that they know, and if it's "Old Joe Clark is a married man," he substitutes someone's name—maybe someone that isn't married—to embarrass them. . . . He changes lines if he's clever enough to do it. (See page 185 for source.)*

WELDON

As a play-party song, Weldon has two kinds of verses: those that give instructions to the players, and those that just fill in while a long figure is in progress. A verse like "Once and a half in Weldon" tells the players to do a grand-right-and-left by turning each oncoming player one-and-a-half times around. Our last verse, "Fare thee well in Weldon," is actually a less-obvious cue to take a new partner. Partly because of the simplicity of making new verses for its one-line stanza, "Weldon" has been used for figures as complex as those in any square dance.

Traditional verses that fill in the time until the next figure include ones like these:

> *Twenty-five miles to London . . . (etc.)*
>
> *Treat 'em all alike in London . . . (etc.)*
>
> *Hooray, boys, in London . . . (etc.)*

Most versions of this song refer to "London," not Weldon—although some mention other places, such as "Ketchem" or "Sundown." There is a Weldon, North Carolina, that is mentioned in an African-American work song, but there's no way to know if that's the same town referred to in this Texas variant.

I WISH I WAS A COWPOKE

"I Wish I Was a Cowpoke" probably originated as a parody of an old hymn, which begins,

> *I want to be an angel,*
> *And with the angels stand,*
> *A crown upon my forehead,*
> *A harp within my hand.*

In 1894, a cowhand named D. J. O'Malley attended a meeting of the Stock Growers Association in Miles City, Montana. He was much amused by the slickly dressed young men seeking cowhand jobs. He published a poem, apparently to be sung to the tune of "I want to be an angel," in the *Stock Grower's Journal,* beginning,

I want to be a cowboy
And with the cowboys stand,
With leather chaps upon my legs
And a six-gun in my hand.
And, while the foreman sees me
I'll make some winter plays,
But I will catch a regular
When the herd's thrown out to graze.

(To "make a winter play" is to try to impress the boss with hard work so the cowhand won't be fired, as most were, when the summer ended. To "catch a regular" means to catch a nap.)

Play-party songs often borrowed the tunes and images of popular songs, changing them to add the necessary dance directions. In the case of this song, a familiar square-dance call was substituted for the second half of O'Malley's stanza.

This song was sometimes used for making new verses. In some of the games, there was no action during the first four lines, and many different occupations were substituted for "cowboy," such as soldier ("with a rifle on my shoulder, and a pistol in my hand") or fireman (ladder, firehose), rich man (money-bag, coin) or schoolboy (satchel, pencil).

A verse about a farmer led to a slightly different form of the song, focusing on farming. Since plains farmers in the late 1800s were called "grangers" (to distinguish them from stock-men or ranchmen), the song became know as "Granger" or "Granger Boy," beginning "I long to be a granger." The verses featured a series of improbable objects on the farmer's shoulder, such as haystacks and corncribs. The term "Granger," by the way, also applies to a member of the "Grange," an organized business cooperative, secret society, and political interest group of farmers, which has been especially interested in the education of farmers and their children.

HOLD MY MULE

Like "Weldon," this song has a simple verse that doesn't require rhyming—making it well-suited for singing dance directions and for improvised entertainment verses. It's no sur-

prise, then, that this song thrived in the play-party environment.

To make a new verse to "Hold My Mule," you just make up one line, repeat it twice more, and tack on the refrain line, which ends every verse. The refrains vary from place to place, often including names of persons or places:

. . . Hail! Oh, Susan Gal!
. . . Swing those ladies lively.
. . . To the O-hi-o.
. . . Down in Arkansas.

Some verses describing dance directions are straightforward, such as these:

Choose your partner and come dance Josie . . .
Get in the ring and let's dance Josie . .

Six in the middle and you'd better get about . . .

Others, however, are more fanciful, portraying the circle as a wheel, or the choosing of partners as marriage and home-making:

One wheel off the old brass wagon . . .
Big white house and nobody living in it . . .
We'll get married and we'll live in it . . .

While figures are being performed, of course, this simple verse-form gives ample opportunity to entertain the party by teasing the individual dancers:

Big foot guy and can't jump Josie . . .
Jump a little higher if you can't dance Josie . . .

Still other verses entertain by describing humorous images, excuses, or requests:

Chicken on the fence post, can't dance Josie . . .
Hole in the floor, and I can't jump Josie . . .
Chew my gum while I dance Josie . . .

This song was so versatile and popular that it was often combined with other songs. Sometimes a slow, pretty prelude would suddenly burst out in "Hold my mule . . ."

OLD JOE CLARK

"Old Joe Clark," often used as a play-party song, is discussed under String Band Songs, page 180.

TIE-INS AND RESOURCES
Curricular Tie-ins

Animals: Mules
Cooperation
Cowhands
Diversity in Social Gatherings
Families: Limit-Setting with Adolescents
Farmers
Hymns: Parodies
Leadership
Making New Verses
Metaphor
Movements: Cultural Attitudes Toward
Musical Instruments: Prohibitions
Music: Social Uses
Parodies
Religion: Prohibitions of Dancing
Romance and Courtship
Social Gatherings
Teasing
Transportation: Wagons
U.S.: Montana
U.S.: North Carolina
U.S.: South
U.S.: Southwest Region
U.S.: Texas
U.S.: West
U.S. History: Frontier
Weddings

Traditional Recordings

A few traditional recordings of play-party songs are included on each of these anthologies:

Rinzler, Kate, ed. *Old Mother Hippletoe: Rural and Urban Children's Songs.* New World Records NW 291. LP. (3 play-party songs)

Ritchie, Jean. *The Ritchie Family of Kentucky.* Folkways Records FA2316. LP. (3 play-party songs)

Williams, Ron, ed. *Skip to My Lou: Traditional Children's Songs and Dances from Southeast Tennessee.* Pine Breeze Records 004. LP. (Pine Breeze Center, Hamilton Avenue, Chattanooga TN 37405) (6 play-party songs)

Resources

Traditional singer Jean Ritchie has made studio recordings of several play-parties from her family tradition (along with other songs):

Ritchie, Jean. *Children's Songs and Games from the Southern Mountains.* Folkways Records FC 7054.

Ritchie, Jean. *Marching Across the Green Grass and Other American Children's Game Songs.* Folkways Records FC 7702. LP.

An entire album of play-parties recorded by revivalist singers is:

Seeger, Pete, Mike Seeger, and Rev. Larry Eisenberg. *American Playparties.* Folkways Records FC 7604. LP.

The following is a videotape of play-parties:

Stu Jamieson Teaches Play-Parties from the Southern Anglo-American Tradition. Washington, DC: Office of Museum Programs, Smithsonian Institution. Videotape. Rental only.

The classic reference on play-parties, which includes the quote about the typical leader (p. 183), is:

Botkin, B. A. *The American Play-Party Song.* New York: Frederick Ungar, 1963. Reprint of 1937.

Among the many collections for teachers and recreation leaders are:

Aaron, Tossi. *Punchinella 47: Twenty Traditional American Play Parties.* Philadelphia: Coda, 1978.

Chase, Richard. *Singing Games and Playparty Games.* New York: Dover, 1967. Reprint of 1949.

Rohrbough, Lynn. *Handy Play Party Book.* Delaware, OH: Cooperative Recreation Service, 1940.

"I Wish I Was A Cowpoke" is based on cowhand poetry. For more cowhand poems and related songs, see:

Lee, Katie. *Ten Thousand Goddam Cattle: A History of the American Cowboy in Song, Story and Verse.* Flagstaff, AZ: Northland Press, 1976.

Ohrlin, Glenn. *The Hell-Bound Train: A Cowboy Songbook.* Urbana, IL: University of Illinois Press, 1973. (Contains bibliography, discography, and an LP with six songs.)

For more about cowhand life, see the section on Cowhand Songs, page 165.

"Hold My Mule," of course, mentions mules. For other songs about mules, see:

Seeger, Ruth Crawford. *Animal Songs for Children.* New York: Doubleday. Pages 18, 62, and 64.

Yolen, Jane. *The Fireside Song Book of Birds and Beasts.* New York: Simon and Schuster, 1972. Pages 34, 36, and 38–40.

For a few tales about mules from various cultures, refer to page 671 of *The Storyteller's Sourcebook* (see page 169).

GAME SONGS

Unlike most work songs, religious songs, and dance songs, children's game songs are the oral tradition of children, not adults. Children learn them at certain ages from other children, pass them on to still others, and then stop playing them at certain ages—often only four or five years later!

Because the generations of children's oral tradition are so short, the details of a game song can change rapidly. At the same time, children's tradition often preserves traces of culture that have vanished from adult culture centuries ago, and that may have even travelled across continents!

Children's game songs may be based on adult songs of any kind. Frequently, they are based on humorous parodies of adult songs, even though the originals may be so long forgotten that no one but a folklorist can appreciate the humor.

Like work songs and dance songs, game songs accompany movements. Generations of children have adapted the words, rhythms, and melodies to suit the actions of the games. As a result, knowing the traditional form of a game can help you make adaptations that still fit the song.

AFRICAN-AMERICAN GAME SONGS

The game songs of children's oral tradition have been replaced in many parts of the world by electronic entertainment and by adult-supervised sports and recreation. Only where these new forms have been slow to penetrate—or where the adult culture consciously values the older entertainments—have large numbers of game songs survived long enough to be recorded by modern folklorists. As a result, most of our examples of game songs come from rural areas, ethnic minorities, or poor urban neighborhoods.

African-American culture has traditionally valued its oral tradition, and well into the twentieth century this culture has been largely restricted from access to newer forms of entertainment. These two factors have resulted in a rich body of children's folklore, documented first in print and later through sound and film recordings.

CHARLIE OVER THE OCEAN

This song has its roots in the political history of the British Isles. England and Scotland were first brought together in 1603, when James Stuart became James I of England. Although his son was forced into exile in France, in 1745 his great grandson, known as "Bonnie Prince Charlie," returned to Scotland in an attempt to regain the throne. Less than a year later, Prince Charlie's Highland supporters were overwhelmed by the government at the Battle of Culloden, and he fled for his life back to France. Although the Stuart cause was lost, its supporters kept their hopes alive with many songs and poems that asked, "Will he no come back again?" from his exile over the water.

As early as 1803, English nursery rhymes referred to these songs and poems, and also to Prince Charlie's reputed fondness for drink:

> *Over the water and over the lea,*
> *And over the water to Charley.*
> *Charley loves good ale and wine,*
> *And Charley loves good brandy . . .*

Similar parodies came to North America with British-Isles immigrants and apparently crossed into African-American tradition. Although children in the United States, Australia, and other English-speaking countries have changed "Charlie" to "Paddy," "Johnny," and even "Froggie," only African-American children have added the characteristically African form of call-and-response, as in the Alabama version given here.

The Alabama children played two games to this song. One game was a version of "Drop the Handkerchief" in which the entire ring skips around while the leader skips in the opposite direction behind the ring. In the other game, a blindfolded leader tries to catch squatting players.

KITTY KASKET

Like "Charlie over the Ocean," "Kitty Kasket" is a uniquely African-American form of a game known throughout the English-speaking world.

In ancient Greece, Pollux described a game in which a rope was dropped behind a squatted player. If the squatter noticed the rope, the squatter chased the dropper around the circle; if not, the squatter was beaten with the rope one time around the circle. A parallel game is described in a medieval Latin manuscript. Although the best-known English version is "Drop the Handkerchief," similar games are known throughout Europe and in India.

Some elaborate forms of the game in the British Isles involve kissing the person chased, and may even conclude with a marriage formula. This feature led some early folklorists to surmise that the game is a relic of an ancient custom called "marriage by capture."

The best-known words in U.S. popular culture are "A tisket, a tasket, a green and yellow basket. . . ," but many variations exist, such as "Wiskit-a-waskit, a green leather basket. . . ." In the various forms of the chasing game, a handkerchief or "letter" may be dropped, but also a rope, a stick, a cap, a doll, or nothing at all.

OLD MR. RABBIT

Unlike the previous two songs, "Old Mr. Rabbit" seems to have originated in African-American culture and spread later to Anglo-American folklore.

A related series of songs contain verses about "Old Mr. Rabbit's" physical peculiarities:

> *Old Mr. Rabbit*
> *Your legs are so long,*
> *Seems to me they're*
> *Put on wrong.*

Some songs combine verses like these with a refrain like our song.

As a game song, "Old Mr. Rabbit" was used with chasing games, partner-stealing games, and even with a play-party game of Missouri whites.

Dozens of songs contain verses about the rabbit with "a mighty bad habit" of eating garden vegetables. Some songs portray the rabbit as a villain, but others see "old cornfield rabbit" as a kind of renegade hero—similar to the trickster rabbit in so many African-American folktales.

TIE-INS AND RESOURCES

Curricular Tie-ins

African Americans: Folklore
Animals: Rabbits
Animals: Fantasies and Fictions
Cross-Cultural Transmissions
England: History
Entertainment: Electronic
Food: Sources and Production
Hope
Parodies
Scotland: History
Tricksters
U.S.: Alabama
Weddings

Traditional Recordings

The version of "Charlie over the Ocean" closest to ours is on:

Courlander, Harold, ed. *Ring Games: Line Games and Play Party Songs of Alabama.* Folkways Records FC 7004. LP.

Related songs are on:

Kaplan, Israel. *When I Was A Boy In Brooklyn.* Folkways Records FG 3501. LP. ("Sally o' the water")

Seeger, Pete, ed. *Skip Rope: Thirty-three Skip Rope Games.* Folkways Records FC 7649. LP. (Also published as Scholastic Records SC 7649). ("Sally over the Water")

No commercially available traditional recording exists of "Kitty Kasket," but other "Drop the Handkerchief" game songs can be heard on:

Edet, Edna Smith, ed. *Caribbean Songs and Games for Children.* Folkways Records FC 7856. LP. ("I Los' My Glove")

Kennedy, Peter, and Alan Lomax, eds. *English Folk Songs. (Columbia World Library of Folk and Primitive Music, Volume III).* Columbia AKL 4943. LP. ("I sent a letter to my love")

Other recordings of African-American children singing traditional game songs include:

Botkin, B. A., ed. *Play and Dance Songs and Tunes.* Library of Congress AFS L9. LP.

Courlander, Harold, ed. *Negro Folk Music of Alabama: Game Songs and Others.* Folkways

Records FE 4474. LP. (Side One of this LP is identical to the entire LP *Ring Games: Line Games and Play Party Songs of Alabama,* FC 7004, listed above.)

Edet, Edna Smith, ed. *Songs for Children from New York City.* Folkways Records FC 7858. LP.

Hawes, Bess Lomax, and Robert Everlein, directed by. *Pizza, Pizza, Daddy-O.* University of California Extension Media Center, Berkeley, CA 94720. Film, 18 minutes.

Lomax, Alan, ed. *Afro-American Blues and Game Songs.* Library of Congress AFS L4. LP.

Ramsey, Frederick, Jr., ed. *Music From the South, Volume 5: Song, Play and Dance.* Folkways Records FA 2654. LP.

Rinzler, Kate, ed. *Old Mother Hippletoe: Rural and Urban Children's Songs.* New World Records NW 291. LP.

Yurchenko, Henrietta, ed. *Johns Island, South Carolina: Its People and Songs.* Folkways Records FS 3840.

Resources

"Charlie over the Ocean" is a descendant of a Jacobite political song. For recordings of Jacobite songs, complete with brief written histories of the Jacobite rebellions, refer to:

Fisher, Archie, Barbara Dickson, and John MacKinnon. *The Fate o' Charlie: Songs of the Jacobite Rebellions.* Trailer Records LER 3002. LP.

MacColl, Ewan. *The Jacobite Rebellions: Songs of the Jacobite Wars of 1715 and 1745.* Topic Records 12T 79. LP.

A unique resource containing ballads about the battles in the rebellion as well as the details of specific battles is:

Brander, Michael. *Scottish and Border Battles and Ballads.* New York: Clarkson N. Potter, Inc., 1975.

On the recording that accompanies this book, "Charlie over the Ocean" is accompanied with piccolo and drum. The arrangement was inspired by a unique African-American fife-and-drum tradition. For more on that tradition, consult:

Gravel Springs Fife and Drum. Center for Southern Folklore (P.O. Box 226, 152 Beale St.,

Memphis, TN 38103; 901-525-3655). 16mm film or videotape. 10 minutes.

Mitchell, George. *Blow My Blues Away.* Baton Rouge, LA: Louisiana State University Press, 1971.

For other songs and story-songs about rabbits, look at:

Jones, Bessie, and Bess Lomax Hawes. *Step It Down: Games, Plays, Songs, and Stories from the Afro-American Heritage.* New York: Harper and Row, 1972. Pages 134, 205, 210.

Seeger, Ruth Crawford. *Animal Songs for Children.* New York: Doubleday. Pages 98, 99, and 100–01.

Yolen, Jane. *The Fireside Song Book of Birds and Beasts.* New York: Simon and Schuster, 1972. Pages 90–97.

African-American narrative tradition, of course, is famous for its tales about rabbits, first brought to mass attention by Joel Chandler Harris. Harris's versions of the folktales (less the more dated portions of his books) are gathered in:

Harris, Joel Chandler. *The Complete Tales of Uncle Remus.* Boston: Houghton-Mifflin, 1955.

Traditional rabbit tales in the Gullah dialect of the Southeast coastal regions have been recorded on:

Emrich, Duncan, ed. *Animal Tales Told in the Gullah Dialect (Three Volumes).* Library of Congress AFS L44, L45, L46. 3 LPs, available separately, with booklets.

Some of these same Gullah tales have been illustrated for children in:

Jacquith, Priscilla. *Bo Rabbit Smart for True: Folktales from the Gullah.* Philomel, 1981.

Other rabbit tales from a traditional teller can be heard on:

Courlander, Harold, ed. *Negro Folk Music of Alabama: Rich Amerson, I.* Folkways Records FE 4471.

For tales about rabbits from a variety of cultures, refer to pages 636–38 (Hare) of *The Storyteller's Sourcebook* (see page 169), and the following anthology:

Purchase, Barbara. *Rabbit Tales.* New York: Van Nostrand Reinhold Company, 1982.

OTHER GAME SONGS

The previous section dealt with game songs from African-American traditions. Of the thousands of other game songs known around the world, here's a small sampling of four, two of which are from English-speaking countries. The final song in this section, "Hill and Gully Rider," does not accompany a children's game at all, but it was sung with a game played traditionally by adults.

AL CITRON

"Al Citron" is a children's stone-passing game from the state of Michoacan, Mexico. Scattered among the nonsense words of its lyrics are a few words with meanings, including *fandango* (the name of a dance) and *citron* (lemon). The traditional game is given in the Rhythm Games chapter as the variation to game #62—Triki (page 48).

Other stone-passing games have been collected in parts of Africa and the West Indies. In Trinidad, stone-passing games are also played by adults at wakes; in Jamaica, adults traditionally play them at picnics and "tea meetings." (See "Hill and Gully Rider," below.)

WINDY WEATHER

This Irish children's game song, like the familiar "Ring Around the Rosie," is taught to young children and toddlers by older children or adults. In the traditional form of the game, all hold hands in a circle and go around faster and faster, usually ending up in a heap. Such games help welcome the youngest ones into the world of the older people.

This version was found in a housing estate (a redevelopment project for city families) in a suburb of Dublin. The older city street games have survived the move to less crowded conditions.

Similar words appear in jump-rope rhymes from Scotland to California, often including words like "All in together," which not only rhyme with "frosty weather," but also signal jumpers to take turns entering the game.

CHE CHE KU LE

This game song from Ghana has words that "translate" easily: they mean nothing in every language! At the same time, like all nonsense words, they follow the linguistic patterns of the language spoken by their creators. In other words, English nonsense words sound like English, and French nonsense words sound like French. When I sang this song to a man from Nigeria, he said, "Yes, that's the way they talk in Ghana."

Each source for "Che Che Ku Le" gives different movements or games. It seems likely, then, that the song is used with different activities, ranging from stationary movements to tag games.

In the discussions of African-American work songs, religious songs, and game songs, I referred to call-and-response as a typically African musical feature. Here's the proof! "Che Che Ku Le" is an African song that uses the most elemental form of call-and-response, in which the group simply repeats each line sung by the leader.

HILL AND GULLY RIDER

In the early 1920s, the enterprising folklorist Martha Beckwith observed Jamaican men and boys in the countryside playing a vigorous game. Starting with all the players holding hands in a curved line, the end player jumps over his own and the second player's linked hands. Followed by the second player, the end player jumps over the joined hands of the second and third players, continuing until all the players are "wound up in a coil." The song included this verse:

> If you tumble down you broke your neck. . .
> If you break your neck you go to hell . . .
> If you go to hell the devil glad. . . .

Games like "Hill and Gully" and stone-pounding games (see "Al Citron," above) were played on holidays, at wakes, at all-day picnics, or at all-night tea-meetings.

The tea-meetings, held in large booths constructed for the occasion, seem to have descended in part from English seasonal folk celebrations and in part from African customs. In addition to games, tea-meetings included the crowning of a "Queen," refreshments, dancing, recitations, and speeches.

Calypso. "Hill and Gully Rider" has also been adopted by calypso singers. Just as the folk games of the Jamaican countryside often represent a blend of British and African elements, calypso combines African, British, Spanish, and French influences. A town-based music, it has spread from an apparent start in Trinidad to much of the Caribbean. Already established by the mid-1800s, calypso songs—often associated with the singing competitions at carnival—can feature call-and-response singing, improvised and/or topical lyrics, and folk tunes that have new words fitted to them.

Since "Hill and Gully Rider" has a call-and-response pattern and easily-built verses, it was a natural folk tune for calypso treatment, and calypso singers have added many verses, making this one of the best-known songs in Jamaica.

TIE-INS AND RESOURCES
Curricular Tie-ins

Africa
African Americans: Folklore
Child Care: History and Lore
Cross-Cultural Transmissions
England
Fruit: Citrus
Ghana
Ireland
Jamaica
Language: Nonsense Syllables
Mexico
Music: Social Uses
New Verses
Social Gatherings

Trinidad
Urban Issues
West Indies
West Indies: Calypso Music

Traditional Recordings

Children from Mexico sing "Al Citron" and other songs on:

Yurchenko, Henrietta. *Latin American Children's Games Songs.* Folkways Records FC 7851. LP.

A different variant of "Windy Weather," along with many other Irish children's songs, can be heard on:

Hamilton, Diane, ed. *So Early in the Morning.* Tradition TLP 1034. LP.

Children from Ghana sing "Che Che Ku Le" on this recording:

U.S. Committee for UNICEF, ed. *Hi Neighbor: Songs and Dances of Brazil, Israel, Ghana, Japan, Turkey.* CMS Records CMS-UNICEF Rec. No. 2. LP.

Of the following two recordings of "Hill and Gully Rider," the first is an unaccompanied traditional recording from Jamaica, whereas the second is by "The Caribbean Chorus" of McGill University, Montreal, Canada:

Roberts, John Storm. *John Crow Say: Jamaican Music of Faith, Work and Play.* Folkways Records FE 4228. LP.

Songs from the British West Indies. Folkways Records FW 8809. LP.

"Hill and Gully Rider" has also been incorporated into some versions of the popular calypso song, "Day-O," such as:

Foodoos, Lord. *Calypso Carnival.* Elektra Legacy Leg 116. LP.

Resources

For stone-passing games from various cultures, consult these sources:

Annan, Ivan. *Ghana Children at Play.* Folkways Records FC 7853. LP. (one stone-passing game, plus a version of "Che Che Ku Le")

Beckwith, Martha Warren. *Jamaica Folk-Lore.* New York: Kraus Reprint Co., 1969. Reprint of 1928. Pages 21–25.

Caribbean Folk Songs & Games. Delaware, OH: Cooperative Recreation Service, Inc. Pages 9 and 13.

Courlander, Harold. *The Drum & the Hoe: Life and Lore of the Haitian People.* Berkeley: University of California Press, 1960. Pages 185–86.

Sharon, Lois & Bram. *Elephant Jam.* Toronto: McGraw-Hill Ryerson, Ltd. 1980.("Al Citron" plus two other stone-passing songs, pages 76–77)

For more Irish children's songs on record, listen to:

The Clancy Brothers & Tommy Makem. *In Person At Carnegie Hall.* Columbia Records CS 8750. LP.

The Clancy Brothers & Tommy Makem & their families. *At Home.* Everest/Tradition Records 2060.

The Clancy Brothers & Tommy Makem & their families. *Irish Folk Airs.* Everest/Tradition Records 2083. LP.

An excellent collection of games, songs, chants, pastimes, and photos from one Dublin neighborhood is:

Brady, Eilís. *All In! All In!* Dublin: Comhairle Bhealoideas Eireann, 1975. (Available from Padraic O' Táilliúir, 93 Muckross Ave., Dublin 12, Ireland)

The wind is an important character in some Irish lore. Two stories featuring the wind are in these books:

Arbuthnot, May Hill. *Time for Fairy Tales, Old and New.* New York: Scott, 1961. ("The Night of the Big Wind," page 360)

MacManus, Seumas. *The Bold Heroes of Hungry Hill.* New York: Pellegrini and Cudahy, 1951. ("The Giant of the Brown Beech Wood," pages 138–57)

For tales about the wind from a variety of cultures, refer to page 731 of *The Storyteller's Sourcebook.* (See page 169.)

For more about the music of Ghana (in addition to the Ivan Annan record mentioned above), refer to:

Africa: Ancient Ceremonies, Dance Music, and Songs of Ghana. Nonesuch Records H-72082. LP.

Warren, Fred, and Lee Warren. *The Music of Africa: An Introduction.* Englewood Cliffs, NJ: Prentice-Hall, 1970.

A bibliography of books for children about Africa devotes pages 29–32 to Ghana and pages 22–27 to West Africa in general:

Cooley, Marcia W., et al. *Africa: A List of Printed Materials for Children.* Information Center on Children's Cultures, United States Committee for UNICEF, 1968.

For more about the cultures and festivals of Ghana, see:

Opoku, A. A. *Festivals of Ghana.* Accra, Ghana (P.O. Box 4348): Ghana Publishing Company, 1970.

Sutherland, Efue. *Playtime in Africa.* New York: Atheneum, 1975.

A classic collection of folktales from what is now Ghana is:

Barker, W. H., and Cecilia Sinclair. *West African Folk-Tales.* Northbrook, IL: Metro Books, Inc., 1972. Reprint of 1917.

For firsthand information on Jamaican folk games and tea meetings (pages 5–7) as well as two other variants of "Hill and Gully Rider" (pages 38–40), see:

Beckwith, Martha Warren. *Jamaica Folk-Lore.* New York: Kraus Reprint Co., 1969. Reprint of 1928.

For scholarly versions of stories and information about Jamaican folklore, including folksongs, see these collections:

Beckwith, Martha Warren. *Jamaica Anansi Stories.* Millwood, NY: Kraus Reprint Co., 1976. Reprint of 1924.

Jekyll, Walter. *Jamaican Song and Story.* New York: Dover Publications, 1966. Reprint of 1907.

Roberts, John Storm. *Black Music of Two Worlds.* New York: William Morrow & Co., Inc., 1974. (Pages 119–32 give an overview of Jamaican music.)

The tea meetings at which "Hill and Gully Rider" was sung involved special booths. For a description of a Jewish celebration held in specially constructed booths, see the section in this chapter on "HaSukkah," page 177.

For children's songs and games from Jamaica, see:

Bennett, Louise. *Children's Jamaican Songs & Games.* Folkways Records FC 7250. LP.

Caribbean Folk Songs and Games. Delaware, OH: Cooperative Recreation Service, n.d.

Lewin, Olive. *Beeny Bud: 12 Jamaican Folk-Songs for Children.* London: Oxford University Press, 1975.

Lewin, Olive. *Brown Gal in de Ring: 12 Jamaican Folk-Songs.* London: Oxford University Press, 1974.

Lewin, Olive. *Dandy Shandy: 12 Jamaican Folk-Songs for Children.* London: Oxford University Press, 1975.

Background on the West Indies for children, with songs composed in West Indian style, is given in:

Perry, Sylvia, and Lillian D. Krugman. *Song Tales of the West Indies.* Far Rockaway, NY: Carl Van Roy Co., 1964.

Jamaican tales for children can be found in:

Carter, Dorothy Sharp. *Greedy Mariani and Other Folktales of the Antilles.* New York: Atheneum, 1974.

Sherlock, Philip. *Anansi, the Spider Man.* New York: Thomas Y. Crowell, 1954.

Sherlock, Philip. *West Indian Folk-Tales.* New York: Henry Z. Walck, Inc., 1966.

To learn more about calypso, consult the essays in any of these:

Attaway, William. *Calypso Song Book.* New York: McGraw-Hill Book Co., 1957. Pages 6–13.

Courlander, Harold. *A Treasury of Afro-American Folklore.* New York: Crown Publishers, Inc., 1976. Pages 100–12.

The Real Calypso. Folkways Records RBF-13. LP. (A reissue of popular calypso songs recorded

1927–46; see the liner notes for an essay on calypso.)

A calypso record for children by an authentic calypsonian is:

> Lord Invader. *West Indian Folksongs for Children.* Folkways Records FC 7744. LP.

For tales about horses from a variety of cultures, refer to pages 642–43 (horses) and page 689 (riding) of *The Storyteller's Sourcebook.* (See page 169.)

BALLADS AND OTHER FOLKSONGS

This category includes the folksongs that aren't included in or accompanied by any particular activity. They are narrative songs, patriotic songs, and entertainment songs. Each one represents an enormous category of world folk music.

BALLADS
DOWN CAME A LADY

"Down Came A Lady" became a children's song only recently. It's actually the first verse of a very old traditional ballad about adultery and murder.

The Ballad. Apparently well known as early as 1611, the ballad of Lord Daniel (known also as Lord Darnell, Arnold, Banner, Vanner, etc.) has been in continuous circulation for well over 300 years. Widely circulated in the British Isles, it crossed the Atlantic with immigrants to North America and spread to English-speaking communities throughout the United States and Canada.

The classic story of adultery and revenge—worthy of an opera—describes Lord Daniel's wife propositioning Little Mathy (also known as Matty Groves, Little Musgrave, Mosie, the Red Rover, etc.). When Mathy objects that she is married, she counters that Lord Daniel is far away hunting. Little Mathy agrees to a rendezvous, but both are unaware that Lord Daniel's page boy has overheard them. The page runs to his master and tells the news. Lord Daniel, approaching his own home, blows his hunting horn. Locked in Little Mathy's arms, Lord Daniel's wife hears the horn, but she dismisses it

as someone else's. Lord Daniel bursts in on them in bed together, and speaks to Mathy in a formulaic dialogue: "How do you like my bed, sir, how do you like my sheets; how do you like my gala wife who lies in your arms asleep?" After Mathy's bold answer ("Right well do I like your bed, sir"), Lord Daniel kills him in a duel, then kills his wife—and in some variants, kills himself as well.

Some versions of the ballad begin with a ball game in which Lord Daniel's wife outplays all the men and boys. Our version, however, starts with a variant of the more popular scene in which women are descending the church steps after services, often complete with a description of their attire. Here's the first verse from a version in which the lord's name is "Lord Barlibas":

> *Down came one drest in black*
> *And one came dressed in brown*
> *And down and came Lord Barlibas'*
> *lady,*
> *The fairest in all the town.*

Our version, whose tune is unrelated to any of the other 73 known traditional tunes, was collected by Miss Alfreda M. Peel in 1923 in Bland, Virginia.

Becoming a Children's Song. In the 1930s, American composer Ruth Crawford Seeger became interested in folk music and began listening to the scratchy aluminum discs of traditional singing stored in the Library of Congress. In 1941, when one of her children enrolled in a cooperative nursery school, she became the "music program" and began to search for American folksongs usable with children. The eventual result was the classic book *American Folk Songs for Children,* the first of its kind and still fresh today.

By treating the first verse of this ballad as a complete song and suggesting activities and ways to change the verse, she transformed a fragment of an adult ballad into a children's song.

Over the years, the song has been included in several anthologies of folksongs for children. In the process, the "oral tradition" of teachers and parents using the song with children seems to have transformed "Lord Daniel's wife" into "old Daniel's wife."

STEWBALL

For a ballad that has become a prison work song, see "Stewball" (Song #20; page 144).

OTHER FOLKSONGS
SO HE PLANTED GINGER

"So He Planted Ginger" is a Bulgarian version of a very old cumulative song. An ancient Jewish version (traditionally associated with the holiday of Passover) speaks of a goat, too, "a kid my father bought for two *zusim.*" A similar English-language nursery rhyme is the "Old Woman and Her Pig." In most of the variants, there is a problem getting an animal to behave: the pig, for example, won't go home. The old woman tries to get a dog to bite the pig. The dog refuses, so the old woman tries to get a stick to beat the dog. The chain of threats continues until someone agrees to do what she wants. Then, the cat chases the mouse, the mouse starts to gnaw the rope, the rope starts to hang the butcher, etc., until the dog starts to bite the pig, who goes home.

The traditional Bulgarian version ends with the water finally quenching the fire, which burns the rifle, which shoots at the wolf, who starts to eat the goat, who finally eats the ginger. This version is strikingly similar to the text of a French-Canadian lullaby, in which the water quenches the fire, which burns the stick, which

beats the dog, which starts to eat the little goat, who is finally glad to eat the cabbage.

I rewrote the Bulgarian song to change the chain of eating and hitting to a chain of reward, using plants and animals native to Europe.

ARIRANG

"Arirang" is a national song of Korea, associated with a legend, with patriotism, and with longing, parting, and sorrow. Many verses exist, some extolling the beauty of Korea, some lamenting betrayal by a faithless loved one.

The Legend. In Kyonggi Do province in Korea, there is a hill named Arirang. According to tradition, four centuries ago a tyrannical emperor hanged 10,000 of his opponents from the top of an enormous pine tree on Arirang hill.

One man, marching up Arirang hill to his death, sang a song of love for his country. He sang of its beauty and his sorrow at saying good-bye to it. The other prisoners began to sing his song with him.

The emperor could not stop people from singing on their way to death. Eventually, it became a tradition that anyone sentenced to execution had a right to first sing the song of Arirang.

The Popularity of the Song. Although contemporary Korea is divided into 14 provinces, traditionally there were eight provinces—each of which has its own hill named Arirang. The popularity of the original Arirang song was so great that other songs were created about the Arirang hill in each province. The Arirang-inspired song from Kangwon province is called "Kangwon Arirang"; each province except for Kyonggi has its own Arirang song with the province's name in the title.

In the middle of the twentieth century, when the Japanese invaded Korea, it became a crime to sing the official Korean anthem. "Arirang" was sung in its place by the resistance fighters. Forty years later, it was still sung in both North and South Korea, the unofficial anthem of Korean unity.

TIE-INS AND RESOURCES

Curricular Tie-ins

Animals: Dogs
Animals: Fantasies and Fictions
Animals: Goats
Animals: Pigs
Animals: Wolves
Bulgaria
Cross-Cultural Transmissions
Death: Attitudes Toward
Defiance
England
Farmers
Food: Harvest
Food: Sources and Production
French Canada (Quebec)
Korea
Leadership
Music: Social Uses
Quebec (French Canada)
Romance and Courtship
U.S.: Virginia
Women: Nontraditional Occupations

Traditional Recordings

"Down Came a Lady" is the first verse of a traditional ballad, "Little Musgrave" (Child ballad number 81). Some U.S. recordings of the full ballad are:

Hornell, Kip, ed. *Virginia Traditions: Ballads from British Tradition.* Ferrum College, Ferrum VA, BRI-002. LP. ("Little Massie Grove")

Joseph Able Trivett. Folk-Legacy Records FSA-2. LP. ("Mathy Grove")

Workman, Nimrod. *Mother Jones' Will.* Rounder Records 0076. LP. ("Lord Daniel")

A complete listing of both written and recorded sources is in:

Bronson, Bertrand Harris. *The Traditional Tunes of the Child Ballads. Four Volumes.* Princeton, NJ: Princeton University Press, 1962. (volume II, pages 267–315)

"So He Planted Ginger" is from Bulgaria. For authentic folk music of Bulgaria, listen to:

Bhattacharya, Deben, ed. *Songs and Dances from Bulgaria.* Argo Records ZRG 562. LP.

Lloyd, A. L., ed, *Folk Music of Bulgaria.* Topic Records 12 T 107. LP.

Raim, Ethel, and Martin Koenig, eds. *In the Shadow of the Mountain: Bulgarian Folk Music.* Nonesuch Explorer Series H-72038. LP.

Raim, Ethel, and Martin Koenig, eds. *Village Music of Bulgaria.* Nonesuch Explorer Series H-72034. LP.

For native Korean recordings of "Arirang," listen to:

Korea: Vocal and Instrumental Music. Folkways Records FE 4325. LP.

Sook, Han Pyung. *Songs of Korea.* Request Records RLP 8031. LP.

Other traditional performances from Korea, including the Arirang-inspired song from Miryang province, can be heard on:

Masu, Genjiro, ed. *Folk Music from Japan, the Ryukyus, Formosa and Korea (Columbia World Library of Folk and Primitive Music, Volume XI).* Columbia Records 91A 02019. LP.

Resources

The complete text of the ballad form of "Down Came A Lady" appears in:

Davis, Arthur Kyle, Jr., ed. *Traditional Ballads of Virginia.* Charlottesville: University Press of Virginia, 1957. Reprint of 1929. Pages 300–01.

For an inexpensive source of traditional Appalachian recordings of ballads, see this book-cassette combination (which contains two printed and one recorded version of "Little Musgrave"):

Burton, Thomas. *Some Ballad Folks.* Johnson City, TN: Center for Appalachian Studies (P.O. Box 70556, Eastern Tennessee State University, Johnson City, TN 37614). Book and cassette.

"So He Planted Ginger" is a cumulative song, related to a widely travelled cumulative story. A song-story version from Appalachia can be heard on:

Lipman, Doug. *Keep On Shaking.* A Gentle Wind 1013. Cassette.

Some cumulative songs are gathered in:

Langstaff, John. *Gather My Gold Together: Four Songs for the Four Seasons.* Garden City, New York: Doubleday, 1971.

Winn, Marie. *The Fireside Book of Fun and Game Songs.* New York: Simon and Schuster, 1974. Pages 10–29.

For more about cumulative stories, see:

Leach, Maria, ed. *Standard Dictionary of Folklore, Mythology and Legend.* New York: Funk and Wagnalls, 1972. Pages 268–89.

Clarkson, Atelia, and Gilbert B. Cross. *World Folktales.* New York: Charles Scribner's Sons, 1980. Pages 223–46.

Withers, Carl. *I Saw A Rocket Walk A Mile.* New York: Holt, Rinehart and Winston, 1965.

Several variants of the original story to "So He Planted Ginger" can be found through *The Storyteller's Sourcebook,* under motif Z41, pages 384–85 (See page 169.). For tales about goats from a variety of cultures, refer to the same source, pages 630–31.

Fresh ginger (as well as candied ginger) is available in Asian grocery stores and in many supermarkets. If you pass a slice around for children to smell, warn them that it's spicy hot if they taste it!

For piano arrangements of "Arirang" and "Kangwon Do Arirang," along with other Korean songs and a discography, consult

Dietz, Betty Warner. *Folk Songs of China, Japan, Korea.* New York: John Day, 1964.

For an inexpensive collection of Korean folksongs, stories, and games, see:

Chai, Hi Chang, et al. *Swing High: Korean Folk Recreation.* Delaware, Ohio: Cooperative Recreation Service, Inc., 1954.

For Korean folktales, see:

Carpenter, Frances. *Tales of a Korean Grandmother.* Rutland, Vermont: Charles E. Tuttle, 1973.

In-Sob, Zong. *Folk Tales from Korea.* New York: Grove Press, 1979. Reprint of 1952 edition.

So-un, Kim. *The Story Bag: A Collection of Korean Folktales.* Rutland, VT: Charles E. Tuttle, 1955.

SOURCES

This section documents the principal sources of the songs and information in this book. For each song, you'll see three types of information (where applicable):

First: where I first learned the song, whether in the version in this book or not.

Closest: the version or versions closest to the one in this book, if different from the "first."

Other: other sources used (including my changes)

For still other versions, recordings, and sources of the songs and background information, see the chapter on Background, Curricular Tie-Ins, and Follow-Up Resources.

The ideas for several of the activities were found in these game and song collections:

Botkin, B. A. *The American Play-Party Song.* New York: Frederick Ungar, 1963 (reprint of 1937).

Brewster, Paul G. *American Nonsinging Games.* Norman: University of Oklahoma Press, 1953.

Opie, Iona, and Peter Opie. *Children's Games in Street and Playground.* Oxford: Clarendon Press, 1969.

Saletan, Tony. *Singing Down the Road.* Los Angeles (1438 North Gower St.): Western Instructional Television, Inc., 1977.

Many of the games described in the present book are based on ideas in these collections of cooperative and other games:

Canfield, Jack, and Harold C. Wells. *One Hundred Ways to Enhance Self-Concept in the Classroom.* Englewood Cliffs, NJ: Prentice-Hall, 1976.

Fluegelman, Andrew. *More New Games!* Garden City, NY: Doubleday & Company, 1981.

Fluegelman, Andrew. *The New Games Book.* Garden City, NY: Doubleday & Company, 1976.

Harrison, Marta, comp. *For the Fun of It! Selected Cooperative Games for Children and Adults.* Philadelphia: Friends Peace Committee, 1975.

Judson, Stephanie, ed. *A Manual on Nonviolence and Children.* Philadelphia: Friends Peace Committee, 1977.

Orlick, Terry. *The Cooperative Sports and Games Book.* New York: Pantheon, 1978.

Orlick, Terry. *The Second Cooperative Sports and Games Book.* New York: Pantheon, 1982.

Schneider, Tom. *Everybody's a Winner: A Kid's Guide to New Sports and Fitness.* Boston: Little, Brown, 1976.

SONG #1—SIT DOWN
First:

Boni, Margaret Bradford. *The Fireside Book of Folk Songs.* New York: Simon and Schuster, 1947.

Other: New words by Doug Lipman.

Landeck, Beatrice. *More Songs to Grow On.* New York: William Sloane Associates, Inc., 1954. Page 26.

Tobitt, Janet E. *The Ditty Bag.* Pleasantville, NY (Box 97), 1946. Page 71.

Winn, Marie. *The Fireside Book of Fun and Game Songs.* New York: Simon and Schuster, 1974. Pages 84–85.

The information on "Easter Rock" came from:

Seale, Lea, and Marianna Seale. "Easter Rock: A Louisiana Negro Ceremony." *Journal of American Folklore* 55 (1942): 212–18.

SONG #2—DOWN CAME A LADY

First:

Seeger, Ruth Crawford. *American Folk Songs for Children.* New York: Doubleday, 1948.

Other:

Davis, Arthur Kyle, Jr., ed. *Traditional Ballads of Virginia.* Charlottesville: University Press of Virginia, 1957. Reprint of 1929. Pages 300–01.

Erdei, Peter, and Katalin Komlos. *150 American Folk Songs to Sing Read and Play.* New York: Boosey and Hawkes, 1974. Page 17.

SONG #3—AL CITRON

First:

Yurchenko, Henrietta, ed. *Latin American Children's Games Songs.* Folkways Records FC 7851. LP.

Other:

Sharon, Lois & Bram. *Elephant Jam.* Toronto: McGraw-Hill Ryerson, Ltd, 1980.

SONG #4—BACK TO MEXICO

First:

Cohen, John, and Mike Seeger, eds. *The New Lost City Ramblers Song Book.* New York: Oak Publications, 1964. Pages 186–87. (Also published as *The String Band Song Book.)*

Other:

Old Time Music at Clarence Ashley's, Volume 1. Folkways Records FA 2355. LP.

The minstrel song verse is from:

White, Newman I. *American Negro Folk-Songs.* Hatboro, PA: Folklore Associates, Inc., 1965 (reprint of 1928). Page 82.

SONG #5—IT'S A SHAME

First:

Leadbelly's Last Sessions, Volume One. Folkways Records FA 2941. LP. ("Ain't It a Shame")

Closest:

Carson, Fiddlin' John. *Old Hen Cackled and the Rooster's Gonna Crow.* Rounder Records 1003. LP.

Other: The English children's rhyme is from:

Parry-Jones, D. *Welsh Children's Games and Pastimes.* Denbigh, Wales: Gee and Son, 1964. Pages 198–99.

Information on the vaudeville version comes from:

Parsons, Elsie Clews. "From Spiritual to Vaudeville." *Journal of American Folklore* 35 (1922): 331.

Puckett, Newbell Niles. *Folk Beliefs of the Southern Negro.* New York: Dover Publications, 1969. Reprint of 1926. Page 71.

SONG #6—WAKE ME, SHAKE ME

First:

Aronoff, Frances Webber. *Music and Young Children.* Holt, Rinehart and Winston, Inc., 1969. Pages 104–05.

Closest:

Work, John W. *American Negro Songs and Spirituals.* New York: Bonanza Books, 1940.

Other:

Davis, Rev. Gary. *Say No to the Devil.* Prestige Bluesville 1049. LP. ("Trying to Get to Heaven in Due Time")

SONG #7—WELDON

First:

Owens, William A. *Swing and Turn: Texas Play-Party Games.* Dallas: Tardy Publishing, 1936. Pages 84–85.

Other: New words by Doug Lipman.

Botkin, B. A. *The American Play-Party Song.* New York: Frederick Ungar, 1963 (reprint of 1937). Page 245.

For the African-American work song mentioning a Weldon, see:

Bass, Robert Duncan. "Negro Songs from the Peedee Country." *Journal of American Folklore* 44 (1931): 420.

SONG #8—I WISH I WAS A COWPOKE

First:

Owens, William A. *Swing and Turn: Texas Play-Party Games.* Dallas: Tardy Publishing, 1936. Page 109.

Other: New words by Doug Lipman.

Botkin, B. A. *The American Play-Party Song.* New York: Frederick Ungar, 1963 (reprint of 1937). Pages 198ff.

Greenway, John. *Folklore of the Great West.* Palo Alto, CA: American West Publishing Company, 1969. Page 195.

Lingenfelter, Richard E., and Richard A. Dwyer. *Songs of the American West.* Berkeley: University of California Press, 1968. Page 331.

SONG #9—SO HE PLANTED GINGER

First:

Kaufman, William I. *UNICEF Book of Children's Songs.* Harrisburg, PA: Stackpole Books, 1970. Pages 54–55.

Other: New words by Doug Lipman.

Barbeau, C. Marius. "Contes Populaires Canadiens." *Journal of American Folklore* 30 (1917): 139–40.

Briggs, Katharine M. *A Dictionary of British Folk-Tales.* Bloomington: Indiana University Press, 1970. Volume one, page 68, and other pages cited there.

For the Passover song, see:

Goodman, Philip. *The Passover Anthology.* Philadelphia: Jewish Publication Society of America, 1961. Page 283.

SONG #10—CHARLIE OVER THE OCEAN

First:

Erdei, Peter, and Katalin Komlos. *150 American Folk Songs to Sing Read and Play.* New York: Boosey and Hawkes, 1974. Page 14.

Closest:

Courlander, Harold. *Ring Games: Line Games and Play Party Songs of Alabama.* Folkways Records FC 7004. LP.

Other: New words by Doug Lipman.

Kennedy, Maureen. *Circle Round the Zero: Play Chants and Singing Games of City Children.* St. Louis: Magnamusic-Baton, 1974. Page 36.

Opie, Iona, and Peter Opie. *The Oxford Dictionary of Nursery Rhymes.* Oxford: Oxford University Press, 1973. Pages 115–16.

Worstell, Emma Vietor. *Jump the Rope Jingles.* New York: Macmillan, 1972 (reprint of 1961). Page 41.

SONG #11—KITTY KASKET

First:

Erdei, Peter and Katalin Komlos. *150 American Folk Songs to Sing Read and Play.* New York: Boosey and Hawkes, 1974. Page 17.

Closest:

Lomax, John A., and Alan Lomax. *Our Singing Country.* New York: Macmillan Company, 1941. Page 77.

Other:

Brewster, Paul G. *American Nonsinging Games.* Norman: University of Oklahoma Press, 1953. Pages 91–92.

Opie, Iona, and Peter Opie. *Children's Games in Street and Playground.* Oxford: Clarendon Press, 1969. Pages 202–03.

Richards, Mary Helen. *The Music Language: Part One.* Portola Valley, CA: Richards Institute of Music Education and Research, 1973. Page 195.

SONG #12—I'M GOING HOME ON THE MORNING TRAIN

First:

Green, Archie, ed. *Railroad Songs and Ballads.* Library of Congress AFS L61. LP.

Other: See the recordings listed in the Background chapter. New words by Doug Lipman.

Cohen, Norm. *Long Steel Rail: The Railroad in American Folksong.* Urbana, IL: University of Illinois Press, 1981. Pages 596, 625, 629, 638–39.

Katz, Bernard. *The Social Implications of Early Negro Music in the United States.* New York: Arno Press, 1969. Page 106–07.

Perrow, E. C. "Songs and Rhymes from the South." *Journal of American Folklore* 26 (1913): 162.

SONG #13—WINDY WEATHER

First:

Hamilton, Diane. *So Early in the Morning.* Tradition TLP 1034. LP.

Closest:

Brady, Eilís. *All In! All In!* Dublin: Comhairle Bhealoideas Eireann, 1975. (Available from Padraic O' Táilliúir, 93 Muckross Ave., Dublin 12, Ireland)

Other: Elizabeth Goldfinger helped with some of the games.

Evans, Patricia. *Rimbles: A Book of Children's Classic Games, Rhymes, Songs and Sayings.* Garden City, NY: Doubleday, 1961. Page 17.

Richards, Mary Helen. *The Music Language: Part One.* Portola Valley, CA: Richards Institute of Music Education and Research, 1973. Page 37.

Ritchie, James T. R. *Golden City.* Edinburgh: Oliver and Boyd, 1965. Page 113.

SONG #14—ROUND THE CORNER

First:

Colcord, Joanna C. *Songs of American Sailormen.* New York: Oak Publications, 1964. Page 41.

Other:

Hugill, Stan. *Shanties from the Seven Seas.* London: Routledge and Kegan Paul, 1961. Page 390.

Terry, Sir Richard Runciman. *The Shanty Book: Part Two.* New York: G. Shirmer, 1926. Page 43.

The information about corn shucking comes from:

Epstein, Dena J. *Sinful Tunes and Spirituals: Black Folk Music to the Civil War.* Urbana, IL: University of Illinois Press, 1977. Pages 161–83.

Jackson, Bruce. *The Negro and His Folklore in Nineteenth-Century Periodicals.* Austin: University of Texas Press, 1967. Pages 110, 168–76.

For "Whiskey Johnny" as a corn song, see:

Whitney, Annie Weton, and Caroline Canfield Bullock. *Folk-Lore from Maryland.* New York: Kraus Reprint Co., 1969 (reprint of 1925). Pages 164–65.

SONG #15—CHE CHE KU LE

First:

Dale, Ralph Alan. *Games to Sing and Play.* New York: Scholastic Book Services, 1971. Page 20.

Closest:

U.S. Committee for UNICEF. *Hi Neighbor Book 2.* New York: United Nations.

Other:

Sharon, Lois and Bram. *Smorgasbord.* Elephant Records LFN 7902. LP. (song #9)

SONG #16—ARIRANG

First:

Kaufman, William I. *UNICEF Book of Children's Songs.* Harrisburg, PA: Stackpole Books, 1970.

Other:

Dietz, Betty Warner. *Folk Songs of China, Japan, Korea.* New York: John Day, 1964.

Haufrecht, Herbert, ed. *'Round the World Folk Sing.* New York: Hollis Music, Inc., 1963. Page 192.

Seeger, Pete. *Folkpeople.* Time Wind F-50006. LP. (Also issued as *Pete Seeger.* Archive of Folk Music FS 201.)

SONG #17—GOOD-BYE, OLD PAINT

First:

Lomax, John A., and Alan Lomax. *Folk Song U.S.A.* New York: New American Library, 1975. Page 273.

Closest:

Sackett, S. J. *Cowboys and the Songs They Sang.* New York: William R. Scott, 1967. Page 67.

Other: See the traditional recordings in the Background chapter.

> Lomax, Alan. *The Folk Songs of North American in the English Language.* Garden City, NY: Doubleday and Company, 1960. Page 378.

SONG #18—OLD JOE CLARK

First: Adapted from many sources over the years!

Other:

> Botkin, B. A. *The American Play-Party Song.* New York: Frederick Ungar, 1963 (reprint of 1937). Page 281.

> Dudley, R. E. and L. W. Payne, Jr., "Some Texas Play-Party Songs." in Stith Thompson, *Round the Levee: Publications of the Texas Folk Lore Society, Number 1.* Dallas: Southern Methodist University Press, 1975 (reprint of 1916). Page 32.

> Lomax, John A., and Alan Lomax. *American Ballads and Folksongs.* New York: Macmillan, 1934. Page 279.

> Randolph, Vance. *Ozark Folksongs, Volume III.* Columbia, MO: State Historical Society of Missouri, 1949. Pages 324ff.

> White, Newman Ivey. *The Frank C. Brown Collection of North Carolina Folklore, Volume V.* Durham, NC: Duke University Press, 1962. Page 64.

The long quotation in the Background chapter about "the typical leader" is from:

> Botkin, B. A. *The American Play-Party Song.* New York: Frederick Ungar, 1963 (reprint of 1937). Page 371.

SONG #19—HOLD MY MULE

First:

> Owens, William A. *Swing and Turn: Texas Play-Party Games.* Dallas: Tardy Publishing, 1936. Page 81.

Closest:

> Erdei, Peter, and Katalin Komlos. *150 American Folk Songs to Sing Read and Play.* New York: Boosey and Hawkes, 1974. Page 52.

Other: New words and melody adapted by Doug Lipman.

> Botkin, B. A. *The American Play-Party Song.* New York: Frederick Ungar, 1963 (reprint of 1937). Pages 80, 169.

> Landeck, Beatrice. *More Songs to Grow On.* New York: William Sloane Associates, Inc., 1954. Page 97.

> McDonough, Nancy. *Garden Sass: A Catalog of Arkansas Folkways.* New York: Coward, McCann and Geoghegan, 1975. Page 178.

> Randolph, Vance. *Ozark Folksongs, Volume III.* Columbia, MO: State Historical Society of Missouri, 1949. Pages 312, 313.

> Scarborough, Dorothy. *On the Trail of Negro Folk-Songs.* Cambridge: Harvard University Press, 1925. Pages 105–06.

SONG #20—STEWBALL

First:

> Lomax, Alan. *The Penguin Book of American Folk Songs.* Baltimore, MD: Penguin Books, 1964. Page 91.

Closest:

> *Leadbelly Sings Folk Songs.* Folkways Records FA 2488. LP.

Other: See the traditional recordings in the Background chapter, as well as the books on Leadbelly (Huddie Ledbetter).

> Jackson, Bruce. *Wake Up, Dead Man: Afro-American Worksongs from Texas Prisons.* Cambridge, MA: Harvard University Press. 1972. Pages 19, 22, 31–33, 102–10.

> Lomax, John A., and Alan Lomax. *American Ballads and Folksongs.* New York: Macmillan, 1934. Page 68.

> Scarborough, Dorothy. *On the Trail of Negro Folk-Songs.* Cambridge: Harvard University Press, 1925. Page 62.

> Seeger, Ruth Crawford. *Animal Songs for Children.* New York: Doubleday. Page 69.

SONG #21—ATSE ZETIM OMDIM

First:

> Steiner, Eric. *Hebrew Songs for the Young Pianist, Book Two.* New York: Mills Music, 1952. Pages 18–19.

Other: Melody adapted (in part, inadvertently!) by Doug Lipman.

Eisenstein, Judith, and Frieda Prensky. *Songs of Childhood.* N.p.: United Synagogue Commission on Jewish Education, 1955. Pages 237–39.

Pasternak, Velvel. *The New Children's Songbook.* Cedarhurst, NY: Tara Publications, 1981. Pages 45–46.

For the information about Tu B'Shvat, see the references in the Background chapter, as well as:

Chill, Abraham. *The Minhagim: The Customs and Ceremonies of Judaism, Their Origins and Rationale.* Second, corrected edition. New York: Sepher-Hermon Press, 1979. Pages 255–56.

Gaster, Theodor H. *Festivals of the Jewish Year: A Modern Interpretation and Guide.* New York: William Morrow, 1952. Pages 255ff.

Trepp, Leo. *The Complete Book of Jewish Observance.* New York: Behrman House, 1980. Pages 137, 154.

SONG #22—JULEY

First:

Colcord, Joanna C. *Songs of American Sailormen.* New York: Oak Publications, 1964. Page 55.

Other:

Hugill, Stan. *Shanties and Sailor's Songs.* London: Herbert Jenkins, 1969. Pages 49–51, 85.

Hugill, Stan. *Shanties from the Seven Seas.* London: Routledge and Kegan Paul, 1961. Page 390.

SONG #23—HILL AND GULLY RIDER

First: Taught to me by Lillian Yaross, a nationally known Orff-Schulwerk teacher from Illinois.

Closest:

Murray, Tom. *Folk Songs of Jamaica.* London: Oxford University Press, 1951. Page 9.

Other:

See the traditional recordings in the Background chapter.

Beckwith, Martha Warren. *Jamaica Folk-Lore.* New York: Kraus Reprint Co., 1969. Reprint of 1928. Pages 21–25.

Hylton-Tomlinson, Ouida. *Mango Walk: Jamaican Folk Songs and Singing Games.* Kingston, Jamaica: Jamaica Publishing House, n.d. Page 10.

Morse, Jim. *Folk Songs of the Caribbean.* New York: Bantam Books, 1958. Page 99.

Nichols, Elizabeth. *Orff Instrument Source Book: Volume II.* Morristown, NJ: Silver Burdett Co., 1971. Page 65.

Paterson, Massie, and Sammy Heyward. *Calypso Folk Sing.* New York: Ludlow Music, 1963. Page 13.

SONG #24—DANCE A BABY DIDDY

First:

Crane, Walter. *The Baby's Opera.* New York: Simon and Schuster, 1981. Page 54.

Other:

Northall, G. F. *English Folk Rhymes.* Detroit: Singing Tree Press, 1968 (reprint of 1892). Page 424.

Opie, Iona, and Peter Opie. *The Oxford Dictionary of Nursery Rhymes.* Oxford: Oxford University Press, 1973. Page 60.

Opie, Iona, and Peter Opie. *The Oxford Nursery Rhyme Book.* London: Oxford University Press, 1975. Page 10.

Weir, Albert E. *Songs the Children Love to Sing.* New York: D. Appleton and Company, 1916. Pages 234–35.

SONG #25—OLD MR. RABBIT

First:

Seeger, Ruth Crawford. *American Folk Songs for Children.* New York: Doubleday, 1948. Page 98.

Closest:

Scarborough, Dorothy. *On the Trail of Negro Folk-Songs.* Cambridge: Harvard University Press, 1925. Page 174–75.

Other: New words by Doug Lipman.

Ames, L. D. "The Missouri Play-Party." *Journal of American Folklore* 24 (1911): 317–18.

Bradford, Louise Larkins. *Sing It Yourself: 220 Pentatonic American Folk Songs.* Sherman

Oaks CA: Alfred Publishing Co., Inc., 1978. Song #76.

Erdei, Peter, and Katalin Komlos. *150 American Folk Songs to Sing Read and Play.* New York: Boosey and Hawkes, 1974. Page 11.

Odum, Howard W. "Negro Folk-Song and Folk-Poetry." *Journal of American Folklore* 24 (1911): 356.

The counting rhyme on page 18 is adapted from:

Perrow, E. C. "Songs and Rhymes from the South." *Journal of American Folklore* 26 (1913): 132.

SONG #26—HASUKKAH
First:

Eisenstein, Judith, and Frieda Prensky. *Songs of Childhood.* N.p.: United Synagogue Commission on Jewish Education, 1955. Page 208.

Other:

Coopersmith, Harry. *Hebrew Songster for Kindergarten and Primary Grades.* New York: Jewish Education Committee of New York, 1948. Page 32.

The information about Sukkot was drawn from the resources listed in the chapter on Background and the books listed in this chapter under "Atse Zetim Omdim," as well as from:

Birnbaum, Philip. *Encyclopedia of Jewish Concepts.* New York: Sanhedrin Press, 1964.

Schauss, Hayyim. *The Jewish Festivals: History and Observance.* New York: Schocken, 1938.

Zevin, Rabbi S. Y. *The Festivals in Halachah, Volume One.* New York: Mesorah Publications, Ltd., 1981.

SONG #27—TRAIN IS A-COMING
First:

Seeger, Ruth Crawford. *American Folk Songs for Children.* New York: Doubleday, 1948. Page 150.

Closest:

Scarborough, Dorothy. *On the Trail of Negro Folk-Songs.* Cambridge: Harvard University Press, 1925. Page 253–54.

Other:

Erdei, Peter, and Katalin Komlos. *150 American Folk Songs to Sing Read and Play.* New York: Boosey and Hawkes, 1974. Page 62.

Grissom, Mary Allen. *The Negro Sings a New Heaven.* New York: Dover Publications, 1969. Reprint of 1930. Pages 48–49.

Hallowell, Emily. *Calhoun Plantation Songs.* Boston: C. W. Thompson & Co., 1907. Page 46.

Odum, Howard W. *The Negro and His Songs.* Westport, CT: Negro Universities Press, 1976. Reprint of 1925. Page 113.

SONG #28—POOR LONESOME COWHAND
First:

Sackett, S. J. *Cowboys and the Songs They Sang.* New York: William R. Scott, 1967. Page 46.

Other: New words and words adapted by Doug Lipman.

Fife, Austin E., and Alta S. Fife. *Cowboy and Western Songs: A Comprehensive Anthology.* New York: Clarkson N. Potter, Inc., 1969. Page 230.

Finger, Charles. *Sailor Chanties and Cowboy Songs.* N.p.: Norwood Editions, 1976. Reprint of 1923. Pages 37–39.

Sandburg, Carl. *The American Songbag.* New York: Harcourt, Brace, Jovanovich, 1955 (reprint of 1927). Page 273.

Tinsley, Jim Bob. *He Was Singin' This Song.* Orlando: University of Central Florida, 1981. Page 217.

SONG #29—SLEEP, BONNIE BAIRNIE
First:

Cass-Beggs, Barbara, and Michael Cass-Beggs. *Folk Lullabies.* New York: Oak Publications, 1969. Page 29.

Other: Melody adapted by Doug Lipman.

Gilchrist, A. G. "Three Northern Lullabies." *Journal of the Folk Song Society, 5.* Number 19, 1915. Page 121.

The meanings of "bairnie" and "bonnie" were found in:

The Compact Edition of the Oxford English Dictionary, Volume I. Oxford: Oxford University Press, 1971. Pages 157, 247.

SONG #30—THERE WAS A LITTLE FROG

First: As a child, I listened over and over to a 78 rpm record of country singer Tex Ritter singing a version of this widespread song.

Closest:

Chroman, Eleanor. *Songs That Children Sing.* New York: Oak Publications, 1970. Pages 10–11.

Other: New words by Doug Lipman.

Cox, John Harrington. *Traditional Ballads and Folk-Songs Mainly from West Virginia.* Edited by George Herzon and Herbert Halpert, 1939, and by George W. Boswell, 1964. Publications of the American Folklore Society, Volume XV, 1964. Pages 179ff.

Evanson, Jacob A., "Folk Songs of an Industrial City," in George Korson, *Pennsylvania Songs and Legends.* Baltimore: Johns Hopkins University Press, 1949.

Opie, Iona, and Peter Opie. *The Oxford Dictionary of Nursery Rhymes.* Oxford: Oxford University Press, 1973. Pages 179ff.

Owens, William A. *Texas Folk Songs.* Dallas: Southern Methodist University Press, 1976. Page 137.

Payne, L. W., Jr. "Some Texas Versions of 'The Frog's Courting.'" In *Rainbow in the Morning,* edited by J. Frank Dobie. Publications of the Texas Folklore Society, Number V. Hatboro, PA: Folklore Associates, Inc., 1965. Reprint of 1926. Page 45.

White, Newman Ivey. *The Frank C. Brown Collection of North Carolina Folklore, Volume III.* Durham, NC: Duke University Press, 1952. Page 160.

INDEX OF RHYTHMIC ELEMENTS

This table is given for the convenience of those who want this kind of information. If it doesn't make sense to you, don't worry! You don't need to know about this to use the songs effectively.

The songs are listed in three sections: duple meter (2/4, 4/4, and cut time), 3/4, and 6/8 meter.

Within each section, the songs are in approximate order of rhythmic complexity.

Please note that the less-common rhythmic elements are not shown here, but are indicated in the right-hand column, "additional rhythms in."

Duple-time songs:

song title	page #	meter	♩	♫	3	𝅗𝅥	▬	♪♪ ♪♪.	♩. ♪	𝄾 ♪	♬	upbeat	additional rhythms
So He Planted Ginger	132	2/4	♩	♫									two-measure repeat
HaSukkah	154	4/4	♩	♫								♫	
Down Came a Lady	123	4/4	♩	♫	3								
Old Mr. Rabbit	153	2/4	♩	♫	3							♪	
Atse Zetim Omdim (first part)	146	4/4	♩	♫		𝅗𝅥							
Train Is A-Coming	155	4/4	♩	♫	3	𝅗𝅥							
Hill and Gully Rider	150	4/4	♩	♫	3			♪♪♪				♫	
Al Citron	124	2/4	♩	♫					♩. ♪			♫	
It's a Shame	126	2/2	♩	♫	3	𝅗𝅥	▬		♩. ♪			♩ ♩	1 measure: 1/2
Back to Mexico	125	¢	♩	♫		𝅗𝅥	▬		♩. ♪				
Juley	148	¢	♩	♫		𝅗𝅥	▬		♩. ♪				
Stewball (verse)	144	4/4	♩	♫						𝄾 ♪		♬	
There Was A Little Frog	159	¢	♩	♫	3	𝅗𝅥				𝄾 ♪		♩ and ♪	
Che Che Ku Le	138	4/4	♩					♪♪♪		𝄾 ♪			
Stewball (refrain)	144	4/4	♩	♫					♩. ♪	𝄾 ♪		♫	
Atse Zetim Omdim (2nd part)	146	4/4	♩	♫				♪♪♪			♬		

song title	page #	meter	additional rhythms
Kitty Kasket	134	2/4	
Windy Weather	136	4/4	in measure 4
Weldon	129	4/4	
Hold My Mule	143	2/4	
I Wish I Was a Cowpoke	130	4/4	
Sit Down (verse)	121	4/4	in measures 2, 8
Sit Down (refrain)	121	4/4	and in measures 2, 3, 7, 9
Wake Me, Shake Me	127	4/4	in measure 5
Old Joe Clark	141	2/4	in measures 4, 7
I'm Going Home on the Morning Train	135	4/4	in every measure!

3/4 time songs:

song title	page #	meter	upbeat	additional rhythms
Poor Lonesome Cowhand	156	3/4		and
Arirang	139	3/4		
Good-bye, Old Paint	140	3/4		in measure 3

6/8 time songs:

song title	page #	meter	upbeat	additional rhythms
Sleep, Bonnie Bairnie	158	6/8		
Round the Corner	137	6/8		
Charlie over the Ocean	133	6/8		in measure 8
Dance a Baby Diddy	151	6/8		in measure 8

INDEX OF MELODIC ELEMENTS

This table is given for the convenience of those who want this kind of information. If it doesn't make sense to you, don't worry! You don't need to know about this to use the songs effectively.

Given in "relative do" terminology. The final note of each song is boxed.

Listed by increasing complexity of scale, beginning with three-tone pentatonic, increasing gradually to seven-tone pentatonic, then going on to scales with fa, then adding ti, finally adding ta (ti-flat).

song title	page	so	la	ti	do	re	mi	fa	so	la	ti	do
Pentatonic songs												
Sit Down (verse)	121				[do]	re	mi					
Old Mr. Rabbit	153		la		do	re	mi					
Al Citron	124	so			do	re	mi					
Che Che Ku Le	138	so			do	re	[mi]					
Down Came a Lady	123	so	la		[do]		mi					
Kitty Kasket	134	[so]	la		do		mi					
Sit Down (refrain)	121	so	la		[do]	re	mi					
Wake Me, Shake Me	127	so	la		[do]	re	mi					
Weldon	129	so	la		[do]	re	mi					
I'm Going Home on the Morning Train	135	so	la		[do]	re	mi					
Round the Corner	137	so	la		[do]	re	mi					
Charlie over the Ocean	133	[so]	la		do	re	mi					
I Wish I Was a Cowpoke (refrain)	130				[do]	re	mi		so			
Windy Weather	136	so			[do]		mi		so			
Good-bye, Old Paint	140	so			[do]	re	mi		so			
HaSukkah	154	so			[do]	re	mi		so			
Arirang	139	so	la		[do]	re	mi		so			
I Wish I Was a Cowpoke (verse)	130	so			[do]	re	mi		so	la		
Back to Mexico	125	so	la		[do]	re	mi		so	la		
It's a Shame	126	so	la		[do]	re	mi		so	la		
Hold My Mule	143	so	la		[do]	re	mi		so	la		
Hill and Gully Rider	150	so	la		[do]	re	mi		so	la		
There Was A Little Frog	159	so	la		[do]	re	mi		so	la		
Train Is A-Coming	155	so	la		[do]	re	mi		so	la		do
Pentatonic plus fa												
Sleep, Bonnie Bairnie	158				[do]		mi	fa	so	la		
Dance a Baby Diddy	151				[do]	re	mi	fa	so	la		
Poor Lonesome Cowhand	156				[do]	re	mi	fa	so	la		
Juley	148	so			[do]	re	mi	fa	so	la		
Pentachordal with ti												
So He Planted Ginger	132	so	[la]	ti	do	re						
Seven-note & other songs												
Stewball	144	so		ta	[do]		mi		so			
Stewball (alternate solfege)	144					re		fa	[so]		ti	re
Atse Zetim Omdim	146	so		ti	[do]	re	mi	fa	so	la		
Old Joe Clark	141	so		ta	[do]	re	mi	fa	so	la	ta	

SUBJECT INDEX

Please See also the Index of Rhythmic Elements and the Index of Melodic Elements.
Certain subjects are grouped together. See especially: animals; body; daily activities; families; feelings; food; geographical features; holidays; language; movements; occupations; science; time

rhythmic, 94-97
rolling, 89
rowing, 89
sequential pulse, 75-83
shaking hands, 7, 95
sitting down, 86, 121
soothing a baby, 71
spinning, 87
in spirituals, 173
while standing in place, 87-88
standing up, 86, 121
static, 92-94
stiffening the body, 22, 91
stretching, 81, 90
swinging partner, 53, 54, 56
tapping, 81
as done on a train, 74
turning, 13, 43, 66, 75, 86
walking, 89
washing a handkerchief, 74
waving, 72, 75
Mud, 45, 116, 134
Music. *See also* Singing; Songs; Work
 songs
 folk, 172, 193
 history of recording industry, 179
 occupational uses, 164, 165, 168,
  170
 social uses, 185
Musical concepts
 accents, 84
 call-and-response, 187, 190
 echo, 81, 84, 190
 fast *vs.* slow, 24, 42, 46, 69, 100
 loud *vs.* soft, 33, 83, 100
 ostinato, 34
 pitch matching, 42
 pulse (beat), 67, 68, 75
 question and answer form, 174
 talent, myth of musical, xii
Musical instruments, xviii, xix, 179, 181
 banjos, 180
 drums, 188
 fiddles, 78, 159, 165, 166, 179,
  180, 183
 fifes, 188
 on frontier, 182
 harps, 183
 Orff instruments, 176
 piccolos, 188
 string band, 179
 triangles, 93

Names, 22, 40, 43, 90, 99, 102, 106,
 112
 used in play-parties, 183
Native Americans, 165
Neighborhoods, 186
New verses, 4, 98, 183. *See also Table
 of Contents;* Activities
 in African music, 172
 movement change with, 74
 in play-parties, 183
 in religious songs, 172
 rhyming, 15, 98, 115-20
 by singing a suggestion, 110-14
 in Spanish, 102
 traditional uses, 165, 184, 190
Nigeria, 190
Noises, 165
Nursery rhymes. *See* Rhymes

Nursery schools, 193

Oceans. *See* Geographical features
Occupations, 110, 184
 accountants, 130
 cowhands, 5, 29, 130, 157, 183,
  186
 engineers (train), 74
 farmers, 18, 47, 58. *See also*
  Farming
 gardeners, 21
 kings, 3
 ministers, 172
 planters, 36
 queens, 3, 190
 sailors, 84, 95
 soldiers, 180
 stevedores, 164
 vaqueras & vaqueros, 157
O'Malley, D.J. (cowhand poet), 183
Orff instruments. *See* Musical instruments

Palestine, 177
Places, 99, 114
Plants. *See also* Trees
 briars, 25
 cabbages, 21, 85
 fantasies and fictions about, 105
 flowers, 113
 ginger, 36, 105
 grass, 91
 hay, 63
 leaves, 9
 lulav bouquet, 75
 seeing inside of, 119
 sorghum, 73
 sugar cane, 73
Plate, 93
Play-parties, 50-56, 182-186
Poetry, 183, 186
Pollux, 187
Props, xvii, 2, 25, 27, 34
 balls, 37, 45, 46, 47, 48
 bean bags, 4, 36, 45, 46, 47, 48
 blindfolds, 25, 27, 28, 29, 31, 32,
  187
Pulleys. *See* Science, ropes & pulleys

Races, horse, 12, 17, 170
Racism, 172, 175, 186
Rain. *See* Science
Recordings. *See* Resources
Religious prohibitions, 180, 182, 183
Resources, where to buy
 folk music recordings, 161
 Jewish books & recordings, 178,
  179
Rhymes
 counting-out, 18, 19, 23, 26, 27
 dandling rhymes, 169
 jump-rope, 189
 nursery rhymes, 162, 167, 187, 194
 rhyming, 15, 98, 115-120
 warning rhymes, 180
Right and left. *See* Directions
Rivers. *See* Geographical features
Rocks, 45
Romance and courtship, 168, 184, 187,
 193
Ropes, 49

Sailing. *See* Transportation
Schools, 193. *See also* Homework
Science
 ashes, 22
 dry *vs.* wet, 22, 91
 ecology, 177
 frost, 136
 gold, 26
 rain, 91, 145
 ropes and pulleys, 84, 164
 weather, 64, 76, 89, 108, 136
 wind, 8, 19, 95, 136, 163, 191
Scotland, 186. *See also* British Isles
Seas and oceans. *See* Geographical
 features
Seasons
 autumn, 154, 177
 spring, 72, 177
 winter, 72, 183
Seeger, Ruth Crawford (composer), 193
Senses, 27, 29, 31
Sequencing, 48, 81
Sex-role stereotypes, 28, 50-51, 163,
 164
Shapes, 8, 92. *See also* Circles; Lines
 arches, 38, 44
 hopping on, 25
 of letters, 93
 spirals, 38
 squares, games in seated circles or,
  14, 15, 16, 26
Singing. *See also* Music; Songs; Work
 songs
 antiphonal, 173
 melodies, singing without, xi
 solo, 28, 97, 110-115
 talent, myth of musical, xii
 work, importance in, 162, 165
Sleep. *See* Daily activities
Social gatherings, 175, 181
 carnivals, 190
 on frontier, 182
 parades, 34
 picnics, 189, 190
 races, horse, 12, 17, 170
 religious rituals, 174
 revival meetings, 98
 tea meetings (Jamaica), 189, 190
 wakes, 189, 190
 weddings, 78, 159, 168
Songs. *See also* Activities; Music;
 Singing; Work songs
 ballads, 123, 145, 170-71, 193-94
 bilingual, 165
 bluegrass, 181
 calypso, 190
 camp-meeting, 173, 175
 cumulative, 132, 194, 195-96
 dance, 179-82
 dandling, 152, 167, 168
 fingerplays, 79
 floating verses in, 174, 180
 folk, value of, xii
 game, 124, 133, 134, 136, 138,
  150, 153, 186-93
 gospel, 127
 hobo, 174
 holiday, 146, 154, 177-79
 hymns, 98, 172, 183
 how to learn, xi, xiii
 for listening, xv